Demystifying Academic Reading

D1608116

Foundational and accessible, this book equips pre-service and practicing teachers with the knowledge, understanding, tools, and resources they need to help students in grades 4–12 develop reading proficiencies in four core academic subjects—literature, history, science, and mathematics. Applying a disciplinary literacy approach, Fang describes the verbal and visual resources, expert strategies, inquiry skills, and habits of mind that students must learn in order to read carefully, critically, purposefully, and with an informed skepticism across genres and content areas. He also shows how teachers can promote language learning and reading/literacy development at the same time that they engage students in content area learning.

With informative synthesis and research-based recommendations in every chapter, this text prepares teachers to help students develop discipline-specific, as well as discipline-relevant, discursive insights, literacy strategies, and ways of thinking, reasoning, and inquiring that are essential to productive learning across academic subjects. It also provides teacher educators with approaches and strategies for helping teacher candidates develop expertise in academic reading instruction. In so doing, the book demystifies academic reading, revealing what it takes for students to read increasingly complex academic texts with confidence and understanding and for teachers to develop expertise that promotes disciplinary literacy. This state-of-the-art text is ideal for courses on reading/literacy methods and academic literacy and eminently relevant to all educators who want their students to become thoughtful readers and powerful learners.

Zhihui Fang is Professor and Head of Literacy and Language Education in the School of Teaching and Learning at the University of Florida, USA. He is the author of several books, including *Demystifying Academic Writing: Genres, Moves, Skills, and Strategies* (2021).

Demystifying Academic Reading

A Disciplinary Literacy Approach to Reading Across Content Areas

Zhihui Fang

Routledge
Taylor & Francis Group

NEW YORK AND LONDON

Designed cover image: © Getty Images

First published 2024
by Routledge
605 Third Avenue, New York, NY 10158

and by Routledge
4 Park Square, Milton Park, Abingdon, Oxon, OX14 4RN

Routledge is an imprint of the Taylor & Francis Group, an informa business

© 2024 Zhihui Fang

The right of Zhihui Fang to be identified as author of this work has been asserted in accordance with sections 77 and 78 of the Copyright, Designs and Patents Act 1988.

Library of Congress Cataloging-in-Publication Data
A catalog record for this title has been requested

ISBN: 978-1-032-55791-5 (hbk)
ISBN: 978-1-032-38688-1 (pbk)
ISBN: 978-1-003-43225-8 (ebk)

DOI: 10.4324/9781003432258

Typeset in Goudy
by Apex CoVantage, LLC

Contents (Brief)

Preface   ix

1 Reading and Learning in Academic Content Areas   1

2 Reading Literature   42

3 Reading History   73

4 Reading Science   121

5 Reading Mathematics   163

6 Developing Teacher Expertise for Academic
   Reading Instruction   213

Index   247

Contents (Detailed)

Preface   ix

1 Reading and Learning in Academic Content Areas   1
   What is Reading?   *1*
   Models of Reading Process   *5*
   Factors Impacting Academic Reading   *13*
   The Challenges of Academic Reading   *17*
   Stages of Reading Development   *21*
   Language, Reading, and Learning   *24*
   Toward a Disciplinary Literacy Approach to Academic Reading   *28*
   Conclusion   *33*
   Reflection and Application   *34*
   References   *34*

2 Reading Literature   42
   Literature in English Language Arts   *42*
   The Challenges of Literary Reading   *44*
   How do Experts Read Literary Texts?   *52*
   Developing Literary Expertise: General Principles and Approaches   *56*
   Teaching Literature in ELA Classrooms: Some Examples   *63*
   Conclusion   *68*
   Reflection and Application   *68*
   References   *69*

3 Reading History   73
   What is History?   *73*
   Reading and Historical Literacy   *75*
   Types of Historical Materials   *78*
   The Challenges of Historical Reading   *81*
   How do Experts Read Historical Texts?   *88*

Developing Historical Literacy Through Reading 90
Conclusion 114
Reflection and Application 115
References 116

4 Reading Science   121
Reading and Science Literacy 121
The Challenges of Science Reading 123
How do Experts Read Science Texts? 128
A Blueprint for Improving Science Reading Ability 132
A Heuristic for Teaching Reading in Science 143
Conclusion 156
Reflection and Application 156
References 157

5 Reading Mathematics   163
What is Mathematics? 163
Reading and Mathematical Literacy 166
The Challenges of Mathematics Reading 169
How do Experts Read Mathematics Texts? 179
Promoting Reading in Mathematics Teaching and Learning 185
Conclusion 205
Reflection and Application 206
References 206

6 Developing Teacher Expertise for Academic
   Reading Instruction   213
Continuing Reading Instruction Beyond Elementary School 213
Who is Responsible for Teaching Academic Reading? 214
What Sorts of Expertise are Needed to Teach Academic Reading? 217
Preparing Teachers for Academic Reading Instruction 225
Conclusion 240
Reflection and Application 241
References 242

Index   247

Preface

Academic reading, or reading done for the purpose of learning and socialization in academic content areas, is a topic of critical importance to K-12 schooling and beyond. Proficiency with academic reading ensures access to the sorts of knowledge, value, and thinking that are privileged in school, workplace, and society. Unlike everyday reading, academic reading is more discipline-specific, purposeful, and critical, requiring more sophisticated and specialized skills, strategies, and habits of mind, as well as effort, practice, and guidance. As students move from elementary school through middle school and into high school and beyond, they are expected to engage with increasingly complex texts in content area learning and disciplinary socialization. This engagement requires reading skills, strategies, dispositions, and proficiencies beyond those students have developed in the elementary grades.

Demystifying Academic Reading: A Disciplinary Literacy Approach to Reading Across Content Areas aims to equip teachers in grades 4–12 with the knowledge, understanding, tools, and resources they need to help their students tackle the new demands of academic reading in curriculum content areas. Specifically, the book discusses what literacy means in different academic disciplines and describes strategies content experts use when reading texts in their disciplines. It also identifies discursive features that make academic and disciplinary texts at once dense, abstract, complex, and difficult to process, illuminating for students the semiotic resources through which meanings are made in genre-specific, discipline-legitimated ways. It then makes pedagogical recommendations for teachers tasked with developing students' advanced literacy in content area learning. Finally, it provides teacher educators with ideas and strategies for helping teachers develop expertise for academic reading/literacy instruction. Throughout the book, the term "content area" (also called "subject area" or "subject matter") is used synonymously with the term "discipline", with the former commonly understood to be the latter recontextualized for pedagogical purposes in the K-12 setting. As such, content areas retain many of the same conceptual, structural, and stylistic features that characterize disciplines.

This book attempts to present a state-of-the-art review of the theory, research, and practice related to academic reading in four core curriculum content areas—literature, history, science, and mathematics. It demonstrates that contrary to popular beliefs, the task of learning to read is by no means complete by the end of third grade, suggesting that even decoding-proficient students still have much to learn about how to read academic and disciplinary texts carefully, critically, purposefully, and with a healthy skepticism in content area learning. Adopting a disciplinary literacy approach—an approach that foregrounds the goals, ethos, methodologies, epistemologies, and practices of academic disciplines and emphasizes building students' understanding of how knowledge within specific disciplines is created, communicated, consumed, and learned, the book describes patterns of semiotic choices that content experts employ to construct texts in their discipline and the heuristics they employ to make sense of and interpret these texts in their reading practice. In so doing, the book demystifies academic reading, showing students how meaning in disciplinary texts is verbally and visually designed and what strategies are effective for engendering text understanding; it also provides evidence-based guidelines and ploys for helping students develop inquiry skills, discursive insights, cognitive strategies, and habits of mind that facilitate meaning making and learning across content areas.

The book is divided into six chapters. Chapter 1 discusses the nature of the reading process, the stages of reading development, the relationship between language and knowledge, the role of reading in content area learning, and the need for a disciplinary literacy approach to academic reading. Key questions addressed in the chapter include the following: What is reading? What is involved in the reading process? What is a text? What does it take to comprehend or understand a text? How does reading develop over the lifespan? How is knowledge construed through language? What is the role of reading in content area learning? How is academic reading similar to and different from everyday reading? What are the challenges involved in academic reading? What is disciplinary literacy? Why is a disciplinary literacy approach needed for academic reading?

Chapter 2 discusses the role of literature in the English language arts (ELA) curriculum, the challenges of literary reading, what it means to be reading like a literary expert, and what teachers can do to promote literary reading. Key questions addressed in the chapter include the following: What is literature? What is the role of literature in the ELA curriculum? What does literary competence mean? What are the types and features of literary texts?

What are the challenges literary texts present to reading and interpretation? What strategies do literary experts use in their reading practice? What are the guiding principles for teaching literature? What can teachers do to promote literary reading and foster literary literacy in the ELA classroom?

Chapter 3 discusses the notion of historical literacy, the role of reading in promoting historical literacy, different types of historical texts, the challenges of historical reading, what it means to be reading like an historian, and what teachers can do to promote historical reading. Key questions addressed in the chapter include the following: What is history? What is historical literacy? What is the role of reading in developing historical literacy? What are the types and features of historical texts? What challenges do historical texts present to reading and understanding? What strategies do historians use in their reading practice? What can teachers do to promote historical reading and foster historical literacy in the history/social studies classroom?

Chapter 4 discusses the notion of science literacy, the role of reading in promoting science literacy, the challenges of science reading, what it means to be reading like a scientist, and what teachers can do to promote science reading. Key questions addressed in the chapter include the following: What is science? What is science literacy? What is the role of reading in developing science literacy? What are the types and features of science texts? What challenges do science texts present to reading comprehension? What strategies do scientists use in their reading practice? What can teachers do to promote science reading and foster science literacy in the science classroom?

Chapter 5 discusses the notion of mathematical literacy, the role of reading in developing mathematical literacy, the challenges of mathematics reading, what it means to be reading like a mathematician, and what teachers can do to promote mathematics reading. Key questions addressed in the chapter include the following: What is mathematics? What is mathematical literacy? What is the role of reading in developing mathematical literacy? What are the types and features of mathematics texts? What are the challenges mathematics texts present to reading, problem solving, and learning? What strategies do mathematicians use in their reading practice? What can teachers do to promote mathematics reading and foster mathematical literacy in the mathematics classroom?

Chapter 6 reiterates the need for continuing reading instruction in secondary school and discusses the roles of reading/literacy teachers versus content area teachers in academic reading instruction, the expertise teachers need to orchestrate effective reading instruction in content areas, and approaches and strategies teacher educators can adopt to increase teacher candidates' expertise in academic reading instruction. Key questions addressed in the chapter include the following: Why is reading instruction still needed beyond elementary schooling? Whose responsibility is it to teach academic reading? What knowledge, skills, and dispositions do teachers need to effectively plan and teach academic reading in content areas? What can teacher preparation programs do to develop teacher candidates' capacities for academic reading instruction in their content area (or across content areas)?

This book can be considered a companion volume to *Demystifying Academic Writing: Genres, Moves, Skills, and Strategies* (Fang, 2021), also published by Routledge, and a sequel to *Reading in Secondary Content Areas: A Language-Based Pedagogy* (Fang & Schleppegrell, 2008), published over a decade ago by the University of Michigan Press. It shows how academic texts are discursively constructed in genre-specific, discipline-legitimated ways and how these texts are read by disciplinary experts in their social practice. It also describes and exemplifies ideas for helping students learn to read academic texts in ways that are consistent with how disciplinary experts interact with these texts. Taking a disciplinary literacy approach, the book offers discursive insights and expert strategies that enable students to cope with the unique challenges of academic reading across content areas. It also shows how teachers can promote language learning and reading/literacy development at the same time that they engage students in disciplinary inquiry and learning across academic content areas. Additionally, it describes ways teacher educators can help teachers develop both motivation for and expertise in academic reading/literacy instruction.

The book does not assume technical knowledge and is written in a style easily accessible to a wide audience. It should be of primary interest to teachers and teacher educators in K-12 contexts. It should also appeal to college reading instructors, as well as scholars and students of academic reading or disciplinary literacy across a range of disciplines. The book can be used in teacher education courses that prepare teacher candidates to teach reading in content area or literacy classes. It can also be used in any course on academic reading/literacy that teaches middle/high school or college students how to read academic texts in content area learning and disciplinary socialization.

I am very grateful to Karen Adler of Routledge, who approached me in 2022 with the invitation to write a book on academic reading. It is her prodding, encouragement, trust, and support that motivated me to complete this book in a timely manner.

1
Reading and Learning in Academic Content Areas

What is Reading?

Reading is a ubiquitous activity in our society. It is important for individual development not only because it is the foundation for academic success and career advancement (Berman & Biancarosa, 2005; Shanahan et al., 2010) but also because it has a strong correlation with personal health and well-being (Bavishi, Slade, & Levy, 2016; Cunningham & Stanovich, 1998). Due to its importance and pervasiveness, reading has been one of the most well researched, albeit still highly controversial, subjects in school. Much is now known about the nature, processes, effects, emergence, development, and uses of reading. Reading is widely understood to be an active process in which the reader constructs meaning based on what s/he sees in print or on screen (Pearson, Palincsar, Biancarosa, & Berman, 2020; Sweet & Snow, 2003). At least three basic elements are involved in this process: the reader, the text, and the task. The reader initiates the interaction with the text for a particular purpose in a specific context. S/he brings to the act of reading his/her knowledge, experiences, beliefs, values, attitudes, worldviews, interests, intentions, identity, capabilities, abilities, and habits of mind, all of which impact his/her level of engagement with the text, the sense s/he ultimately makes of the text, and the uses to which s/he puts the meaning that has been constructed.

The text is, broadly speaking, any object that can be "read". This object represents "any configuration of signs that provide a potential for meaning" (Smagorinsky, 2001, p. 137). It can be a newspaper article, a poem, a textbook, a movie, a television show, a person, a piece of art (e.g., sculpture, building, photograph, painting), a political cartoon, a song, a map, a traffic sign, an online advertisement, or a mathematical equation. Each of these objects has structure, coherence, function, development, and character at the same time (Halliday, 2002). They can be looked at, examined, made sense of, analyzed, interpreted, interrogated, and renovated because they

DOI: 10.4324/9781003432258-1

"have causal effects upon, and contribute to changes in, people (beliefs, attitudes, etc.), actions, social relations, and the material world" (Fairclough, 2003, p. 8).

A text is typically constructed using verbal and/or visual resources. Verbal resources refer to natural language with its lexis (vocabulary) and grammar. Visual resources consist of images such as tables, figures, photos, mathematical symbols (e.g., %, Σ, φ, β), drawings, maps, sonograms, and videos. Verbal texts are governed by "the logic of time and of sequence in time", and they represent the world through telling (Kress, 2003, p. 2). Reading verbal texts, thus, involves making sense of the world told/narrated. Visual texts, on the other hand, are governed by "the logic of space" and "the simultaneity of elements in spatial arrangements", and they represent the world by showing (Kress, 2003, p. 2). Reading visual texts, thus, involves making sense of the world shown/displayed. Most texts today are multimodal, with some more heavily reliant on verbal resources and others more heavily dependent on visual resources to convey meaning. Reading these texts, therefore, entails the ability to make sense of the world told *and* shown.

A text can be print/paper-based or screen-based. With print/paper-based texts, reading is typically a linear and continuous process, with the reader expected to begin at a certain point in the text clearly marked by the author (e.g., title, paragraph, section, chapter) and then proceed to an end that is also clearly marked by the author. The reading path—from the beginning to the end of the text—is to a large extent determined by the author, whose choice of verbal and/or visual resources positions the reader to follow a route carefully laid out by the author. Screen-based texts can be traditional texts displayed on a digital device—such as a computer, an e-reader, a tablet, or a smart phone—instead of on paper. Reading these texts is similar to reading paper-based texts in that it is a largely sequential process. However, research has shown that when people read on screen, they usually do not understand what they have read as well as when they read the same text in print (see Delgado, Vargas, Ackerman, & Salmeron, 2018 for a research review). The advantage of paper-based reading is greater in time-constrained reading than in self-paced reading and with informational texts than with narrative texts. This advantage can be explained by two factors. First, we tend to read faster on screen. This habit hinders us from absorbing the ideas in the text, particularly when we are interacting with an academic or disciplinary text, where ideas are often densely packed and hierarchically structured. Second, we do a lot of scrolling when reading on screen. This scrolling back and forth makes us lose a sense of place in the text (e.g., a particular paragraph, page, section, or chapter), which is important to remembering and recall. Moreover, scrolling up and down a page takes quite a bit more mental work than reading a still page because our eyes cannot focus on the words but have to keep chasing them as we scroll up and down the page.

More often, however, screen-based texts exist in an online environment populated with hyperlinks, digital references to other objects or files that the reader can follow by clicking. These texts, called hypertexts, transcend the linear quality of traditional texts. They provide access to a vast amount of information that may or may not be reliable or relevant, compelling the reader to play a more active role in deciding what to read next (i.e., which hyperlinks to click) and how much time to spend on each hyperlink. Although the author is the one who decides how many and which hyperlinks to embed in a text, the reader has to determine the relationships between linked texts and images as well as among various hyperlinks so that s/he can choose a reading path that best suits his/her purpose and satisfies his/her curiosity. In this sense, reading hypertexts, or online reading, is a non-linear, or discontinuous, process that does not follow a specific order and requires a new set of skills not commonly associated with the reading of conventional texts, or offline reading. These skills include, for example, filtering (becoming more selective in choosing what to read in the text), skimming (actually reading less of the text), pecking (reading passages in no particular sequence), imposing (imposing readers' frameworks on the texts they peruse), filming (deriving significant meaning more from graphics than from words), trespassing (loosening of textual boundaries, with readers becoming textual burglars), de-authorizing (lessening sense of authorship and authorly intention), and fragmenting (breaking texts into fragments so that they can be reassembled in ways that satisfy the reader's intention) (Sosnoski, 1999).

A text can also be classified according to its purpose, to wit, genre. Three major categories of school-based genres have been identified: person, factual, and analytical (Martin, 1989). Personal genres, which include recount and narrative, (re)create personal experiences. Factual genres, which include procedure, biography, and report, present factual information about a process, a person, or a thing. Analytical genres, which include explanation and exposition, present analysis and argument. Each of these genres consists of a series of schematic stages, or macrostructural elements, that are unique to the genre and is constructed with a distinct set of lexical and grammatical resources that are not only functional for making it the kind of text it is but also appropriate for a particular context. Successful engagement with these genres requires, among other things, mature control over the schematic, lexical, and grammatical resources that construct them.

Finally, the task includes purpose (why the reader reads), process (what mental activity the reader engages in while reading), and consequence (what the reader learns or experiences as a result of reading) (Sweet & Snow, 2003, p. 2). It also impacts reading in tangible ways. For example, reading for leisure or entertainment is a different sort of experience and engenders a different sort of outcome than reading for specific information to be recalled later or reading to analyze and evaluate an argument. When reading for leisure, the reader may scan and skim a text, sampling passages that sound interesting, that relate to personal experiences, or that evoke empathy, without the pressure to learn or memorize anything in particular. When reading for specific information, the reader will need to be more intentional in his/her search for particular passages or sections, with the goal of identifying, processing, and remembering detailed information in these text segments for later recall. When reading for critical analysis and evaluation, the reader needs to pay close attention to the author's verbal/visual choices, think critically about the ideology (e.g., values, beliefs) imbued in these choices, assess the quality of evidence and the strength of argument, make intertextual connections, identify who is (dis)advantaged by the text message, and determine what course of action to take in light of this message. The amount and intensity of mental work involved in each of these three readings is clearly different.

To summarize, reading is a complex process involving (a) understanding written text, (b) developing and interpreting meaning, and (c) using meaning as appropriate to type of text, purpose, and situation (Pearson, Palincsar, Biancarosa, & Berman, 2020, p. 26). This process is seen by some (e.g., Goodman, 1986; Smith, 2004) as natural, similar to reading faces or learning to speak, but by others (e.g., Fletcher & Lyons, 1998; Stanovich, 2000) as unnatural and, for many children, laborious and difficult. Regardless of how the process is viewed, there appears to be a general consensus among scholars from different camps that reading is simultaneously social, cognitive, semiotic, and critical (Fang, 2012a). It is social in the sense that it involves the transaction between the reader and the author via text for a specific purpose and in a specific context. It is cognitive in that it involves the use of mental processes, strategies, and procedures in comprehending and meaning making. It is semiotic in that it involves the decoding and processing of verbal and/or visual signs in a text. It is critical in that it involves constant evaluation of the messages in the text and formulation of responses to these messages. The ability to read is a tremendous feat that gives us access to knowledge, values, worldviews, habits of mind, capital, and power that are otherwise not readily accessible, making us become a more informed, thoughtful, and active participant in our academic, professional, and social lives. Developing this ability is, as will be shown in this book, a multifaceted process that requires considerable investment in time, commitment, resources, and support.

Models of Reading Process

Reading, or reading comprehension, has been defined as "the ability to extract and construct linguistically based meaning, both literal and inferred, from written text" (Tunmer & Hoover, 2019, p. 77). Exactly how comprehension happens during reading has been the subject of much debate. Many models of reading process have been proposed to explain how meaning is made during the act of reading or what it takes to comprehend a text. Two models are currently popular and being hotly contested—the simple view of reading and the complex (or multidimensional) view of reading. Although Hoover and Tunmer (2021) contended that the simple view of reading, as it was originally conceptualized by Gough and Tunmer (1986), is "a model of the cognitive capacities needed for reading and not the cognitive processes by which reading is accomplished" (p. 400), they also acknowledged that the two (cognitive capacities vs. cognitive processes) are inextricably intertwined in that a description of the relationships among various cognitive capacities (abilities or competencies) inevitably involves an explanation of the mechanisms, or processes, that underlie their interaction and the outcome of this interaction (i.e., comprehension).

Simple View of Reading

The simple view of reading, or SVR, posits that reading is the product of two basic but independent components—decoding and listening comprehension (Gough & Tunmer, 1986; Tunmer & Hoover, 2019). Their relationship can be expressed in a formula as:

$$D \ (decoding) \ x \ LC \ (listening \ comprehension) = RC \ (reading \ comprehension)$$

Here, decoding means efficient word recognition, to wit, the ability to read words quickly, accurately, and silently. Listening comprehension refers to the ability to derive meaning from spoken words in sentences. It is sometimes, and perhaps misleadingly (because word recognition is also a linguistic/ language process that contributes to comprehension), called "linguistic comprehension" or "language comprehension", especially in the more recent descriptions of SVR. For example, Tunmer and Hoover (2019) presented an updated version of SVR, called the Cognitive Foundations Framework, in which reading comprehension is conceptualized to be dependent on two necessary and equally important cognitive capacities—word recognition and language comprehension. Word recognition is defined as "the ability to derive accurately and quickly a representation from printed input that allows access to the appropriate word meaning contained in the internal mental lexicon" (p. 78). It is an alphabetic coding skill that encompasses concept about print, letter knowledge, and phonemic awareness. Thus, word recognition has two components. One is the ability to recognize the shape, size, look, and other orthographic features of a word without necessarily knowing its meaning. For example, we can recognize someone (e.g., facial features, hair style, body structure) without necessarily knowing who that person really is (e.g., his/her name, age, place of birth, profession, habits, preferences). Another dimension of word recognition is the ability to turn graphs/letters (after initial recognition) into sounds. Being able to sound out a word does not necessarily mean that the reader will understand what the word means, unless this word is already in his/her listening vocabulary (that is, oral language repertoire). For example, it is possible that a reader is able to sound out a word like "Huawei" or "Auschwitz" but does not know what it means or represents. Language comprehension, on the other hand, refers to "the ability to extract and construct literal and inferred meaning from linguistic discourse represented in speech" (p. 78). It includes linguistic (phonological, syntactic, semantic) knowledge, background knowledge, and inferencing skills. In this sense, language comprehension means understanding what a word (or text) means in context. When we have "comprehended" someone, we know who that person is (e.g., his/her name, profession, habits, dispositions, cravings, tendencies, and so on). Word recognition relates to language comprehension in that if one can identify, or recognize, a word quickly and effortlessly, s/he can then channel his/her cognitive resources to constructing meaning from words, sentences, and paragraphs—i.e., to comprehend.

These two essential components of reading comprehension are further unpacked by Scarborough (2001), who used a rope to visually illustrate the different strands or components that are woven into skilled reading. The Rope Model similarly sees skilled reading as the outcome of fluent execution and coordination of word recognition and language comprehension. Word recognition in this model includes phonological awareness (i.e., awareness at the word, syllable, and phoneme level), decoding (i.e., phonics—alphabetic principle and spelling-sound correspondence), and sight recognition of familiar words. Language comprehension consists of background knowledge (e.g., facts and concepts about a topic), vocabulary (breadth and depth of knowledge about a word), language structures (e.g., syntax and semantics), verbal reasoning (i.e., the ability to make inferences and interpret metaphor), and literacy knowledge (e.g., print concepts, genre knowledge). As word recognition becomes increasingly automatic and language comprehension becomes increasingly strategic, the reader is said to become increasingly skilled or proficient in reading. Like the original SVR, the Rope Model of Reading also lumps together everything else besides word recognition that impacts reading comprehension into the basket called "language comprehension" (cf., Duke and Cartwright [2021, p. 533], which reconfigures the components of language comprehension but in a way that is not too drastically different from what the Rope Model does). From this perspective, then, if another component of reading comprehension (e.g., background knowledge) were to be emphasized, the SVR can conceivably be revised to be "background knowledge x language comprehension = reading comprehension", with "language comprehension" again being the all-encompassing category that captures everything else—both linguistic (e.g., decoding, vocabulary, syntax) and non-linguistic (e.g., strategy use, motivation)—that impacts reading comprehension.

In essence, what the SVR presumes is that once the words in a written text are decoded, the reader would apply the same mechanism s/he uses in listening comprehension to written text comprehension. In other words, the SVR grafts the reading process into the listening process, such that reading is seen as involving the conversion of written language into spoken language, where meaning is presumed to be more readily accessible. According to the model, it is possible to have strong listening/language comprehension and still be a poor reader if there is difficulty with decoding. Similarly, it is possible to be strong in decoding and still be a poor reader if listening/language comprehension is weak.

The SVR demonstrates that to achieve reading comprehension, the reader must have strong word recognition and strong language comprehension. It suggests that improvement in word recognition and language comprehension will lead to improvement in reading comprehension. The implication of this suggestion for pedagogy is that reading instruction should focus on word recognition and language comprehension. In reading instruction, efforts to improve automaticity and fluency in word recognition typically focus on phonological awareness and phonics. This emphasis is highlighted in recent discussions of what is referred to as "the Science of Reading" (Snowling, Hulme, & Nation, 2022), a term loaded in tone as well as in meaning because scholars from different research traditions tend to define and approach "science" very differently (see, for example, Reinking, Hruby, & Risko, 2023 for a poignant commentary on this topic and

Goodwin & Jimenez, 2020 for a special issue of *Reading Research Quarterly* on the same topic). Unlike word recognition, which is believed to be "a teachable skill" because "it involves a narrow scope of knowledge (e.g., letters, sounds, words) and processes (decoding)" (Kamhi, 2007, p. 28), language comprehension "is not a skill and is not easily taught" because it is "a complex of higher-level mental processes" that are domain/content-specific and "include thinking, reasoning, imagining, and interpreting" (Kamhi, 2007, p. 28). In reading instruction, efforts to improve language comprehension typically focus on vocabulary (seen as a proxy for knowledge) and background knowledge. This emphasis is reflected in the recent push, by scholars like Hirsch (2005, 2006) and Willingham (2006), for knowledge-based, or content-rich, school curricula, the most famous of which is the Core Knowledge Curriculum Series (https://www.core knowledge.org/curriculum/), provided by the Core Knowledge Foundation, a not-for-profit organization founded by E. D. Hirsch, a professor emeritus of education and humanities at the University of Virginia, USA.

Complex view of reading

There is no doubt that the ability to recognize, decode, and aurally comprehend words in sentences is important to reading comprehension. The SVR is an adequate model for beginning reading, that is, the initial stage of learning to read. The texts that young children are expected to read typically deal with topics that are near and dear to them (i.e., topics with which they are familiar) and the language (e.g., vocabulary, sentences) that presents this topic is akin to the everyday language children use in their daily social interaction with peers and family members. Two examples of such texts can be found in Text 1.1 and Text 1.2. Text 1.1 is an excerpt from "Arthur's TV Trouble", which is part of Marc Brown's Arthur Adventure book series, a favorite of children. Text 1.2 is a brief excerpt about the fights in a late-night band show from *Diper Overlode*, which is one of the "Diary of a Wimpy Kid" series by popular children's book writer Jeff Kinney.

Text 1.1

Ads for Treat Timer were everywhere. Now Arthur really wanted one.

Arthur counted his money. D.W. helped. "Even with all of my birthday money," he said, "I only have ten dollars and three cents."

"I know what you're thinking," said D.W. She ran to protect her cash register.

Arthur decided to ask Dad for an advance on his allowance.

"Gee, I'd love to help," said Dad, "but my catering business is a little slow right now."

Arthur knew Mom would understand. "Money doesn't grow on trees," said Mother, "and I think Pal likes treats from you, not a machine." (Brown, 2004, pp. 174–177)

Text 1.2

The crowd was starting to get annoyed, and they let the band know it by pelting them with chicken wings. But I was dealing with a BIGGER issue. People started lining up to use the porta-potty, and I couldn't do anything to STOP them. Thankfully, the club ran out of chicken wings, and the audience started to head home. And that was a good thing, because Billy got Buffalo sauce in his eye and couldn't read the lyrics off his phone anymore. (Kinney, 2022, pp. 108–109)

Thanks to familiarity with the topics of the two texts, children who are native speakers of English would normally be able to comprehend both texts if they can hear the words and sentences read aloud. In other words, the vocabulary and syntax of the two texts are within children's oral language repertoire and, thus, their listening comprehension capability. This means that the main challenge for reading and understanding this sort of text is word recognition, and the SVR simply highlights the extreme importance of word recognition in this early stage of reading acquisition.

However, when children start to read texts in curriculum content areas, or academic disciplines recontextualized for the purpose of K-12 schooling, where topics become more unfamiliar and the language that presents these topics becomes more unlike the everyday language that they use in their mundane social life, the SVR becomes too simplistic and not robust enough to account for comprehension of more advanced academic and disciplinary texts. In a literary text such as Robert Frost's (1915) "The Road Not Taken", for example, students would typically have little trouble decoding and understanding individual words in this narrative poem; however, many of them are likely to struggle with comprehending or, rather, interpreting the overall meaning, or theme, of the poem, which is about the importance of choices in our journey through life. Many of us have experienced tremendous challenges when trying to comprehend academic or disciplinary texts that are read aloud to us, recognizing that these texts often need to be read silently, slowly, and closely in order to ensure comprehension and understanding. Two cases in point are Texts 1.3 and 1.4, presented below.

Text 1.3

After a lengthy description of how integration was a Communist/Socialist plot to destroy America and how the mixing of races would ruin our nation, Brady unknowingly foreshadowed the Emmett Till case thirteen months before it happened: . . . This warning from Brady put segregationists in Mississippi on the lookout for smart-talking Negro boys from Northern cities who would soon come to the South to harass white women and ultimately destroy segregation and the Southern way of life.

Text 1.4

Over the last 40 years, Europe and North America have been leaders in reducing particulate air pollution from industry, autos, energy, and other sources. The increasing absence of human-caused air pollution in the Northern Hemisphere, estimated to be a 50-percent drop in concentration from 1980 to 2020, has led to surface warming over the tropical Atlantic Ocean, which contributes to more frequent tropical cyclones. Without significant amounts of particulate pollution to reflect sunlight, the ocean absorbs more heat and warms faster. A warming Atlantic Ocean has been a key ingredient to a 33-percent increase in the number of tropical cyclones during this 40-year period, Murakami said. (https://www.noaa.gov/education/resource-collections/weather-atmosphere/weather-systems-patterns)

Text 1.3 is an excerpt from Chris Crowe's (2003, p. 31) *Getting Away with Murder*, an award-winning social studies trade book about the kidnapping and killing of a Black teenage boy (Emmett Till) and the subsequent trial and acquittal of his two White killers (Milam and Bryant). Text 1.4 is an excerpt from an online article about weather systems and patterns. Both texts deal with topics that are not commonsensical and, thus, likely less familiar to children. The language used to present these topics is more technical, abstract, dense, and hierarchically structured than the language that children are accustomed to using in their daily social interaction. Simply being able to recognize and decode words in these texts does not ensure their comprehension. Moreover, the sort of knowledge needed for understanding these passages goes beyond the commonsense knowledge to which young children are exposed daily. The texts are difficult to comprehend when listened to. That is, it is beyond the listening comprehension capability of typical adolescents or adults. This is why some reading scholars have argued to move beyond the SVR to embrace a more complex view of reading (CVR), where other factors impacting comprehension—such as domain knowledge, academic language proficiency, knowledge of disciplinary conventions, strategy use, motivation, interest, identity, purpose, and context—become more relevant or prominent in reading comprehension and are given greater attention.

An example of this more complex view of reading can be found in the DRIVE model described by Cartwright and Duke (2019), where reading is compared to driving. Specifically, the DRIVE model tries to explain what happens during reading by likening the reader reading a text to the driver operating a motor vehicle, as shown in Figure 1.1. It identifies many cognitive and sociocultural contributing factors related to the three elements involved in reading—the reader, the text, and the context, drawing particular attention to the roles of the reader, the purpose for reading, and the characteristics of the text being read.

The CVR dovetails with the multidimensional view of reading espoused by other scholars. Kucer (2014), for example, argues that reading is not a monolithic or generalized skill that can be applied unproblematically across contexts (e.g., school vs. home vs. community) or content areas (e.g., science vs. literature vs. music); rather, it is simultaneously cognitive, linguistic, sociocultural, and developmental. Each of these dimensions emphasizes a particular aspect of reading. The linguistic dimension emphasizes text features (e.g., discourse genre, grammatical complexity, format of presentation) that impact the reading process. The cognitive dimension emphasizes the mental processes involved in comprehension and meaning making. The sociocultural dimension emphasizes what the reader brings to the reading task, such as funds of knowledge, prior experience, identity, stamina, interest, motivation, and purpose. The developmental dimension emphasizes the patterns and trajectories of, as well as the support needed for, reading development. Similarly, Lee (2014) identified four dimensions of reading that she believed should receive more attention in K-12 schools: (a) the role of culture in reading, (b) the social and emotional dimensions of such reading, (c) the complexities entailed in such reading, and (d) the infrastructure demands of promoting such reading. Taken together, these dimensions provide us with a deeper, more comprehensive understanding of reading. They can better inform not only our explanations of children's reading successes and failures but also our pedagogical responses to their reading achievements.

In essence, the CVR recognizes that reading is much more than just a cognitive activity; it is deeply embedded in the socioeconomic, cultural, historical, political, racial, and gendered identities of the reader (Paugh & MacPhee, 2023; Yaden & Rogers, 2022). While the CVR seeks to encapsulate "almost anything and everything" that impacts the process of reading, it can get a little too complicated such that its relevance or applicability to classroom

Reading	Driving
Purpose for reading	Destination
Texts	Roads
Text types	Road types
Text structure	Traffic patterns
Organizational signals	Road signs
Other text features	Other road features
Text content	Route
Number of texts	Number of lanes
Reader	Driver and vehicle
Concepts of print and graphics	Knowledge of how vehicle transportation works
Reading motivation & engagement	Ignition & gas
Knowledge for word recognition	Wheels
Word recognition strategies	Tires
Phonological awareness	The treads
Reading fluency	Axles
Vocabulary and morphological knowledge	Struts and shock absorbers
Syntactic knowledge	Chassis
Discourse knowledge	Seats
Text structure knowledge	Traffic pattern knowledge
Content knowledge	Route knowledge
Reader's emotional state	Driver's emotional state
Critical reading	Road reviews
Comprehension monitoring	Dashboard
Strategic reader	Strategic driver
Executive function skills and reading	Multitasking drive
Context for reading	Context for driving
Past & upcoming context	Rearview mirror and headlights
Reading conditions	Weather conditions
Setting for reading	Scenery for driving
Culture of reading	Rules of the road

Figure 1.1 Reading–Driving Analogy (Cartwright & Duke, 2019)

instruction is diminished (or not readily apparent). In other words, if reading involves what is perceived to be "almost anything and everything", as described in, for example, Cartwright and Duke's (2019) CVR, then what should the focus of instruction be, since reading teachers are not likely to have the time or expertise to attend to "almost anything and everything" in the classroom? For this reason, some scholars like Kamhi (2007) have proposed to reject a complex view of reading in favor of a simple view of reading, arguing that the scope of reading should be limited to word recognition only because "it is a skill that can be taught to every typically developing child and to most students with language and learning disabilities" (p. 29). (For a different view on this issue, see, for example, Reinking and Reinking [2022], who contended that phonics in English is incredibly complex and, thus, cannot be fully understood, taught, learned, or applied, cautioning that "mastering phonics in English is a fluid and dynamic process of coordinated concessions to complexity, not checking off mastery of items in a random set of generalizations" [p. 18]). Comprehension, on the other hand, is seen as a much more fluid, variable construct that depends heavily on content knowledge and other variables. In the words of Frank Smith (2004), "comprehension and learning are fundamentally the same, relating the new to the already known" (p. 13). For this reason, Kamhi (2007) and others have suggested that the task of building content knowledge (and by implication, expanding vocabulary)—that is, improving comprehension—should be left to domain-specific content areas such as history/social studies, science, literature, and mathematics. This implies that the responsibility for teaching comprehension belongs to content area teachers (see Chapter 6 for further discussion of this issue).

Factors Impacting Academic Reading

Academic reading, or reading done for the purposes of learning and socialization in academic content areas, is a meaning-making process that involves interaction between the skills and cognitive processes of the reader and the linguistic/discursive characteristics of a text (van den Broek, 2010). According to Kintsch (1998), reading comprehension involves three levels of representation: *the surface, the textbase,* and *the situation model.* When interacting with a text, the reader engages with the surface structure of the text, by processing words and sentences, to construct propositions (concepts or ideas) presented in the text. The propositions are then stitched together to form a textbase of meanings. The textbase formed by these propositions is integrated with the reader's schemata (prior knowledge and experience) to create the situation model, which is an in-depth mental representation consisting of actions and relations described in the text. This construction-integration theory of text comprehension suggests that the extent to which a reader understands a text is influenced by at least four factors (Fang, 2008).

The first is the reader's familiarity with text language and text genre. Fluency with text language at the word, phrase, and sentence levels enables efficient processing of text and contributes substantially to comprehension. Research (e.g., Lonigan, Burgess, & Schatschneider, 2018; Uccelli et al., 2015) has consistently demonstrated a significant, positive relationship between language skills and reading ability among both first and second language learners. For example, Uccelli et al. (2015) found that grades 4–6 children who are more skillful at unpacking morphologically complex words and dense sentences, resolving anaphoric reference, understanding discourse connectives, and recognizing academic register scored higher on reading comprehension measures than those with poorer academic language skills. Similarly, knowledge of text genres (e.g., narrative vs. informational) impacts comprehension in that readers who understand the schematic structure and linguistic features of a text tend to perform better on comprehension and recall tasks than those who do not (Denton et al., 2015). Sadoski, Goetz, and Rodriguez (2000) reported that concrete texts (i.e., texts using concrete/familiar language and non-technical content) result in "overwhelmingly better" gist recall and reading engagement than do abstract texts (i.e., texts using abstract/unfamiliar language and technical content) and that the effect of concreteness is greater for narrative and persuasive texts than for literary stories and expository texts. Osterholm (2006) found that students read mathematical texts with symbols and mathematical texts without symbols differently because symbols have "both a semantic meaning (like ordinary words) and an operational meaning" (p. 341) and students with greater facility in detaching the semantic component of the symbols can work much more quickly with the symbols. In short, familiarity with text characteristics facilitates mental representations of the propositional relations in the text, or the textbase, which can then be integrated with the reader's pre-existing schemata to create the situation model.

The second factor is the reader's prior, or background, knowledge about the topic of the text. This knowledge includes both mundane knowledge about our everyday social/cultural lifeworlds and domain-specific knowledge about specialized topics. Every text makes lexical and grammatical choices that are inherently ambiguous and takes for granted the reader's familiarity with a wide range of unspoken and unwritten facts about the natural and social worlds. It is prior knowledge (about the topic and the context) that enables the reader to clarify potentially ambiguous words or sentences, fill semantic gaps, make intertextual connections, draw reasonable inferences, establish conceptual coherence, and attain a deeper understanding of the text (Willingham, 2017). In other words, prior knowledge helps the reader construct the situation model of what the text is about, including its events, actions, circumstances, and relationships. And because human brain stores knowledge of different topics in separate blocks, the more knowledge a particular block already has, the more new knowledge the block attracts, leading to a wealth of knowledge base on the topic that renders subsequent encounters with the same topic less challenging. This "knowledge attracts knowledge" principle (Willingham, 2006) explains why a student who is knowledgeable about, say, modern Chinese history, is better able to comprehend and interpret texts on the Opium Wars than those who lack knowledge of this historical period. Recent research reviews (Cervetti & Wright, 2020; Smith et al., 2021) attest to this principle, concluding that (a) high levels of background knowledge enable children to better comprehend a text, (b) the effect of knowledge is larger with expository text than with narrative text, (c) knowledge has a compensatory effect on comprehension, meaning that readers weak on word recognition (or language proficiency in general) can still perform well on comprehension if they have sufficient prior knowledge about the text topic, and (d) students tend to rely more heavily on prior knowledge than on the text when information in the text contradicts their prior knowledge. This is perhaps what led Marilyn Adams (2011), a renowned reading researcher, to declare that "knowledge truly is the most powerful determinant of reading comprehension" (p. 10).

The third factor impacting text understanding is the use of cognitive strategies, which facilitates integration of text information with the reader's existing knowledge to form a coherent mental representation of the meaning of the text. Two types of cognitive strategies can be differentiated. One is comprehension strategies. These are generic strategies that can be applied to all texts (regardless of content domains) and are, thus, relevant to all disciplines. They include predicting, inferring, monitoring, summarizing, and questioning. These strategies engender surface-level understanding of text. They help the reader activate prior knowledge, sustain attention, focus on task-relevant goals, suppress irrelevant information, monitor and evaluate text understanding, and regulate reading behaviors for the purpose of constructing meaning (Almasi & Fullerton, 2012; Arrington et al., 2014). The other type is interpretative strategies. These strategies are more discipline-specific and require considerable expertise in specialized domains. They engender deeper, more sophisticated understanding of text that goes beyond literal understanding, or comprehension. Such strategies include, for example, reattention in literary reading (see Chapter 2), contextualization in historical reading (see Chapter 3), transduction in science reading (see Chapter 4), and translation in mathematics reading (see Chapter 5).

Effective use of cognitive strategies hinges on the degree to which the reader understands the text language and the text genre, is familiar with the text topic, and has the motivation to engage with the reading task (Fang, 2008). In fact, there is a symbiosis among knowledge level, language proficiency, and strategy use (Alexander & Judy, 1988). For example, readers who know something about a topic are likely to be familiar with the words/concepts in the text and will be better able to engage in the kind of reading behaviors that can help them delve more deeply into the text and learn more; and these strategic behaviors will, in turn, result in knowing more about the topic and developing greater vocabulary and language skills.

The fourth factor—the reader's motivation, engagement, and agency—also influences the comprehension outcomes of reading. When the reader is motivated to read, s/he becomes more engaged with the plots, ideas, and arguments presented in the text; and this, in turn, results in a better overall understanding of the text (Barber & Klauda, 2020). Texts on topics that relate to the reader's prior experiences, are meaningful to his/her life, or pique his/her interests tend to be more appealing and have the potential to engender deeper engagement with the text. We all know of children who struggle with or detest school-based texts (e.g., textbooks) but are avid readers of popular culture texts (e.g., Pokemon cards, online instructions for video games, rap lyrics), where vocabulary and syntax can be just as challenging as, if not more challenging than, those of school-based textbooks. Because motivation resides in the interaction between the reader and the text (Turner & Paris, 2005), readers who are more familiar with the text topic and the text language/genre and confident in their reading ability are likely to be more motivated to read the text and become more engaged while reading, which, in turn, leads to better overall comprehension outcomes (Guthrie, Wigfield, & Perencevich, 2004; Wolters et al., 2014).

A reader's sense of agency can, likewise, influence his/her transaction with the text. For example, Wiesner, Weinberg, Fulmer, and Barr (2020) studied how an undergraduate student of calculus and a science professor read a calculus textbook excerpt, demonstrating how reading experience was influenced by not only the demands of the text being read but also by the reader's sense of power and authority in relation to the textbook and his/her values surrounding disciplinary knowledge and understanding. Specifically, the researchers found that the science professor positioned himself as someone who has the authority and freedom to critique and tinker with the textbook excerpt because of his role as a college instructor who regularly evaluated textbooks and created curriculum materials, whereas the student participant approached the same excerpt as someone who is expected to fol-low the book's instructions to learn new materials because he did not have a strongly agentive relationship with the textbook. In addition, while the professor focused on "big ideas" and skimmed over known concepts during reading, the student gave uniform attention to the entire text, paying close attention to procedures and facts.

To summarize, a broad array of skills, strategies, knowledge, and disposition interact in synergic ways to bring about an understanding of text. As the knowledge students are expected to engage with becomes more specialized and complex over the years of schooling, the texts they are expected to read also become more abstract, dense, and complex. At the same time, the goal of reading in academic content areas typically becomes more sophisticated, going beyond surface understanding (i.e., comprehension) to include other aspects of understanding such as analysis, evaluation, interpretation, and follow-up action. According to Luke and Freebody (1999), for example, the ability to read academically means not just being able to process verbal or visual signs in the text (code breaker) and to participate in thoughtful con-versation with the text (meaning maker), but also being able to use the text for specific purposes and contexts (text user) and to critically analyze, chal-lenge, and transform the text (text critic). To develop this multi-dimensional ability requires progressively more specialized content knowledge, more ad-vanced language skills, and more sophisticated cognitive strategies, as well as discipline-relevant experiences and motivation (Fang, 2020). In the words of Marilyn Adams (2011), "the capacity to understand and learn from any text depends on approaching it with the language, knowledge, and modes of thought, as well as the reading skill, that it presumes" (p. 9).

The Challenges of Academic Reading

Texts in academic content areas are constructed in patterns of language that differ markedly from those that construct the everyday texts students en-counter in the early years of schooling. This difference is a main source of reading difficulty for many students. It is now well documented, for example, that many children who have been making steady reading progress during the early years of schooling (e.g., K-3) experience a sudden drop in read-ing interest, reading fluency, and reading achievement around fourth grade, and the decline precipitates during the middle and high school years, espe-cially among children who come from low-income families or linguistically minoritized backgrounds. This phenomenon, often referred to as "the fourth-grade slump" (Chall, Jacobs, & Baldwin, 1991), has been attributed, in large part, to students' unfamiliarity with academic texts in curriculum content areas. In early grades, students are exposed primarily to commonsense knowledge, and the texts they read typically deal with topics that are near and dear to them and with events that involve specific individuals and occur in specific times and places. The language that constructs this knowledge is commonsensical and dynamic, close to the language students use in everyday spontaneous conversation with friends, family members, and others with shared experiences and communal understanding.

However, as they advance to upper elementary grades and beyond, students are expected to engage with an increasingly larger volume of academic texts in science, social studies, and other content areas. These texts present more advanced, abstract, and complex knowledge that students are expected to not only assimilate and reproduce but also question and critique. The language used to construct and challenge this specialized knowledge thus becomes more uncommonsensical and static—to wit, technical, dense, abstract, metaphoric, and hierarchically structured (Fang & Schleppegrell, 2008). In this literacy development trajectory, students are expected to develop increasingly sophisticated control over language during the school years, moving from the language of everyday talk to the language for construing and challenging disciplinary knowledge (Christie, 1998; Halliday, 2007; Schleppegrell, 2004). The new demands on both knowledge and language in academic reading augur the need for readers to develop more advanced language skills and more sophisticated literacy strategies so that they can process abstract discourses, bridge semantic gaps, draw inferences, make intertextual connections, and deepen understanding.

To demonstrate the new challenges posed by academic reading, let's compare the two excerpts below, one dealing with a commonsense topic (Text 1.5) and the other an uncommonsense topic (Text 1.6). Text 1.5 is the opening paragraph in *Defiance* (Hobbs, 2005, p. 9), a trade book for elementary students about an 11-year-old boy, Toby Steiner, who is determined to do normal things on his vacation rather than return to hospital for cancer treatment. Text 1.6 is an excerpt from a U.S. high school biology textbook (Biggs et al., 2006, p. 211).

Text 1.5

Toby knew he was in trouble, but the cow didn't. She just kept gazing at him with her huge brown eyes, like she was in love or something. So he went on petting her, even though he wasn't supposed to be there. His mother would have a fit if she knew. She was always having a fit about something, even out here in the country, where they were supposed to be having a vacation.

The cow was really big, and at first, when he'd stopped his bicycle to get a closer look, Toby was a little bit afraid of her. Didn't even know it was a "her" until he saw what was underneath, her huge pink udder swollen with milk. It made him think about the time at the hospital when he was just a little kid, eight or nine. How his eyes kept sliding over to the box of doctor gloves by the side of the sink. He knew very well that he wasn't supposed to touch anything, but they'd left him alone in the examining room for such a long time.

Text 1.6

The cell cycle is controlled by proteins called cyclins and a set of enzymes that attach to the cyclin and become activated. The interaction of these molecules, based on conditions both in the cell's environment and inside the cell, controls the cell cycle. Occasionally, cells lose control of the cell cycle. This uncontrolled dividing of cells can result from the failure to produce certain enzymes, the overproduction of enzymes, or the production of other enzymes at the wrong time. Cancer is a malignant growth resulting from uncontrolled cell division. This loss of control may be caused by environmental factors or by changes in enzyme production.

Text 1.5 describes what Toby did, thought, and felt during his vacation, an ordinary topic to which a child reader can generally and readily relate. The vocabulary is colloquial, consisting mostly of everyday words that elementary-age children typically have little trouble recognizing and understanding. The structure of the sentences is similar to that of the sentences that children use in their everyday lifeworld, with each sentence consisting of 2–3 simple clauses linked together by coordination or subordination. The verbs are in active voice, putting the focus of each sentence on the actor, which is one of the main characters in the story (e.g., *Toby, his mother, the cow*). These characters become the main grammatical participants in the story. They are constructed in simple nouns and subsequently referred to as pronouns (e.g., *he, she*). As a whole, the text unfolds in a natural sequence of events depicting these main characters' thoughts, feelings, and actions.

Text 1.6, on the other hand, deals with a topic that is specialized (i.e., *cell cycle*), requiring domain-specific knowledge to ensure comprehension. It uses scientific vocabulary words that are technical (e.g., *cyclin, protein, enzymes*) or semi-technical (e.g., *division, factors*). More significantly, the text uses many abstract nouns, including *interaction, dividing, failure, production, overproduction, growth, loss,* and *changes.* These nouns, called nominalizations because they derive from verbs (e.g., *interact, divide, fail, produce, grow, lose, change*), enable condensation of chunks of information into grammatical 'things' that then participate in the processes of cell division. Some of these nouns are combined with other grammatical elements (e.g., demonstrative, adjective, prepositional phrase) to form noun phrases (e.g., *the interaction of these molecules*, *this uncontrolled* dividing *of cells*, *this* loss *of control*) that summarize or distill previously presented information and serve as the grammatical subject for the next sentence, in effect creating a discursive flow that contributes to the cohesive texture of the text. Each sentence in the text typically consists of two noun phrases linked by a verb. Some of these noun phrases are long and complex (e.g., *a set of enzymes that attach to the cyclin and become activated*, *a malignant growth resulting from uncontrolled cell division*), containing a large amount of semantic data that increases the informational density of the sentence. The use of passive voice (e.g., *is controlled, be caused*) enables the author to foreground particular concepts or ideas and maintain focus throughout the text. Hedging devices such as *may* and *occasionally* increase the precision of information and the rigor of argument. Overall, the text reads much more technical, abstract, dense, and removed from personal experiences, making it considerably more challenging for students to read and comprehend than Text 1.5.

Adding to the linguistic challenge of academic reading is that most academic texts today are multimodal, juxtaposing verbal, visual, and audio resources, often with digitally integrated hyperlinks. Reading and comprehending multimodal texts requires not only deep knowledge about how verbal grammar constructs meaning, as shown in the analysis above, but also an acute understanding of the structures, or grammar, of visual design—color, perspective, salience, framing, and composition (Kress & van Leeuwen, 2021). Despite repeated calls for greater attention to multimodal reading (e.g., New London Group, 1996; Serafini, 2014), students continue to be challenged by multimodal texts, with many reporting problems such as having difficulty connecting or reconciling information presented verbally versus that presented aurally or visually; becoming navigationally disoriented; getting overwhelmed, confused, and fatigued by the amount of available information; having trouble staying focused and remembering the information in the text; lacking strategies to effectively glean needed information or construct meaning from visual representations; not knowing how to evaluate credibility of sources; and having difficulty detecting authorial voice or ideology in the information presented on digital platforms (Delgado, Vargas, Ackerman, & Salmeron, 2018). These challenges suggest that students need to develop explicit knowledge about how images (e.g., photos, drawings, tables, symbols, diagrams, charts) and layout (e.g., borders, typography, and other graphic design features) can be structured in different ways to make or foreground/

background different kinds of meanings and how verbal, visual, and audio resources are used in electronic formats across different contexts (Kohnen, Mertens, & Boehm, 2020; Unsworth, 2001).

Stages of Reading Development

Going from being able to read Text 1.5 (or Texts 1.1 and 1.2) to being able to read Text 1.6 (or Texts 1.3 and 1.4) does not happen overnight. Rather, the transition is a developmental process that takes many years. During this process, students develop domain knowledge, understanding of disciplinary norms, academic language proficiency, cognitive maturity, genre mastery, reasoning skills, and other capacities that enable them to better cope with the more advanced discursive practices of generalization, abstraction, distillation, interpretation, and argumentation that characterize disciplinary meaning making. Jeanne Chall (1983), the late Harvard reading professor, divided this developmental process into six distinct but potentially overlapping stages—Stage 0 (Pre-reading), Stage 1 (Decoding), Stage 2 (Confirmation and Fluency), Stage 3 (Reading for Learning the New), Stage 4 (Multiple Viewpoints), and Stage 5 (Construction and Reconstruction).

Specifically, Stage 0 is typically attained by children between 6 months and 6 years of age (i.e., birth through kindergarten). In this stage, children pretend to read the text, engaging in what is referred to as "emergent reading" (Sulzby, 1985). Relying heavily on pictures and memory, they are able to retell a brief story or describe specific objects/actions when looking at pages of a picture book previously read to them. They are also able to name letters of the alphabet and recognize environmental print (e.g., the word "stop" in the traffic sign STOP). These abilities are typically developed as a result of being read to by an adult (or an older child) and immersed in a print-rich environment, where they are encouraged to play with books, paper, pencils, crayons, blocks, and letters.

Stage 1 is typically attained by children at the ages 6 and 7 (i.e., first and second grade). In this stage, which is called decoding, children learn the relationship between letters and sounds and between spoken and written words. They are able to read simple texts containing high frequency (or sight) words (e.g., *the, we, can, now, had, that, like*) and phonically regular words (e.g., *mat, hat, cat*). These abilities are typically developed through direct instruction in phonics (letter–sound relationships), independent practice in reading simple or decodable texts, and guided practice in reading slightly more challenging texts.

Stage 2 is typically attained by children between the ages of 7 and 8 years old (i.e., second and third grade). In this stage, children start to consolidate basic decoding skills, sight vocabulary, and use of contextual cues, which enables them to read simple, familiar texts with increasing fluency (i.e., speed, accuracy, and intonation). This ability is developed through direct instruction in more advanced decoding skills, wide reading of interesting/familiar texts at the instructional and independent levels, and guided reading at more challenging levels.

If Stages 0–2 are the "learning-to-read" phase of reading development, as is commonly believed, Stage 3 is often considered the beginning of the "reading-to-learn" phase, when children between the ages of 9 and 13 years old (i.e., grades 4 through 8) are expected to use the reading skills and strategies they have acquired thus far to learn new ideas, develop new knowledge, experience new feelings, and learn new attitudes, albeit generally from one viewpoint. This ability is typically developed through systematic vocabulary study, reading of increasingly more complex narrative and expository texts, and guided study of texts that contain new information and unfamiliar vocabulary and syntax (e.g., textbooks, reference works, trade books, newspapers, magazines).

Stage 4 emerges around the ages of 15–18 years old (i.e., grades 9–12). In this stage, children begin to develop multiple viewpoints. They can appreciate works arguing different points of view. They can also decide how quickly or slowly to read and whether to skim or closely study a text. These abilities are typically developed through systematic study of academic vocabulary words, as well as wide reading and close study of complex texts in a broad range of content areas (e.g., science, mathematics, history), newspapers, and magazines.

Stage 5 is typically associated with adulthood, 18+ years old (i.e., college and beyond). During this stage, students become mature, efficient readers. They can read and analyze multiple texts, assimilate and evaluate information, synthesize across sources to form their own understanding, critique the knowledge presented in the text, and create new knowledge. They know what to read versus what not to read as a means of efficiently meeting the goals of their reading. These abilities are typically developed through wide reading and close examination of difficult materials and writing from multiple sources to demonstrate knowledge integration and multiple perspectives.

According to Chall, all children go through these stages, albeit at different rates. This means that although the suggested stages are general trajectories that all normally developing children go through, they do not necessarily reach the same stage at the same time. For example, while a 6-year-old child is typically expected to be an emergent reader (stage 0), another child of the same age may already be reading at the decoding (stage 1) or even fluency stage (stage 2). Moreover, children do not go through these stages in a discrete, linear, or sequential order; instead, the development is recursive and spiral, with boundaries between the stages often becoming indistinct. A child's reading performance depends on a multitude of factors, including the difficulty level of the text (e.g., language complexity, content familiarity), the purpose of the task (e.g., reading for enjoyment vs reading for specific information), the child's interest in and motivation for the task, and the amount and quality of support provided to the child.

More recently, Shanahan and Shanahan (2008) proposed a pyramid-like, but much less nuanced, model of reading/literacy development for PreK-12 contexts. The base of the pyramid represents "basic literacy", which consists of a set of highly generalizable basic skills that underlies virtually all reading tasks. These skills include concepts about print (e.g., knowledge about book orientation and directionality of print; understanding that print conveys a message; distinction among letters, words, and sentences; knowledge of the alphabetic system; awareness of common punctuation marks such as comma, period, and exclamation), phonological awareness, basic decoding, knowledge of high frequency words, being able to read simple texts with appropriate speed and prosody, and understanding basic text structure for stories versus informational texts. These skills are typically mastered by children before the end of third grade; but for some students, the development may last well into middle school.

In upper elementary grades, students begin to develop "intermediate literacy", which occupies the middle portion of the pyramid, by adding more sophisticated literacy skills that are common to many, but not all, reading tasks. These skills "are not as widely applicable to different texts and reading situations, but nor are they particularly linked to disciplinary specializations" (p. 44). They include decoding multisyllabic words, recognizing less common punctuation marks (e.g., colon, split quotes), knowledge of a larger corpus of vocabulary terms, greater cognitive endurance to maintain attention to more extended discourse, generic comprehension strategies (e.g., inferencing, monitoring, rereading, looking for context clues), understanding more varied genres and more complex forms of text structure (e.g., circular plots, problem–solution, cause–effect). These skills are typically mastered by students toward the end of middle school, but it is not uncommon to see some high school students still struggling to develop them.

Finally, during middle and high schools, students begin to develop more advanced literacy skills that are anchored in specific disciplines such as science, mathematics, history, and literature. These specialized reading routines and language uses, which Shanahan and Shanahan (2008) called "disciplinary literacy" and are represented in the top portion of the pyramid, are needed to cope with the more demanding texts of content area learning. The difficulty of disciplinary texts lies not only in the content they construe, which is technical and complex, but also in the way language and other semiotic resources are used to package and present this content. Comprehending these texts requires not only basic and intermediate literacy skills but also understanding of the knowledge, assumptions, routines, skills, and habits of mind that experts within specific disciplines use in constructing and interpreting meaning.

The pyramid model of reading/literacy development illustrates the increasing specialization of reading skills. It shows that as the knowledge that students are expected to engage with becomes less commonsensical and more specialized, the reading skills needed for interacting with and comprehending these texts also become more sophisticated, moving from the more basic and generalizable to the less generalizable and more specialized. This developmental trajectory mirrors the developmental path charted by Chall (1983), and both have been influential in shaping the discussion about academic reading and ways to promote its development.

Language, Reading, and Learning

School or disciplinary knowledge is presented to students primarily through written texts. These texts are constructed in patterns of language that become progressively more technical, abstract, dense, and metaphoric as the knowledge students are expected to learn becomes less mundane and more specialized. To learn school/disciplinary knowledge, students must be able to read (and write) the texts that present this knowledge; and to read/write these texts effectively, students must develop the capacity to handle the language that is often the primary medium for constructing the texts. As Hasan (1996) wrote, "Academic disciplines are, after all, largely a constellation of certain types of discourse, and in the end, what counts as knowing a discipline is the ability to participate successfully in the discourses of that discipline" (p. 398). Halliday (2016) echoed this point, noting that "[t]he core of all subject learning in school is the language that is used to learn with and to teach with" (p. 75). In discussing science, Lemke (2002) spoke of the intertwined nature of language and content, noting that "[t]here is no science without language, and no mastery of scientific English separate from the comprehension of some set of scientific concepts" (p. 42). For this reason, literacy, narrowly defined in this book as the ability to read and write, is considered a language-based practice and justifiably treated as part of language development.

According to Halliday (2006), for example, there are three critical moments of language development in children. The first moment emerges during infancy, at the ages of 1–2, when children move from infant protolanguage to mother tongue. During this process, children start to construe classes, developing the ability to generalize from proper names (e.g., *Charlie*) to common names (e.g., *pet/dog*). These common names refer to phenomena that are directly accessible to the senses, making possible commonsense theories of knowledge. The second critical moment occurs at 4–6 years, when children move from the grammar of everyday spoken language to the grammar of written language (i.e., language for reading and writing). During this process, children reconstrue experience in more abstract ways, demonstrating a capacity to handle entities that have no perceptual correlates (e.g., *friendship*, *idea*). This capacity for abstraction signals the onset of literacy, suggesting that children in this stage can process abstract signs such as written language and are ready to move into educational forms of knowledge. The third critical moment of language development takes place around puberty, at the ages of 9–13, when children move from the grammar of written language to the language of academic content areas, also referred to as academic language, disciplinary language, or metaphoric language. During this process, children develop the ability to use grammatical metaphor, that is, to replace one grammatical class (e.g., adjective: *frequent*; verb: *the pain grows*) with another (e.g., noun: *frequency*; adjective: *the growing pain*). They learn to reconstrue experience in a more theoretical, or metaphoric, mode, one that is grammatically incongruent with the commonsense construal of the world. For example, in the congruent (i.e., everyday) construal of experience/knowledge, happenings are realized grammatically as verbs, qualities as adjectives, things as nouns, and logical relations as conjunctions; but in non-congruent construals, qualities (e.g., *diverse*) are realized as nouns (e.g., *diversity*), happenings (e.g., *to increase water supply*) as nouns (e.g., *the increase in water supply*) or adjectives (e.g., *the increasing water supply*), and logical relations (e.g., *because*) as nouns (e.g., *the reason*), verbs (e.g., *trigger*), or prepositions (e.g., *with, for*). This capacity for metaphoric construal of experience suggests that children are ready to engage with the technical knowledge of academic content areas.

These three critical moments of language development have been characterized by Halliday (2006) as "three successive waves of energy", with each wave enlarging children's meaning potential and at the same time taking them one step away from their concrete everyday experience. As children move from one wave to the next, they do not let go of their previously learned grammar. Rather, the three kinds of grammar coalesce and are "enshrined in the grammatical construction of the text" (p. 46). From this perspective, literacy development can be viewed as the braiding of these three strands of language, represented in Figure 1.2 (Fang, 2012b). During the preliteracy stage (roughly ages birth through 4), children learn the mother tongue (i.e., everyday spoken language) for construing commonsense knowledge. This language development takes place primarily at home in interaction with family members. During the basic, or functional, literacy stage (roughly ages 4 through 9), children learn to control written language and the abstract mode of meaning that enable them to participate functionally in a print-literate culture. This language development takes place mainly from pre-school through third grade, with family and peer groups playing an equally important role. During the advanced, or disciplinary, literacy stage (roughly ages 9 through 18), children begin to cope with discourse that is grounded in grammatical metaphor. This type of discourse is typically found in the academic subjects of secondary and tertiary schooling, where specialized, technical knowledge becomes the focus of study. Advanced literacy builds on, rather than excludes, the language skills (e.g., generalization, abstraction)

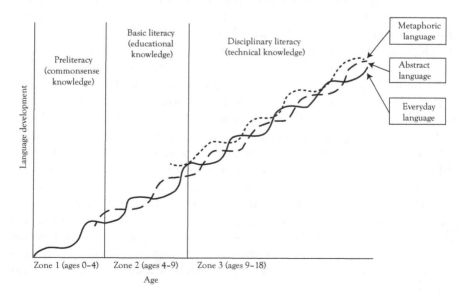

Figure 1.2 Language and Literacy Development (Fang, 2012b, p. 22)

and knowledge (commonsense, educational) that have been developed during the preliteracy and basic literacy stages and are continuing to develop throughout adulthood. In fact, every use of language (i.e., text) is a product of simultaneous braiding of the three language strands, with some texts (or certain parts of a text) drawing more or less heavily on certain strand(s) than do others (Fang, 2012b). The demarcation lines among the three stages are often blurry, meaning that there is considerable variability among the same-age children in their language and literacy development.

Not only does language become progressively more abstract and metaphoric as the knowledge children are expected to engage with becomes more advanced and specialized across the school years, it also varies from one academic discipline to another and among the subfields within the same discipline. As Macken-Horarik, Love, and Unsworth (2011, p. 17) stated, "Language resources don't just become more complex and abstract as students progress through the years; they pattern and co-pattern at all levels of choice in distinct ways" in response to changing contextual configurations related to subject matter, social relations, and modes of communication. While it is widely recognized that each academic discipline has its own lingo, it is not always apparent to people that the grammar is also different across disciplines (Fang & Schleppegrell, 2008). For example, poets create multilayered language play with graphology, phonology, words, syntax, and semantics in their texts (see Chapter 2). Historians, on the other hand, use abstract language to enable the shift from chronological retelling of past events to evidence-based interpretations of these events (see Chapter 3). Scientists construe theoretical explanations about the natural world through dense nominal syntax with technical and abstract vocabulary (see Chapter 4), and mathematicians prove axioms, theorems, lemmas, corollaries, and relationships by drawing simultaneously on the resources of natural language, mathematics symbols, and visual displays (see Chapter 5). These discursive differences reflect the fundamental differences in the ways different disciplines create, communicate, consume, and critique knowledge, as the next four chapters of this book will demonstrate.

Research has suggested a robust relationship between language/reading skills and content area learning. For example, Espin and Deno (1993) examined the relationship between reading proficiency and content area learning among 121 tenth-grade students in a rural U.S. high school. They found moderate to high correlations between students' reading measures (reading of multiple English and science textbook passages and a standardized reading test) and their performance on a classroom study task, grade point average, and a variety of achievement test scores. Demps and Onwuegbuzie (2001) found that Georgia high school seniors' eight-grade scores on a standardized reading test were significantly related to their performance on the writing, language arts, math, social studies, and science subtests of the Georgia High School Graduation Test. Internationally, Korpershoek, Kuyper, and Van Der Werf (2015) reported that Dutch secondary students' reading skills were positively related to their final exam grades on mathematics, physics, and chemistry. Taken together, these and numerous other studies suggest that students with lower levels of reading proficiency face challenges in content area learning, whereas those excelling in reading are more likely to achieve success in schooling and throughout life.

Toward a Disciplinary Literacy Approach to Academic Reading

A language-based theory of learning, as described above, implies that the process of learning to read does not end in third grade or even elementary schooling; rather, students need to continue to develop their reading ability in order to handle the more technical and specialized content, as well as the more abstract, dense, and metaphoric language, of academic texts in curriculum content areas. Berman and Biancarosa (2005) spoke to this need when they wrote that while most adolescent learners can read simple, everyday texts, many "frequently cannot understand specialized or more advanced texts" and "are unprepared to meet the higher literacy demands of today's colleges and workplaces" (p. 6).

There is no doubt that students need continuing support beyond third grade or elementary school in their reading development. Such support has traditionally been provided through an approach called content area literacy (e.g., Readence, Bean, & Bean, 2019; Vacca, Vacca, & Mraz, 2016). The approach uses conceptual and instructional frameworks that are grounded in literacy theory, seeing reading/literacy as a set of tools or strategies to be imported into the disciplines to improve reading/writing in content area classrooms (Dillon et al., 2010). It is rooted in the beliefs that the cognitive requirements for reading and learning from texts are essentially the same regardless of content domains and that the primary difference among school subjects is in their content (Shanahan & Shanahan, 2012). As such, content area literacy emphasizes the acquisition of basic reading skills (e.g., decoding, vocabulary, fluency) and comprehension strategies (e.g., identifying main ideas, predicting, summarizing, annotating, making inferences, concept mapping, questioning, visualizing), as these skills and strategies are believed to aid students in extracting information from texts in any content area and hence the learning and retention of content in school subjects.

The approach, with its focus on literacy goals and its disregard for disciplinary ideologies and epistemologies, has contributed to bifurcation of reading/literacy from content area learning, creating an artificial divide between reading/literacy teachers, who are seen as responsible for teaching students to learn to read/write academic and disciplinary texts, and content area teachers, who see themselves as merely responsible for teaching students to master the content of their discipline. For example, Chandler-Olcott, Doerr, Hinchman, and Masingila (2015) found that secondary mathematics teachers made selective use of curriculum materials to bypass or reduce these materials' literacy demands by "mining the materials for particular problems, reading to and interpreting texts for students, and supplementing investigations in ways that undermined the materials' investigative orientation and instructional goals" (p. 455). The approach, according to Hinchman and O'Brien (2019), "undermines the intended purposes for subject-area study in schools, and, thus, subject-area teachers' maintenance of expertise, student interest, and engagement" (p. 527). As a result, it has paid limited dividends. For example, results from the 2019 National Assessment of Educational Progress (see Table 1.1) show that roughly two-thirds of students in grades 4, 8, and 12 are still struggling with academic reading—i.e., reading below the proficiency level, with proficiency for grade 12 defined as the ability to "locate and integrate information using sophisticated analyses of the meaning and form of the text" and to "provide specific text support for inferences, interpretive arguments and comparisons within and across texts" (https://www. nationsreportcard.gov/highlights/reading/2019/). These statistics have not changed substantially over the past 25 years.

In response to this stagnation in reading growth, scholars (e.g., Fang & Schleppegrell, 2008, 2010; Moje, 2008; Shanahan & Shanahan, 2008) have called for a different approach to promoting academic reading in content areas. The approach, called disciplinary literacy, uses the conceptual and instructional frameworks grounded in disciplinary learning theory. It views reading/writing not merely as a set of tools or strategies for learning from texts but as an integral part of disciplinary practices. It recognizes that disciplines

Table 1.1 National Assessment of Educational Progress 2019 Reading Achievement Data

Grade Level	Below Basic	Basic	Proficient	Advanced
Fourth	34%	31%	26%	9%
Eighth	27%	39%	29%	4%
Twelfth	30%	33%	31%	6%

differ not only in content but also in the ways this content is produced, communicated, critiqued, and consumed. It promotes the development of students' ability to "engage in social, semiotic, and cognitive practices consistent with those of content experts" (Fang, 2012b, p. 19). As such, the approach focuses more on disciplinary outcomes (e.g., learning key concepts, big ideas, unifying themes, core practices, and habits of mind related to a discipline) rather than discrete literacy outcomes (e.g., learning academic vocabulary, identifying main ideas, looking for context clues, drawing inferences, using a graphic organizer, making comparison and contrast, providing a summary). It abandons the "one-size-fits-all" model of basic skills and generic strategies commonly seen in content area literacy instruction and places, instead, an emphasis on learning to employ the same habits of mind used by disciplinary experts in their literate practices. These habits of mind include discipline-legitimated ways of engaging in reading, writing, listening, speaking, thinking, reasoning, and problem solving within a given discipline. Thus, instead of focusing on basic skills and generic strategies, disciplinary literacy emphasizes the teaching of discipline-specific, as well as discipline-relevant, knowledge, understanding, skills, strategies, practices, and habits of mind (International Literacy Association, 2017). A summary comparison between content area literacy and disciplinary literacy instructional approaches is presented in Table 1.2.

This shift toward a discipline-based approach to academic reading/literacy instruction reflects the growing recognition within the reading/literacy education community that literacy practices vary across disciplines and that these practices are best learned and taught within each discipline (Hinchman & O'Brien, 2019). According to noted sociolinguist Ken Hyland (2020), academic disciplines are highly specialized fields of inquiry where people with shared norms and habits of mind engage in similar professional practices. They differ in the extent of consensus on structure of inquiry and the knowledge it produces. "Mature" sciences, such as physics and mathematics, are those with well-developed paradigms, and they have clear and unambiguous ways of defining, ordering, and investigating knowledge; on the contrary, disciplines such as sociology and literature are characterized by a high level of disagreement with respect to what constitutes knowledge, what appropriate methods of inquiry are, what criteria are applied to determine acceptable findings, what theories are proven, and the importance of problems to study (Bernstein, 2000). Thus, each discipline is a distinct discourse community with its own ways of producing, structuring, communicating, critiquing, teaching, and learning knowledge. Members within the same discourse community have shared goals, assumptions, values, worldviews, methods, rhetorical conventions, stylistic preferences, and other patterns of

Table 1.2 Comparing Content Area Literacy and Disciplinary Literacy Approaches to Academic Reading

Content Area Literacy	Disciplinary Literacy
Recognizes that disciplines differ only in content	Recognizes that disciplines differ not just in content but also in the ways this content is produced, communicated, and consumed
Views reading/writing as a set of tools or strategies to be imported into the disciplines to improve content learning from texts	Views reading/writing as an essential and integral part of disciplinarians' social practices
Believes that the cognitive requirements of reading and learning from texts are essentially the same regardless of content areas	Believes that each discipline is a distinct discourse community with its own ways of generating, structuring, communicating, evaluating, teaching, and learning knowledge
Uses the conceptual and instructional frameworks grounded in literacy learning theory	Uses the conceptual and instructional frameworks grounded in disciplinary learning theory
Focuses on discrete literacy outcomes such as identifying main ideas, learning academic vocabulary, drawing inferences, asking questions, and making comparison/contrast	Focuses on disciplinary outcomes such as learning core concepts, big ideas, essential practices, unifying themes, and habits of mind
Emphasizes building content knowledge about the discipline	Emphasizes building an understanding of how knowledge is created, communicated, and consumed in the discipline

interaction. They have a unifying purpose, address "similar problems about a similarly conceived external world", adopt similar approaches, establish incentives and forms of cooperation around a subject matter and its problems, and display "similar preferences for particular argument forms, lexical choices and discourse structures" (Hyland, 2004, p. 177). In the words of Christie and Maton (2011, p. 5),

> Membership in a disciplinary community offers shared, intersubjective bases for determining ends and means, approaches and procedures, ways to judge disciplinary findings, the bases on which to agree or disagree, and problems apprehended (if not always solved, since many require hard work and are at times intractable), as well as providing shared

pleasures in intellectual pursuits and the excitements of possible new understandings emerging from jointly constructed knowledge of many kinds.

In other words, each community of experts establishes and maintains its own set of concepts, principles, processes, standards, and genres for inquiries and debates in knowledge building. These discipline-legitimated conventions shape—and evolve in response to—new developments in the discipline. They reflect the unique epistemology, methodology, and goals that characterize each discipline. Induction into a disciplinary community, therefore, involves learning "the organization of knowledge and of intellectual and educational practices for its creation, teaching and learning" (Christie & Maton, 2011, p. 4). Becoming literate in a discipline means not only the acquisition of a body of content knowledge about the discipline but also an understanding of how this body of knowledge is produced, shaped, communicated, renovated, and understood.

For this reason, Shanahan and Shanahan (2008) have proposed that as students advance in their schooling, reading/writing instruction "should become increasingly disciplinary, reinforcing and supporting student performance with the kinds of texts and interpretive standards that are needed in the various disciplines or subjects" (p. 57). Similarly, McConachie and Petrosky (2010) argued that reading (and literacy) at the secondary level "must be anchored in the specifics of individual disciplines" (p. 15) and its development should involve simultaneous engagement with disciplinary content (e.g., core concepts, big ideas, key relationships) and disciplinary habits of mind (e.g., ways of reading, writing, viewing, representing, listening, speaking, thinking, reasoning, and problem solving consistent with those of content experts). This approach to academic reading, clarified Rainey and Moje (2012), "does not seek to make experts of teenage students"; rather, it "begins to help students to read, write, and think in ways that are aligned with experts in the field" (p. 74). At the same time, it recognizes the challenges of, and, thus, does not advocate, wholesale importation of professional disciplinary practices to content area classrooms. These challenges include the content problem (e.g., certain content or practices of the discipline may be too difficult for adolescents to grasp), the resource problem (e.g., K-12 schools may not have the personnel, tools, or other resources to engage in some of the activities that are productive for disciplinary experts), the ethical problem (e.g., some practices of the disciplinary community that contribute to the growth of the discipline may be ethically problematic to replicate in the classroom), and the goals problem (e.g., activities or practices that may be useful for the production of disciplinary knowledge—such as those taking months or years to complete—may be inappropriate or detrimental for promoting student growth in the classroom). A more detailed discussion of these problems in the context of mathematics teaching and learning can be found in Weber, Dawkins, and Mejia-Ramos (2020).

A disciplinary literacy approach to academic reading has several distinct benefits. Because the approach pays due respect to disciplinary goals and ways of knowing, it is more likely to be embraced by content area teachers, who are expected to teach reading in their subject but have perennially been resistant to the responsibility. It is also more likely to entice and engage students in disciplinary study and promote their content learning and advanced literacy development at the same time. Ultimately, it will help usher students into discipline-legitimated ways of thinking, knowing, communicating, critiquing, and consuming, which are essential to productive, powerful learning and socialization in the disciplines. As noted literacy education scholar Judith Langer (2011) opined, understanding and using disciplinary markers of literacy not only "fosters a sense of belonging within a discipline and contributes to the confidence a learner needs in order to explore and question ideas that go beyond the given" but also "permits individuals to understand the oral and written texts they encounter more deeply and helps them connect and build larger constructs, question faulty ones, hone their thinking within the field, and connect and use their knowledge across disciplines and life contexts" (p. 3).

Conclusion

Reading is fundamental to the development of both academic competence (i.e., the ability to effectively learn and perform in academic subjects) and social understanding (i.e., the ability to empathize with others' emotion, cognition, and motivation). It is a complex process impacted by a multitude of factors related to the text (e.g., linguistic and conceptual complexities), the reader (prior knowledge, identity, language proficiency, strategy use, motivation), and the context (e.g., purpose, task demand, support). Past efforts to improve students' academic reading have yielded limited dividends, leading to calls for alternative approaches. One of these new approaches is disciplinary literacy. The approach recognizes that "[e]ach form of knowledge has a distinctive set of 'big ideas', of warrants, and of ways to represent ideas and evidence and thus requires students to navigate across different genres and discourse communities" (Bain, 2012, p. 515). It foregrounds the goals, the ethos, the epistemologies, and the methodologies of the disciplines, helping students learn discipline-legitimated ways of producing and consuming texts and of creating and renovating knowledge. It values "teachers' perspectives, compelling inquiry, authentic disciplinary texts, supportive practices, [and] gradually withdrawn scaffolds" and sees students as capable of using available resources to engage in new learning (Hinchman & O'Brien, 2019, p. 532). As such, the approach is believed to be a more promising way of promoting advanced literacy development, with the potential to not only deepen students' content learning but also develop their ability to read and write academic/disciplinary texts in more powerful ways. As Langer (2011) noted, a disciplinary literacy approach to academic reading creates more authentic, motivating contexts in which students can engage productively in "learning the content, language, and ways of thinking and communicating that are considered signs of 'knowing' within each discipline" (p. 157). The rest of this book demonstrates how this approach can be enacted across the core school-based subjects of literature, history, science, and mathematics.

Reflection and Application

1. What is reading? How does an individual's reading ability develop over his/her lifespan?
2. What is a text? What does it take to comprehend or understand a text? How is academic reading similar to and different from everyday reading?
3. What is the relationship among language, reading, and content area learning? Why can reading/literacy be considered part of language development?
4. What is disciplinary literacy? Why is a disciplinary literacy approach needed in academic reading instruction? What are the affordances and challenges associated with the approach? In what ways is the approach different from (and more advantageous than) the traditional approach to teaching reading in academic content areas?
5. How does the discussion of "simple view of reading" versus "complex view of reading" in the chapter illuminate—and help you make sense of—the current debates around "the science of reading" or other pedagogical recommendations for reading?

References

Adams, M. (2011). Advancing our students' language and literacy: The challenge of complex texts. *American Educator*, winter issue, 3–11, & 53.

Alexander, P., & Judy, J. (1988). The interaction of domain-specific and strategic knowledge in academic performance. *Review of Educational Research*, 58, 375–404.

Almasi, J., & Fullerton, S. (2012). *Teaching strategic processes in reading* (2nd ed.). New York: Guilford Press.

Arrington, N., Kulesz, P., Francis, D., & Fletcher, K. (2014). The contribution of attentional control and working memory to reading comprehension and decoding. *Scientific Studies of Reading, 18*(5), 325–346.

Bain, R. (2012). Using disciplinary literacy to develop coherence in history teacher education: The clinical rounds project. *The History Teacher, 45*(4), 513–532.

Barber, A., & Klauda, S. (2020). How reading motivation and engagement enable reading achievement: Policy implications. *Policy Insights from the Behavioral and Brian Sciences, 7*(1), 27–34.

Bavishi, A., Slade, M., & Levy, B. (2016). A chapter a day: Association of book reading with longevity. *Social Science & Medicine, 164,* 44–48.

Berman, I., & Biancarosa, G. (2005). *Reading to achieve: A governor's guide to adolescent literacy.* Washington, DC: NGA Center for Best Practices.

Bernstein, B. (2000). *Pedagogy, symbolic control and identity: Theory, research, critique* (rev. ed.). London: Rowman & Littlefield.

Biggs, A., Hagins, W., Kapicka, C., Lundgren, L., Rillero, P., Tallman, K., Zike, D., & National Geographic Society (2006). *Biology: The dynamics of life* (Florida Edition). Chicago, IL: McGraw-Hill/Glencoe.

Brown, M. (2004). *The world of Arthur and friends: Six Arthur adventures in one volume.* New York: Little, Brown and Company.

Cartwright, K., & Duke, N. (2019). The DRIVE model of reading: Making the complexity of reading accessible. *The Reading Teacher, 73*(1), 7–15.

Cervetti, G., & Wright, T. (2020). The role of knowledge in understanding and learning from text. In E. Moje, P. Afflerbach, P. Enciso, & N. Lesaux (Eds.), *Handbook of Reading Research* (Vol. 5, pp. 237–260). New York: Routledge.

Chall, J. (1983). *Stages of reading development.* New York: McGraw-Hill.

Chall, J., Jacobs, V., & Baldwin, L. (1991). *The reading crisis: Why poor children fall behind.* Cambridge, MA: Harvard University Press.

Chandler-Olcott, K., Doerr, H., Hinchman, K., & Masingila, J. (2015). Bypass, augment, or integrate: How secondary mathematics teachers address the literacy demands of standards-based curriculum materials. *Journal of Literacy Research, 47*(4), 439–472.

Christie, F. (1998). Learning the literacies of primary and secondary schooling. In F. Christie & R. Mission (Eds.), *Literacy and schooling* (pp. 47–73). London: Routledge.

Christie, F., & Maton, K. (2011). *Disciplinarity: Functional linguistic and sociological perspectives.* London: Bloomsbury.

Crowe, C. (2003). *Getting away with murder: The true story of the Emmett Till case.* New York: Phyllis Fogelman Books.

Cunningham, A., & Stanovich, K. (1998). What reading does for the mind. *American Educator*, Spring/Summer, 1–8.

Delgado, P., Vargas, C., Ackerman, R., & Salmeron, L. (2018). Don't throw away your printed books: A meta-analysis on the effects of reading media on reading comprehension. *Educational Research Review, 25*, 23–38.

Demps, D., & Onwuegbuzie, A. (2001). The relationship between eighth-grade reading scores and achievement on the Georgia High School Graduation Test. *Research in the Schools, 8*(2), 1–9.

Denton, C., Enos, M., York, M., Francis, D., Barnes, M., Kulesz, P., & Carter, A. (2015). Text processing differences in adolescent adequate and poor comprehenders reading accessible and challenging narrative and informational text. *Reading Research Quarterly, 50*(4), 393–416.

Dillon, D., O'Brien, D., Sato, M., & Kelly, C. (2010). Professional development and teacher education for reading instruction. In M. Kamil, D. Pearson, E. Moje, & P. Afflerbach (Eds.), *Handbook of reading research* (Vol. 4, pp. 629–660). New York: Routledge.

Duke, N., & Cartwright, K. (2021). The science of reading progresses: Communicating advances beyond the simple view of reading. *Reading Research Quarterly, 56*(S1), S25–S44.

Espin, C., & Deno, S. (1993). Performance in reading from content area text as an indicator of achievement. *Remedial and Special Education, 14*(6), 47–59.

Fairclough, N. (2003). *Analysing discourse: Textual analysis for social research*. London: Routledge.

Fang, Z. (2008). Going beyond the 'Fab Five': Helping students cope with the unique linguistic challenges of expository reading in intermediate grades. *Journal of Adolescent and Adult Literacy, 51*(6), 476–487.

Fang, Z. (2012a). Approaches to developing content area literacies: A synthesis and a critique. *Journal of Adolescent and Adult Literacy, 56*(2), 111–116.

Fang, Z. (2012b). Language correlates of disciplinary literacy. *Topics in Language Disorders, 32*(1), 19–34.

Fang, Z. (2020). Toward a linguistically informed, responsive, and embedded pedagogy in secondary literacy instruction. *Journal of World Languages, 6*(1–2), 70–91.

Fang, Z., & Schleppegrell, M. (2008). *Reading in secondary content areas: A language-based pedagogy*. Ann Arbor, MI: The University of Michigan Press.

Fang, Z., & Schleppegrell, M. (2010). Disciplinary literacies across content areas: Supporting secondary reading through functional language analysis. *Journal of Adolescent and Adult Literacy, 53*(7), 587–597.

Fletcher, J., & Lyons, R. (1998). Reading: A research-based approach. In W. Evers (Ed.), *What's gone wrong in America's classrooms?* (pp. 50–77). Stanford, CA: Hoover Institution Press.

Goodman, K. (1986). *What is whole in whole language?* Portsmouth, NH: Heinemann.

Goodwin, A., & Jimenez, R. (2020). The science of reading: Supports, critiques, and questions. *Reading Research Quarterly, 55* (S1), S7–S16.

Gough, P., & Tunmer, W. (1986). Decoding, reading, and reading disability. *Remedial and Special Education, 7*(1), 6–10.

Guthrie, J., Wigfield, A., & Perencevich, K. (2004). *Motivating reading comprehension: Concept-oriented reading instruction.* Mahwah, NJ: Erlbaum.

Halliday, M. (2006). *The language of science* (edited by J. Webster). New York: Continuum.

Halliday, M. (2007). *Language and education* (edited by J. Webster). London: Continuum.

Halliday, M. (2002). On grammar and grammatics. In J. Webster (Ed.), *On grammar* (Vol. 1 in *Collected works of M.A.K. Halliday*, pp. 384–417). London: Continuum.

Halliday, M. (2016). *Aspects of language and learning.* London: Springer.

Hasan, R. (1996). Literacy, everyday talk and society. In R. Hasan & G. Williams (Eds.), *Literacy in society* (pp. 377–424) London: Longman.

Hinchman, K., & O'Brien, D. (2019). Disciplinary literacy: From infusion to hybridity. *Journal of Literacy Research, 51*(4), 525–536.

Hirsch, E.D. Jr. (2005). Reading comprehension requires knowledge—of words and the world. In Z. Fang (Ed.), *Literacy teaching and learning: Current issues and trends* (pp.121–130). Columbus, OH: Pearson.

Hirsch, E.D. (2006). *The knowledge deficit: Closing the shocking education gap for American children.* Boston, MA: Houghton Mifflin.

Hobbs, V. (2005). *Defiance.* New York: Farrar Straus & Giroux.

Hoover, W., & Tunmer, W. (2021). The primacy of science in communicating advances in the science of reading. *Reading Research Quarterly, 57*(2), 399–408.

Hyland, K. (2004). *Disciplinary discourses: Social interactions in academic writing.* Ann Arbor, MI: University of Michigan Press.

Hyland, K. (2020). *Disciplinary identities: Individuality and community in academic discourse.* Beijing: Foreign Language Teaching and Research Press.

International Literacy Association (2017). *Content area and disciplinary literacies: Strategies and frameworks.* Newark, DE: Author.

Kamhi, A. (May, 2007). Knowledge deficits: The true crisis in education. *The ASHA LEADER*, pp. 28–29.

Kinney, J. (2022). *Diary of a wimpy kid: Diper Overlode*. New York: Amulet Books.

Kintsch, W. (1998). *Comprehension: A paradigm for cognition*. Cambridge, MA: Cambridge University Press.

Kohnen, A., Mertens, G., & Boehm, S. (2020). Can middle schoolers learn to read the web like experts? Possibilities and limits of a strategy-based intervention. *Journal of Media Literacy Education, 12*(2), 64–79.

Korpershoek, H., Kuyper, H. & Van Der Werf, G. (2015). The relation between students' math and reading ability and their mathematics, physics, and chemistry examination grades in secondary education. *International Journal of Science and Mathematics Education, 13*(5), 1013–1034.

Kress, G. (2003). *Literacy in the new media age*. London: Routledge.

Kress, G., & van Leeuwen, T. (2021). *Reading images: The grammar of visual design* (3rd ed.). London: Routledge.

Kucer, S. (2014). *Dimensions of literacy: A conceptual base for teaching reading and writing in school settings* (4th ed.). New York: Routledge.

Langer, J. (2011). *Envisioning knowledge: Building literacy in the academic disciplines*. New York: Teachers College Press.

Lee, C. (2014). The multi-dimensional demands of reading in the disciplines. *Journal of Adolescent and Adult Literacy, 58*(1), 9–15.

Lemke, J. (2002). Multimedia semiotics: Genres for science education and scientific literacy. In M. J. Schleppegrell & M. C. Colombi (Eds.), *Developing advanced literacy in first and second language: Meaning with power* (pp. 21–44). Mahwah, NJ: Lawrence Erlbaum.

Lonigan, C., Burgess, S., & Schatschneider, C. (2018). Examining the Simple View of Reading with elementary school children: Still simple after all these years. *Remedial and Special Education, 39*, 260–273.

Luke, A., & Freebody, P. (1999). A map of possible practices: Further notes on the four resource models. *Practically Primary, 4*(2), 5–8.

Macken-Horarik, M., Love, K., & Unsworth, L. (2011). A grammatics 'good enough' for school English in the 21st century: Four challenges in realizing the potential. *Australian Journal of Language and Literacy, 34*(1), 9–23.

Martin, J. (1989). *Factual writing*. Oxford University Press.

McConachie, S., & Petrosky, T. (2010). *Content matters: A disciplinary literacy approach to improving student learning*. San Francisco: Jossey-Bass.

Moje, E. (2008). Foregrounding the disciplines in secondary literacy teaching and learning: A call for change. *Journal of Adolescent and Adult Literacy, 52*(2), 96–107.

New London Group (1996). A pedagogy of multiliteracies: Designing social futures. *Harvard Educational Review, 66*(1), 60–92.

Osterholm, M. (2006). Characterizing reading comprehension of mathematical texts. *Educational Studies in Mathematics, 63,* 325–346.

Paugh, P., & MacPhee, D. (2023). *Learning to be literate: More than a single story.* New York: Norton.

Pearson, D., Palincsar, A., Biancarosa, G., & Berman, A. (2020). *Reaping the rewards of the Reading for Understanding Initiative.* Washington, DC: National Academy of Education.

Readence, J., Bean, T., & Bean, R. (2019). *Content area literacy: An integrated approach* (11th ed.). Dubuque, IA: Kendall Hunt Publishing.

Rainey, E., & Moje, E. (2012). Building insider knowledge: Teaching students to read, write, and think within ELA and across the disciplines. *English Education, 45*(1), 71–90.

Reinking, D., Hruby, G., & Risko, V. (2023). Legislating phonics: Settled science or political polemics? *Teachers College Record, 125*(1), 104–131.

Reinking, D., & Reinking, S. (2022). Why phonics (in English) is difficult to teach, learn, and apply: What caregivers and teachers need to know. *Journal of Reading Recovery, 22*(1), 5–19.

Sadoski, M., Goetz, E., & Rodriguez, M. (2000). Engaging texts: Effects of concreteness on comprehensibility, interest, and recall in four text types. *Journal of Educational Psychology, 92*(1), 85–95.

Scarborough, H. (2001). Connecting early language and literacy to later reading (dis)abilities: Evidence, theory, and practice. In S. Newman & D. Dickinson (Eds.), *Handbook of early literacy research* (pp. 97–110). New York: Guilford.

Schleppegrell, M. J. (2004). *The language of schooling: A functional linguistics perspective.* Mahwah, NJ: Erlbaum.

Serafini, F. (2014). *Reading the visual: An introduction to teaching multimodal literacy.* New York, NY: Teachers College Press.

Shanahan, T., Callison, K., Carriere, C., Duke, N., Pearson, D., Schatschneider, C., & Torgesen, J. (2010). *Improving reading comprehension in kindergarten through 3rd grade* (NCEE 2010–4038). Washington, DC: National Center for Education Evaluation and Regional Assistance, Institute of Education Sciences, U.S. Department of Education.

Shanahan, T. & Shanahan, C. (2008). Teaching disciplinary literacy to adolescents: Rethinking content-area literacy. *Harvard Educational Review, 78*(1), 40–59.

Shanahan, T., & Shanahan, C. (2012). What is disciplinary literacy and why does it matter? *Topics in Language Disorders, 32*(1), 1–12.

Smagorinsky, P. (2001). If meaning is constructed, what is it made from? Toward a cultural theory of reading. *Review of Educational Research, 71*(1), 133–169.

Smith, F. (2004). *Understanding reading* (6th ed.). Mahwah, NJ: Erlbaum.

Smith, R., Snow, P., Serry, T., & Hammond, L. (2021). The role of background knowledge in reading comprehension: A critical review. *Reading Psychology, 42*(3), 214–240.

Snowling, M., Hulme, C., & Nation, K. (2022). *The science of reading: A handbook* (2nd ed.). New York: Wiley.

Sosnoski, J. (1999). Hyper-readers and their reading-engines. In G. Hawisher & C. Selfe (Eds.), *Passions, pedagogies and 21st century technologies* (pp. 161–177). Boulder, Colorado: University Press of Colorado and Logan, UT: Utah State University Press.

Stanovich, K. (2000). *Progress in understanding reading: Scientific foundations and new frontiers.* New York: Guilford.

Sweet, A., & Snow, C. (2003). *Rethinking reading comprehension.* New York: Guilford.

Sulzby, E. (1985). Children's emergent reding of favorite storybooks: A developmental study. *Reading Research Quarterly, 20*(4), 458–481.

Tunmer, W., & Hoover, W. (2019). The cognitive foundations of learning to read: A framework for preventing and remediating reading difficulties. *Australian Journal of Learning Difficulties, 24*(1), 75–93.

Turner, J., & Paris, S. (2005). How literacy tasks influence children's motivation for literacy. In Fang, Z. (Ed.), *Literacy teaching and learning: Current issues and trends* (pp. 31–39). Columbus, OH: Pearson.

Uccelli, P., Gallloway, P., Barr, C., Meneses, A., & Dobbs, C. (2015). Beyond vocabulary: Exploring cross-disciplinary academic language proficiency and its association with reading comprehension. *Reading Research Quarterly, 50*(3), 337–356.

Unsworth, L. (2001). *Teaching multiliteracies across the curriculum: Changing contexts of text and image in classroom practice.* Buckingham: Open University Press.

Vacca, R., Vacca, J., & Mraz, M. (2016). *Content area reading: Literacy and learning across the curriculum* (12th ed.). Boston, MA: Pearson.

van den Broek, P. (2010). Using texts in science education: Cognitive processes and knowledge representation. *Science, 328*(5977), 453–456.

Weber, K., Dawkins, P., & Mejia-Ramos, J.P. (2020). The relationship between mathematical practice and mathematics pedagogy in mathematics education research. *ZDM Mathematics Education 52*, 1063–1074.

Wiesner, E., Weinberg, A., Fulmer, E., & Barr, J. (2020). The roles of textual features, background knowledge, and disciplinary expertise in reading a calculus textbook. *Journal for Research in Mathematics Education*, *51*(2), 204–233.

Willingham, D. (Spring, 2006). How knowledge helps. *American Educator*, *30*(1), https://www.aft.org/periodical/american-educator/spring-2006/how-knowledge-helps

Willingham, D. (2017). *The reading mind: A cognitive approach to understanding how the mind reads*. San Francisco, CA: Jossey-Bass.

Wolters, C., Denton, C., York, M., & Francis, D. (2014). Adolescents' motivation for reading: Group differences and relation to standardized achievement. *Reading and Writing: An Interdisciplinary Journal*, *27*(3), 503–533.

Yaden, D., & Rogers, T. (2022). Section 7: Literacies and languages. In R. Tierney, F. Rizvi, & K. Ercikan (Eds.). *International encyclopedia of education* (4th ed., pp. 7001–8000). Elsevier.

2

Reading Literature

Literature in English Language Arts

English language arts, or ELA for short, is a school subject whose boundaries have always been loose, open to discursive inputs from a variety of disciplines that include philosophy, rhetoric, literary criticism, applied linguistics, psychology, cultural studies, and media studies. Historically, the goals of ELA were contested and shifting (Christie & Macken-Horarik, 2011; Purves & Pradl, 2003). During the nineteenth century, the focus of ELA was on the teaching of basic, often discrete, skills of reading (e.g., phonics, vocabulary), writing (e.g., spelling, literary techniques, and rhetorical moves), and grammar (e.g., parts of a sentence). The literature used for this purpose, if any, is largely religious texts emphasizing moral values or anthologies with bowdlerized versions of certain literary classics believed to have the potential to inculcate moral values. This focus, which reflects a functional literacy ideology (Cadiero-Kaplan, 2002), emphasizes the learning of basic skills, forms, processes, and procedures for comprehending and creating texts. It is making a comeback over the past few years as the back-to-the-basics movement, rebranded today as "the science of reading" (Goodwin & Jimenez, 2020; Snowling, Hulme, & Nation, 2022), regains its popularity among certain sectors of the education world.

From the beginning of the twentieth century, the focus of ELA became the transmission of moral and cultural values. The literature used for this purpose is largely that which belongs to a literary, and primarily Western, canon— a body of texts considered to be most important and influential to a particular culture at a particular time and in a particular place. These texts, seen as "Great Books" to be celebrated and revered for eternity because of their enduring moral and cultural values, feature classical and modern literary works such as *The Odyssey* by Homer (750 BC), *The Divine Comedy* by Dante Alighieri (1320), *The Canterbury Tales* by Geoffrey Chaucer (1400),

DOI: 10.4324/9781003432258-2

Macbeth by William Shakespeare (1606), *Pride and Prejudice* by Jane Austen (1813), *Frankenstein* by Mary Wollstonecraft Shelley (1818), *The Scarlet Letter* by Nathaniel Hawthorne (1850), *A Tale of Two Cities* by Charles Dickens (1859), *War and Peace* by Leo Tolstoy (1869), *The Adventures of Huckleberry Finn* by Mark Twain (1884), *Ulysses* by James Joyce (1920), *The Great Gatsby* by F. Scott Fitzgerald (1925), *The Grapes of Wrath* by John Steinbeck (1939), *1984* by George Orwell (1949), *The Catcher in the Rye* by J.D. Salinger (1951), *Lolita* by Vladimir Nabokov (1955), *To Kill a Mockingbird* by Harper Lee (1960), and *One Hundred Years of Solitude* by Gabriel Garcia Marquez (1967) (see Bloom, 1994, for a more expansive list). For most of the twentieth century, this Western canon held sway in ELA instruction, with newer, more contemporary books added to the list over time, such as *Beloved* by Toni Morrison (1987) and *Gilead* by Marilyn Robinson (2004). This focus on "Great Books", which reflects a cultural literacy ideology (Cadiero-Kaplan, 2002), emphasizes the learning of cultural and moral content in certain literary texts. It can now also be found in the Core Knowledge Curriculum endorsed by E.D. Hirsch and his associates (see Chapter 1).

After World War II, a more progressive ideology informed the ELA curriculum, leading to an emphasis on personal growth. This emphasis recognizes that "our traditional focus on 'great' literature and our narrow conception of literacy do not adequately serve the need of our students today" (Yagelski, 1994, p. 34). It promotes, instead, creativity and ownership and encourages the use of more contemporary, non-canonical texts with themes and topics that better connect with students' everyday lives, such as young adult novels and trade books about traditionally marginalized groups. Toward the end of the twentieth century and into the twenty-first century, ELA began to embrace a critical literacy ideology (Cadiero-Kaplan, 2002), emphasizing the importance of developing the capacity to evaluate and critique what is read. This focus encourages exploration of the situatedness and constructedness of text, the hidden ideologies in literature, and the affordances of visual and verbal resources in representing experiences and communicating ideas. It invigorates interests in cultural studies, new literacy studies, and multiliteracies, further expanding students' textual diets to include popular culture texts (e.g., graphic novels), films, and other media (e.g., raps, video games). Yagelski (1994) went so far as to suggest that in order to make ELA as a school subject meaningful and useful to students, literature "should be removed from the center of the secondary English curriculum and become part of the study of language that should be at the center of that curriculum" (p. 35). He argued that the primary purpose of ELA at the secondary level "should be, first, to give students meaningful experiences in using written and oral language in a variety of ways for a variety of purposes, and second, to help them come to understand the social, rhetorical, situated nature of all language use" (p. 34). Along this vein, he recommended that literature, if it must be taught, should be taught in ways that help students better understand language and language use in diverse contexts.

These shifts and changes contribute to the perception that ELA is a "weakly classified" field with a fragmented identity whose boundaries are permeable to a range of disciplines (Bernstein, 2000). In fact, ELA is often not considered an academic discipline because it lacks a unifying theoretical paradigm or methodology and a clearly definable and stable object of study. Despite its evolving foci and purposes, as well as the wide range of texts used, ELA has consistently remained a school subject where reading, writing, and language figure prominently (Smagorinsky & Flanagan, 2014), with literature often, albeit not always, serving as the springboard for the learning of all three curricular strands. For example, learning to read literature is seen in many ELA classrooms as involving learning to analyze the rhetorical structures (e.g., narrative, rhyme scheme, dramatic structure) and literary techniques (e.g., alliteration, allusion, repetition, foreshadowing, symbolism, theme, plot, characterization) employed in different types of literary work (e.g., sonnets, novels, plays), with the goal of generating a plausible interpretation of text. At the same time, literary texts often serve as model compositions for contextualizing the discussion of writing crafts, genre features, and language usage. In effect, literature functions as the nexus that connects reading, writing, and language studies in ELA classrooms.

The Challenges of Literary Reading

Because the content of ELA is relatively ill-defined, a broad range of texts have been valued and used in the school subject. These include poetry, short stories, novels, periodicals, memoirs, biographies, historical documents, reference materials, magazines, news reports, films, musical lyrics, letters, and essays. This chapter focuses on one broad category of texts that students are regularly asked to read and respond to in ELA classrooms—literary texts, leaving other categories of texts to the next two chapters (on history and science), where they figure more prominently. Arguably the core of the literature curriculum in ELA, literary texts are the sort of literature whose primary purpose is to entertain rather than inform and which can support sustained, multiple (though not infinite) interpretations. They include prose fiction (e.g., short stories, novels, novellas), poetry (e.g., free verse, sonnet, epic), and drama (e.g., play, ballet, opera). These genres feature aesthetic, poetic, and playful use of language. They have aesthetic, artistic, and epistemic values, giving readers pleasure, provoking their imagination, eliciting their thoughts and feelings, broadening their horizons, promoting debates about controversial social issues, and ultimately helping them better understand themselves and others around them.

Literary reading is "a constructive act, often requiring one not only to decode texts but also to encode meaning in them based on prior experiences" (Smagorinsky, 2015, p. 144). This means that reading a literary text is about more than comprehending setting, characters (e.g., their internal states and motivations), and plot (e.g., chronological and causal links among actions); rather, it is essentially an interpretive process requiring the reader to draw on his/her prior knowledge and experiences to notice important signals, impose significance or meaning to these signals, dwell on figuration and imagery, make and confirm conjectures, establish intertextual links, conduct detailed analysis, perform critical evaluation, seek meaning patterns, and distill themes (Goldman et al., 2016). As Warren (2011) observed, expertise in literary reading "does not consist solely of the ability to approach a text cold and interpret it satisfactorily; rather, of equal or greater importance is the ability to interweave pertinent contextual information with close textual analysis" (p. 368).

Students face several challenges in developing this sort of literary expertise. One main challenge in reading literature is that students may not have the knowledge about the social, cultural, geopolitical, and historical contexts in which the literary work was produced. Because literature is a medium for representing people's life experiences, some knowledge of the context of its production is key to understanding these experiences. It helps the reader identify "author's generalizations" (Hillocks & Ludlow, 1984)—abstract generalizations the author presumably made about the world beyond the text, to wit, the theme of the text. Many literary texts used in ELA classrooms, especially the classical ones, describe human experiences, dilemmas, and social values to which most students today could not easily relate or were cast in settings of long ago with which students have little familiarity. For example, John Steinbeck's (1939) *The Grapes of Wrath* narrates the experiences of Tom Joad and his family as they migrated westward from Oklahoma to California in search of a better life. To understand the story and appreciate the hardship experienced by the Joads, it would be helpful to have some background knowledge about two overlapping events in U.S. history: the Dust Bowl of the 1930s, a time of severe drought that caused dust storms and destroyed livelihoods across the Great Plains (a region covering parts of Kansas, Oklahoma, Nebraska, New Mexico, Colorado, Texas, and other midwestern and southwestern states of the U.S.), and the Great Depression (1929–1939), a period of worldwide economic calamity that originated in the U.S. and caused drastic decline in economic output, severe unemployment, and acute deflation around the world. Similarly, in reading William Shakespeare's (1806) Macbeth—a powerful tragedy over 400 years old based on the events in the life of a real historical figure, knowing something about the historical context (e.g., the Elizabethan and Jacobean periods in British history—an era of relative stability sandwiched between decades of uncertainty and turmoil) is important for understanding why Shakespeare wrote the drama the way he did and how he used and twisted history to make a better play and to address the political agenda of his royal patron King James I of England. Many contemporary works of young adult literature, as well as literary classics, make repeated references to ancient gods, monsters, mortals, and warriors (Hamilton, 1999). An appreciation of these texts requires some background knowledge about Greek mythology or other civilizations.

Another challenge in reading literary texts is to recognize and understand the literary devices used in these texts. Literature is an artistic creation; and as such, it typically employs a range of literary and linguistic techniques that add nuances to, contradict, or create image for meaning. These devices include allegory, allusion, anaphora, characterization, conflict, irony, epistrophe, euphemism, flashback, foreshadowing, hyperbole, imagery, mood, motif, paradox, parallelism, personification, plot, point of view, pun, satire, symbolism, theme, understatement, and dozens of other terms and techniques that can help with the interpretation of text. Pursuing and understanding these devices is crucial to literary interpretation and appreciation (Lee & Spratley, 2010). Returning to The Grapes of Wrath, we can see quite a few examples of allusion, symbolism, and foreshadowing. Steinbeck named the original place that the Joads lived Dustbowl, which alludes to the desert of Egypt in the Bible—a dry, uninhabitable place. The term foreshadows the plight that the Joad family would encounter in their westward journey. Route 66 is, likewise, religious symbolism in that it alludes to the treacherous journey that the Israelites took to escape the desert in Egypt (and associated oppression and slavery) to the Promised Land where freedom and a better life can be found. Thus, the road symbolizes hope for the Joad family since they too were embarking on a journey, similarly filled with trials and tribulations, to an expectedly better life in the fertile land of California. There are also many instances in the novel where blood is used to symbolize death (e.g., the death of the Joad family dog, the fight with the police, blood from the work being done on the farm). Herman Melville's (1851) Moby Dick, a story about a group of seamen hunting a gigantic sperm whale called Moby Dick, is another novel that uses many literary devices, including, for example, alliteration, allusion, conflict, first-person narration, foreshadowing, hyperbole, imagery, metaphor, motif, parallelism, paradox, personification, repetition, simile, and symbolism. These literary devices help add depth to meaning, create more vivid pictures of what the author tried to convey, build connections between characters and themes on a deeper level, and keep the reader actively engaged with the unfolding plot. While many of these literary devices can also be found in everyday texts (e.g., newspaper articles, hip-hop lyrics), students may not be familiar with how they are used in canonical literary texts and will, thus, require guidance (Lee & Spratley, 2010).

While literary devices provide a helpful way to generate textual interpretation, they may not be present in all texts, as writers sometimes do not use these devices in their work. This means that students will have to find alternative ways of generating a reasonable interpretation of text. One alternative is to systematically examine patterns of language in a text to accumulate evidence that leads to a particular interpretation of the text's motifs and authorial stance. For example, drawing on the discourse analysis tools provided by a functional theory of language called systemic functional linguistics (Halliday & Matthiessen, 2014), researchers (e.g., Adams & Fang, 2020; Eggins, 2004; Huisman, 2016; Lukin, 2003) have shown how close attention to patterns of lexical and grammatical choices in poems or stories can help reveal meanings that may otherwise not be transparent to the reader and generate evidence to support a particular interpretation. Developing the expertise to conduct this sort of detailed linguistic analysis can, however, be challenging for students (Fang et al., 2014).

A further challenge with literary reading is that each genre of literature has its own discursive norms and conventions. Being able to read a short story does not ensure similar successes with poetry or drama, and vice versa. An awareness and understanding of the structure, language, and discursive traditions of each genre helps the reader navigate the text for meaning patterns. It also enables the reader to identify "structural generalizations" (Hillocks & Ludlow, 1984), that is, to explain how parts of the text operate together to produce certain meanings and achieve certain effects. Each genre (or its subgenre) has a distinct set of structural elements that helps it achieve its purpose. For example, a poem aims to paint a picture of what the poet feels about a thing, a person, an idea, a concept, or an object through the creative use of language. As such, it can be unstructured or structured. An unstructured poem is, as the name implies, a free verse that follows no formal organizational patterns. A structured poem, on the other hand, has formal structural elements, including intentional line breaks and stanza breaks, a consistent rhyme scheme, and an adherence to the rules of meter. Different poems use these elements in somewhat different ways to fulfil each poet's intentions. A haiku, for example, consists of three lines, the first having five syllables, the second seven, and the third five again. It does not typically rhyme. A sonnet, on the other hand, must have 14 lines in length, with typically 10 syllables per line, and is usually written in iambic pentameter. Its rhyme scheme can vary, but its last two lines typically form a rhyming couplet. Reading a poem requires close attention to all of these structural elements, as the poet makes deliberate language choices to convey meaning and add nuances to his/her work.

A story has a plot structure that typically consists of some combination of the following elements: orientation, initiating event(s), complication(s), climax, falling action(s), and denouement. In orientation, the author introduces the characters, establishes the setting, and foreshadows the primary conflict of the story. The initiating event is an inciting incident that creates the conflict and escalates tension as the story unfolds. When the tension or conflict reaches the most intense point, the story is said to be in the climax, when the main character is forced to make a life-altering decision. The decision triggers a series of actions aimed at resolving the conflict or diffusing tension. The story is brought to a happy or tragic ending (denouement) depending on whether the conflict is satisfactorily resolved and tension successfully diffused. Different kinds of stories (e.g., fantasy, tall tale) or the same kind of story from different cultures (Greek mythology vs. Chinese mythology) tend to have somewhat different structural elements and characterization that help accomplish the different purposes of the genres and reflect the differences in cultural traditions.

A drama usually consists of a prologue, a series of acts that are further divided into scenes, and an epilogue. A prologue, similar to the pregame show of a football game, is the opening segment that introduces the rest of the drama. It provides important background information about the main characters and their situations. For example, Shakespeare's *Romeo and Juliet* opens with 14 lines that set the scene, telling the audience that the drama will be about two families of equal wealth living in the city of Verona, Italy. An act is a large section of a drama. Just like how an actual football game can be divided into two halves (or four quarters), a drama can be made up of one or more acts. *Romeo and Juliet*, for example, has five acts. Each act consists of one or more scenes, similar to how each half or quarter of a football game consists of a series of offensive, defensive, and special team plays. These acts together tell a story that has some type of conflict, which develops until it reaches the climax and is later resolved in some way. Similar to the postgame show in football, an epilogue is a scene that takes place after the climax. It is usually a short speech given by the narrator character to the audience at the end of a play. It serves as a conclusion to the play, showing what becomes of its major characters.

Not only do literary genres differ in schematic structure, they also differ in the ways they deploy lexical and grammatical resources of language. Different ways with words create different degrees of challenge for readers. For example, many classical texts of long ago contain archaic or seldom used vocabulary (and syntax) that students today may find foreign. Some such words found in Geoffrey Chaucer's *Canterbury Tales* are "drey" (*the nest of a squirrel*), "indite" (*to produce a literary work*), "parvis" (*courtyard*), "joust" (*fight*), "yore" (*time long past*), "choleric" (*angry*), "mirth" (*excitement*), and "votary" (*priest or priestess*). Other literary texts use a substantial amount of dialect, which can make them less accessible to students, who are used to reading texts written in standard/conventional English. Mark Twain's *Huckleberry Finn* uses accents and slangs to bring his characters to life, as can be seen in this dialogue from Jim, a slave: "*Well, he sot up a bank, en say anybody dat put in a dollar would git fo' dollars mo' at de en' er de year*" (chapter 8). The use of dialect here vividly portrays, albeit in a seemingly racialized way, Jim's lack of education and of his ability to pronounce some words "correctly"; however, it can also disrupt the flow of reading and impede comprehension, rendering the reading experience potentially less enjoyable for some students.

In general, drama and prose fiction use language in ways that are easier to understand than poetry. Drama uses mostly dialogue because it is meant to be performed (i.e., spoken and acted out) on stage. As such, its language generally sounds colloquial and more everyday-like, making it comparatively easier to process and comprehend than that of prose fiction or poetry. In prose fiction, stories are largely told through everyday language. They are typically written in complete sentences that conform to grammatical conventions; and these sentences are linked to form paragraphs, and paragraphs combine to form chapters. There is also a considerable amount of dialogue in prose fiction. For poetry, language is more compressed and unconventional; and its interpretation often requires close attention to both its graphological structures (e.g., perimeter, block, line, character) and its phonological structures (e.g., tone, foot, syllable, phoneme). As Peskin (1998) noted, because poetry emphasizes image formation and a consistent rhyming scheme, it "often disregards syntax, the connectives and linear order of language," with the consequence that "the construction of meaning when reading poetry will make far greater demands on the inferential process" (p. 236). A case in point is "A Total Stranger One Black Day" (see Text 2.1), a poem by e.e. cummings, one of the most popular American poets of the twentieth century whose body of work includes nearly 3000 poems and has inspired countless readers. The poem has an unorthodox, ungrammatical, fragmented style that creates a special effect of dissonance and strangeness and contributes to the idea that humans are vulnerable and complex. Students who are unaware of the discursive conventions of poetry may read this poem as little more than an odd-looking prose.

Text 2.1

a total stranger one black day
knocked living the hell out of me—

who found forgiveness hard because
my(as it happened)self he was

—but now that fiend and I are such
immortal friends the other's each

The added demand on the inferential process is not unique to poetry reading, however. Even though prose fiction uses language that generally follows grammatical conventions, it tends to show, rather than tell, when portraying a character's feelings/emotions or conveying the author's message. That is, a character's feeling is often conveyed subtly or indirectly through showing what the character does or says (e.g., *Harry pounded his right fist on the desk and yelled obscenities at Dudley. I was pacing back and forth on the floor before my beam routines.*), rather than explicitly or directly through telling (e.g., *Harry was really mad at Dudley. I was very nervous before the gymnastics competition started.*). This means the reader must go beyond the apparent, surface-level meaning when reading literature. In literature, there is usually no topic sentence or topic paragraph, where the main idea or thesis is presented and subsequently elaborated with description, examples, explanations, or evidence. Thus, to understand what the character truly thinks/feels or what the author's stance is, the reader often must make inferences based on the concrete actions/events described. This can be challenging, especially for those not equipped with relevant prior knowledge/experience or not used to this way of communicating ideas.

In the following excerpt (Text 2.2) from Louis Sachar's (1998) *Holes*, an award-winning young adult novel, Miss Katherine Barlow, a white school teacher, has a crush on Sam, a young African-American onion farmer, who is called upon to repair the school building. However, her interest in, or love for, him is not explicitly stated. Instead, her sentiment toward him is conveyed through detailed descriptions of their interactions during his work on the schoolhouse. If students cannot make inferences based on these concrete descriptions, they would have trouble understanding why Miss Katherine "was sad when the roof was finished", why she was "the only person who wasn't happy with it", or why running out of things needing to be fixed became problematic, as getting a broken schoolhouse fixed is, by any reasonable measure, a good thing and should make the teacher happy.

Text 2.2

It took Sam a week to fix the roof, because he could only work in the afternoons, after school let out and before night classes began. Sam wasn't allowed to attend classes because he was a Negro, but they let him fix the building.

Miss Katherine usually stayed in the schoolhouse, grading papers and such, while Sam worked on the roof. She enjoyed what little conversation they were able to have, shouting up and down to each other. She was surprised by his interest in poetry. When he took a break, she would sometimes read a poem to him. On more than one occasion, she would start to read a poem by Poe or Longfellow, only to hear him finish it for her, from memory.

She was sad when the roof was finished . . .

The next time she saw him, she mentioned that "the door doesn't hang straight," and she got to spend another afternoon with him while he fixed the door.

By the end of the first semester, Onion Sam had turned the old rundown schoolhouse into a well-crafted, freshly painted jewel of a building the whole town was proud of. People passing by would stop and admire it. "That's our schoolhouse. It shows how much we value education here in Green Lake."

The only person who wasn't happy with it was Miss Katherine. She'd run out of things needing to be fixed. (pp. 109–111)

To summarize, literary texts vary in terms of their schematic structures, rhetorical conventions, literary traditions, language use, and knowledge demands. They present a range of challenges for students, who are expected to not only comprehend but interpret the texts they read in the ELA classroom. These challenges are difficult to quantify; they defy popular measures of text complexity or text difficulty such as Lexile (Schnick & Knickelbine, 2000), Coh-Metrix (Graesser, McNamara, & Kulikowich, 2011), and other readability formulas. Developing the capacity to cope with these challenges requires experience and support, a topic to which we shall return later in the chapter.

How do Experts Read Literary Texts?

To help students cope with the challenges of literary reading, it is useful to first examine how literary experts read the texts in their discipline and what they value in their reading. An understanding of the strategies literary experts use to tackle challenges and construct meaning during reading would provide important insights that can inform efforts to promote effective literary reading and develop literary literacy among students. A number of studies have explored what literary experts do when reading literary, albeit primarily poetic, texts. Some of these studies compare literary experts' reading to literary novices' reading. In these studies, the term "expert" is loosely defined, ranging from English professors working within or outside their domain of expertise to graduate students majoring in English.

Zeitz (1994) explored differences in the ways literary experts (13 graduate students in English) and novices (24 high school students and 16 engineering graduate students) cognitively processed and represented two significant but unfamiliar pieces of literature—a poem and a short story. Participants were asked to read and recall a poem and a short story and then answer seven questions requiring analyses of these two texts. The researcher found that experts were superior to novices in gist-level recall (for poem) and recognition of multilevel sentences (i.e., sentences containing similes, metaphors, references to symbols, and irony) (for short story), but not in verbatim-level recall (for poem) and recognition of plot-level sentences (i.e., sentences consisting of simple accounts of actions) (for short story). Experts were better at moving from a mundane, literal, detailed, basic level of representation to a more abstract, principled level of representation. They also surpassed novices in reasoning skills in that they were able to produce more evidence to support their claims and organize it into arguments with greater hierarchical depth and more complex comparisons. The researcher concluded that what advantaged experts was their extended experience with literature, which led to the development of a rich knowledge base organized by highly abstract structures that enhances their memory, analysis, and reasoning with literary texts.

The important role of knowledge in literary interpretation is affirmed by Peskin (1998), who asked eight doctoral candidates in English (experts) and eight undergraduates in their first two years of English studies or advanced high school students who had received intensive poetry instruction (novices) to think aloud as they attempted to make sense of two unfamiliar period poems (a metaphysical poem and an Elizabethan love sonnet). She found that experts had a deeply rich structure of knowledge that enabled them to easily allude to other literary texts, to place the poems in proper literary contexts, to anticipate the content, and to explore poetic significance in greater depth. They attended more frequently to structural and linguistic cues (e.g., wordplay, rhythm, rhyme scheme) in order to find patterns of meaning or to contextualize and categorize the poems. They also made far more spontaneous comments reflecting their enjoyment and appreciation of the poems. On the other hand, novices, due to a lack of knowledge about the conventions specific to the particular form, school, and period of poetry, used few productive interpretive strategies (e.g., scanning to contextualize, looking for meaning at the locus of binary opposition, attending to linguistic cues), had trouble identifying poetic significance and thematic unity, and frequently expressed frustration with reading. The researcher concluded that "knowledge is an important component of poetic communication, not only in the construction of meaning but in the resultant pleasure experienced when reading a poem" (p. 253).

Differences between experts and novices in strategy use are also reported by Reynolds and his colleagues (Reynolds & Rush, 2017; Reynolds, Rush, Lampi, & Holschuh, 2021), who asked four college freshmen (novices) and four English professors (experts) to read two literary texts (a poem and a short story) and perform a think-aloud protocol to articulate their thinking as they read. The researchers found that when reading, experts engaged in the recursive process of generating, weaving, and curating. First, they generated ideas about the text by making predictions, asking questions, noticing unfamiliar words or concepts, and observing elements of structure and examples of literary terms. They then wove the ideas they had generated with their own personal background and disciplinary knowledge by making connections between what they knew and what was on the page. This allowed them to connect discrete pieces of information and make sense of the text. Finally, they revisited and evaluated the connections, as well as their earlier predictions and questions, until they were ready to proffer their final interpretation of the text. There are, however, differences between experts and novices in how they interacted with literary texts. While both groups used the strategies of hypothesizing, noticing vocabulary, and questioning in their reading, experts used these strategies much more frequently and in qualitatively different ways than did novices. Specifically, experts engaged in recursive and constant hypothesizing about the relationship between characters, about tone, and about other meanings in an effort to build a coherent interpretation, whereas novices tended to hypothesize about plot structure and characterization. Moreover, while both groups asked comprehension-based questions that probed what was happening in the text, they used these questions in qualitatively different ways. Specifically, experts used comprehension-based questions as a way of engaging in literary conversations that help build an overall interpretation, whereas novices used these questions to seek answers related to basic plot elements. And when encountering an unfamiliar vocabulary word, experts wrestled with it to figure out its meaning or significance, but novices used it as an excuse for stopping engagement with the text.

Other studies focused on experts without comparing them to novices. Warren (2011), for example, asked eight English professors to think aloud as they read four lyric poems of varying familiarity. He found that regardless of whether they were reading familiar or unfamiliar poems, participants produced "open" readings in which they assumed different perspectives, reveled in ambiguities, and sought originality in interpretation. When reading familiar poems, participants produced longer protocols and richer interpretations, drawing heavily on their knowledge of the poem's scholarship, historical context, and author, as well as their prior readings. When reading unfamiliar poems, participants recognized their lack of relevant knowledge but tried to work around it for as long as they deemed appropriate. They knew when to stop trying, what additional information was needed, and where to find it. The researcher concluded that it is the possession of both "generic" and "specific" expertise—to wit, general knowledge about poetry and specific knowledge about a particular poem or poet—that contributed to the participants' productive engagement with text and their ability to understand its "point(s)".

Chapman (2015) examined how three university professors read texts in their own areas of specialization. One of the participants in the study, Dr. Carroll, is a literary scholar with expertise in children's literature. He was asked to think aloud as he read an unfamiliar text of his own choice that related to his specialization—Patricia Crain's (2000) *The Story of A: The Alphabetization of America from the New England Primer to The Scarlet Letter*, a book that explores the history of the alphabet as a text genre for children and of alphabetization as a social and educational practice in America. Data from Dr. Carroll's reading think alouds and follow-up discussions of the think alouds, as well as semi-structured interviews, reveal that Dr. Carroll used a range of strategies during reading. These include setting a purpose for reading (e.g., reading to see if the book could be a resource for a graduate seminar and for a book writing project), sourcing (i.e., paying attention to the author and the publisher of the book), contextualizing (i.e., wanting to know when and how the work came into existence), making connections (to other texts, to his own work, and to possible future work), predicting (as a way of testing his own conjectures about the text and its significance), summarizing (i.e., paraphrasing what was just read as a way of confirming or monitoring his own understanding), annotating (e.g., underlining challenging or important parts of text and taking notes so that he could refer back to them in his own research later), close reading (e.g., rereading portions of the text that he considered to be of great importance), and engaging with paratext (i.e., attending to and appreciating the book's title, table of contents, front matter, back matter, illustrations, inscriptions, and binding, as well as markings and annotations by previous readers). These strategies helped him comprehend, interpret, evaluate, and make use of the text in ways that aligned with his research goals and teaching needs.

Unlike the cognitive approach taken by researchers in the aforementioned studies, Rainey (2016) focused on the social and cultural practices of literary studies that mediate the cognitive processes of reading. She probed, through interviews, how a group of 10 university-based literary scholars (i.e., professors and doctoral candidates) read and reasoned with literary texts. She found that literary reading is fundamentally social and problem-based. Specifically, literary scholars viewed seeking patterns as a central part of their meaning making, emphasized the importance of noticing/exploring surprising or confusing aspects of text, engaged deeply with the text, considered various types of contexts and secondary sources, and worked rigorously toward building an original interpretation of text. These practices reflect the shared norms, assumptions, and values that literary scholars hold about what counts as knowledge in literary studies and how knowledge is collectively produced and communicated.

To summarize, literary reading is purpose-driven and interpretive in nature. The interpretation of literature involves both "exploring the literary text" and "expounding the perspective from which that text is explored" (Huisman, 2019, p. 110). Literary experts do not just focus on basic plot elements of the text in their reading; instead, they move beyond surface-level comprehension to analysis, evaluation, and description, attempting to offer an original way of thinking about the central theme or puzzle featured in the text. They predict, reread, backtrack, examine, underline, annotate, connect, imagine, summarize, source, and contextualize as they seek to both decipher the plain sense of the text and explore its deeper meaning and literary significance. They draw on their extensive knowledge about literary traditions and disciplinary standards to help them identify patterns of meaning, clear up confusions, and wrestle with interpretive problems. At the same time, they also actively attend to linguistic and discursive features to appreciate the artistry of the text and to seek clues that may suggest a particular angle for reading or support a particular interpretative lens. And they gain both satisfaction and joy from the hard work of trying to generate a robust interpretation with the ring of originality.

Developing Literary Expertise: General Principles and Approaches

Unlike the manner in which literary experts interact with disciplinary texts, secondary students generally have a very different kind of reading experience in ELA classrooms. They typically read a text, answer some literal or inferential questions, work on vocabulary, and identify themes (Reynolds & Rush, 2017). As a consequence, many adolescents have trouble going from surface comprehension to rigorous interpretation in their literary reading. For example, Harker (1994) studied how 15 tenth-grade students deemed by their teachers as particularly capable of literary interpretation read two poems (lyrics) from a tenth-grade poetry anthology. The students recorded their think-aloud protocols as they read and responded to the poems at their own pace. Analysis of the reading responses revealed that the students focused on the literal meanings of the poems, rather than their potentially rich and varied poetic significance. More specifically, they frequently requested the meanings of words they did not understand and worked hard to attain the plain sense, or overt meaning, of the poems, instead of pursuing the imaginative possibilities that the poems evoke. They lacked sufficient prior knowledge of poetic conventions to make mental connections among the different parts of a text and to notice and ponder a particular word, line, or stanza of poetic or unusual significance. Moreover, they rarely engaged in the strategy of "reattention"—i.e., constant refocusing of attention on the text in an effort to make sense of it on its own terms—that would lead to progressive refinement of meaning and eventual construction of a rigorous interpretation.

Developing the sort of expertise demonstrated by literary experts takes a considerable amount of time, experience, and support. It is certainly not the goal of literature instruction in K-12 contexts to make literary experts of adolescents. Rather, a disciplinary literacy approach to literature aims to help students develop the capacity to read and reason with literary texts in ways that are aligned with how literary scholars interact with literature, including setting appropriate purposes for reading, recognizing and using literary tools and conventions, evaluating and critiquing claims made by others in the field, and generating and communicating sophisticated and nuanced interpretations that are also evidence-based (Rainey & Moje, 2012). More specifically, students are expected to able to (a) engage in close reading of texts, using literary strategies to identify plot elements and rhetorical devices, (b) synthesize within and across texts to construct generalizations about theme and characterization, (c) recognize key structural and linguistic choices made by the author and understand the functions of these choices, (d) use academic language to construct written arguments with claims, evidence, and warrants, (e) establish criteria for judging interpretive claims and arguments, and (f) demonstrate understanding that there are multiple interpretive possibilities for every text (Goldman et al., 2016, p. 11). These literary literacy goals are consistent with what the Common Core State Standards recommended for the study of literature (see Table 2.1 for sample literature standards for high school) (NGA & CCSSO, 2010).

Table 2.1 Common Core State Standards for 11th and 12th Grade Literature

Strands	Standards
Key Ideas & Details	• Cite strong and thorough textual evidence to support analysis of what the text says explicitly as well as inferences drawn from the text, including determining where the text leaves matters uncertain.
	• Determine two or more themes or central ideas of a text and analyze their development over the course of the text, including how they interact and build on one another to produce a complex account; provide an objective analysis of the text.
	• Analyze the impact of the author's choices regarding how to develop and relate elements of a story or drama (e.g., where a story is set, how the action is ordered, how the characters are introduced and developed).
Craft & Structure	• Determine the meaning of words and phrases as they are used in the text, including figurative and connotative meanings; analyze the impact of specific word choices on meaning and tone, including words with multiple meanings or language that is particularly fresh, engaging, or beautiful.
	• Analyze how an author's choices concerning how to structure specific parts of a text (e.g., the choice of where to begin or end a story, the choice to provide a comic or tragic resolution) contribute to its overall structure and meaning as well as its aesthetic impact.

(Continued)

Strands	Standards
	• Analyze a case in which grasping a point of view requires distinguishing what is directly stated in a text from what is really meant (e.g., satire, sarcasm, irony, or understatement).
Integration of Knowledge & Ideas	• Analyze multiple interpretations of a story, drama, or poem, evaluating how each version interprets the source text.
	• Demonstrate knowledge of 18th, 19th, and early 20th century foundational works of American literature, including how two or more texts from the same period treat similar themes or topics.

To achieve these disciplinary learning goals in the teaching of literature, ELA teachers need to establish a classroom culture that promotes communal reading and guided discussion of text (Elliott, 2021). That is, students need opportunities to read and reread a wide range of literary texts, paying close attention to textual details such as setting, characterization, plot structure, language choices, literary devices, and contextual references. However, textual encounter alone is rarely sufficient for literary learning. Students also need time to talk about what they have read, engaging in conversation that uses textual evidence to explore questions about characters, plots, themes, motifs, contexts, and values (Elliott, 2021). After all, knowledge in literature is not constructed in isolation, but created "through argument with others, whether real or imagined, as we work through possible interpretations and make the case for our own particular take on a text" (Elliott, 2021, p. 12). This means that teachers need to create space for students to share and discuss the different interpretations they have individually generated. It is through active engagement with one another's ideas and viewpoints that students begin to clear up their confusions, clarify their thinking, deepen their understanding, formulate their own interpretations, explain their positions, propose counter arguments, and expand their perspectives.

In classrooms where literature is conceived of as "a conversation within and between students, texts and teachers" (Elliott, 2021, p. 11), students are encouraged to make text-to-self, text-to-text, and text-to-world connections, pose questions based on what puzzles or mystifies them, explain characters' traits and actions, restory texts, adopt perspectives other than their own, and explore multiple perspectives and multiple interpretations (Beach, Appleman, Fecho, & Simon, 2020). In these classrooms, the teacher is no longer considered the only one who knows the meaning of literature. Rather, there is usually more than one valid interpretation of text because what students bring to the reading task—their identity, their prior knowledge and experiences, and their intention and level of interest—is valued. It is now commonly understood that what the text means can vary from one reader to another because different readers bring with them different sets of beliefs, knowledge, assumptions, theoretical lenses, biases, and purposes (Rosenblatt, 1978). At the same time, however, not all interpretations are equally valid or valued, as the "correctness" or validity of any interpretation lies in the quality of evidence provided and in the ways such evidence is used and presented to justify or support the interpretation (Christie & Dreyfus, 2007; Elliott, 2021). It is worth bearing in mind that the process for generating an interpretation is just as important as the final interpretation that is rendered.

To promote communal reading and guided discussion of literature, teachers can adopt the critical inquiry approach proposed by Beach, Thein and Webb (2015). The approach emphasizes critical engagement with literature through collaborative exploration of a meaningful issue or an intriguing problem that piques students' interest. It encourages students to draw on their prior knowledge and experience, make intertextual connections, construct identities, collaborate with others, ponder the significance of particular details or the overall work, use digital tools and apps to respond to and create texts, and share responses as they read, analyze, and critique literary works of common interest. For example, Bintz and Ciecierski (2021) described how critical engagement with crossover literature—a genre of literary texts that cross age boundaries—can facilitate meaningful discussions on controversial issues or challenging real-life situations (e.g., death, child abuse, sexual orientation, incarceration, family separation, illegal drugs, divorce, pornography, depression, homelessness) in ELA classrooms, suggesting that such engagement "helps readers develop self and social awareness and gain new knowledge that allows them to better understand their own lives and the lives of others" (p. 34).

Teachers can also use some of the strategies that Hicks and Steffel (2012) recommended for the teaching of literature. One strategy is to have a whole-class unit on a specific text. In this unit, all students read and discuss the same literary text and at the same time receive direct instruction that helps guide them toward understanding certain aspects of the text. Another strategy is to use literature circles. Students are divided into small groups. Members in each group read and share responses to or reflections on a book of common interest. The teacher monitors, encourages, and guides small group discussions. Each group also completes a culminating project (e.g., multimedia presentation, a diorama, a book report) that showcases their understanding of the book they have read or their appreciation of the author's craft. A third strategy is to have students examine literary fiction thematically, providing them with an opportunity to identify literary techniques used to construct stories and compare/contrast the ways in which the theme is developed across different types of fiction.

When guiding literary discussions or literary responses, it is important for teachers to, according to the literary scholars in Rainey (2016), encourage students to identify, pursue, and communicate about significant literary puzzles or questions. More specifically, teachers should invite students to consider rich questions or puzzles, making sure that these questions/puzzles can be answered in multiple ways. They also need to show students how to construct literary puzzles that explore the significance of a particular feature of a text or question how different parts of a text work together as a system to achieve its central purpose. Additionally, teachers can help students learn to (a) use formal elements such as setting, plot, meter, characterization, and rhyme to identify the theme of the text, (b) look for paradox, ambiguity, irony, tension, and other rhetorical signals to help establish, among other possibilities, the most unified or plausible interpretation of the text, and (c) analyze language choices to see how they contribute to characterization, convey authorial attitude, and have particular effects on the reader. More importantly, teachers should coach students through cycles of literary inquiry, sharing a text with students, prompting them to identify strange or surprising moments in the text, posing a literary puzzle or question, considering multiple interpretive possibilities, and generating original or otherwise productive claims with supporting evidence (Rainey, 2016).

Another way of supporting students to develop literary expertise is through what Lee (1995, 2001) referred to as "cultural modeling". Cultural modeling is a framework for designing a curriculum and learning environment that leverages students' everyday language and literacy practices to teach literary literacy and language practices, with a particular focus on racial/ethnic minority groups, especially youth of African descent. It encourages teachers to identify potential points of synergy and differences between problem solving in an everyday domain and problem solving within an academic subject such as literature and then draw on what students already know and are capable of doing to help accomplish their instructional goals. It requires teachers to conduct careful analysis of students' routine everyday social practices, examining the modes of reasoning, concepts, strategies, heuristics, and habits of mind that students use in their everyday problem solving. For example, when a high school ELA teacher found that her low-achieving African-American students had trouble interpreting symbols in canonical literary texts even though they routinely encountered and made sense of metaphor and symbols in a variety of out-of-school contexts (e.g., church, street), she chose texts from African-American youth culture (e.g., rap lyrics, rap videos, short films, film clips), which are rife with symbols with which students are familiar, to teach them how to identify literary symbolism and construct logical, warrantable claims in literary interpretation. She helped students recognize the similarities between what they did to interpret youth culture texts and what they could do to interpret canonical literature that also involves major attention to symbolism. She showed how her students' tacit understanding of how to reason about symbolism in out-of-school contexts can be scaffolded to teach literary reasoning and interpretation in her ELA class.

It is worth emphasizing that the end goal of literary reading is to develop an interpretation of the work being studied. To help students generate an interpretation and to promote multiple perspectives in interpretation, teachers may also consider explicit teaching of contemporary literary theories, such as reading response theory, formalism, Marxism, critical race theory, new historicism, gender studies/feminist theory, psychoanalysis, cultural studies, postcolonialism, deconstructionism, poststructuralism, postmodernism, and deconstructionism (Appleman, 2015). Each of these theories provides a different lens that gives readers an alternative way of looking at literature, helping them uncover themes, ideologies, and other invisible workings of the text. For example, reading response theory, which informs much of the current K-12 literature teaching practice, underscores the point that students may have different interpretations of the same text due to differences in their background knowledge and prior experiences. Marxist theory gives students tools for exploring literature through the prism of social class, enabling them to better understand issues of ideology, class, and power, as well as the political, social, and economic dimensions of the society. Critical race theory helps students see how the racist behaviors or attitudes depicted in a piece of literary work reflect not just the individual bias or prejudice but also the institutionalized racial discriminations in public policies and legal systems. Postcolonial criticism enables students to interpret literature in light of European colonialism and imperialism. Appleman (2015) explained that the purpose of teaching multiple literary theories is not to turn adolescents into critical theorists, but to give them tools for exploring literature from multiple perspectives. She argued that "learning different literary theories provides students with different lenses to look at literature, enabling them to have critical encounters with literature that can lead to multiple and differing interpretations of text while simultaneously creating a multiplicity where students can see different perspectives" (p. 11). Teaching students different literary theories is, therefore, key to avoiding what Reynolds et al. (2021, p. 589) called "interpretive monism", the idea that there is only one known interpretive answer (held by the teacher) and the task of students is to find and defend that answer.

To help students learn to generate justifiable interpretations, teachers also need to model the practice of close reading, showing students its value in literary reading. Close reading is, in the words of Kathleen McCormick (1994), "a method of reading literary texts that involve[s] detailed analytical interpretation as if the words on the page spoke directly and profoundly to the reader" (p. 34). It requires careful, exacting scrutiny of words, sentences, paragraphs, and visuals to explore their significance in the text. The analysis often involves noting the author's craft and thinking about how the semiotic (verbal/visual) and rhetorical choices the author made contribute to the overall meaning of the text and may affect the reader's responses to the text. This method can help students "overcome the purely private nature of literature as a school subject" (Halliday, 1982, p. 12), enabling them to generate interpretations based on concrete textual evidence rather than merely on private intuition or personal feeling.

For example, Eggins (2004) presented a detailed analysis of Kate Chopin's (1984) *The Story of an Hour*, a famous short story featuring a female protagonist who feels liberation at the news of her husband's death, showing how close attention to the cohesive resources in a text—references, conjunctions, and lexical strings (i.e., a list of all sequentially occurring content-bearing words that are semantically related, either taxonomically or through an expectancy relation)—can add significant depth to patterns that are detected in a surface reading and at the same time reveal additional insights. The analysis enables her to uncover thematic and metaphorical meanings that are not immediately obvious when the text is taken at face value until all the related words are strung together. For example, her analysis of references shows that "the patterns of reference chains help to realize Chopin's suggestion that conventional marriage deprives women of self-possession of their own bodies" (p. 40), and her analysis of lexical strings reinforces this finding, revealing that Chopin "is much concerned with a woman's control of her body as an essential component of her self-possession" (p. 40). This example shows that close reading through systematic cohesion analysis can help readers identify major or minor human participants and their relative importance in the text and unpack dense webs of semantic links in a text to better understand the meaning being made.

Similarly, Lukin (in Fang & Schleppegrell, 2008) demonstrated how close reading of an untitled sonnet by the great American poet Edna St. Vincent

Millay can help students generate linguistic evidence to support a particular interpretation of the poem. The poem involves an address by a female speaker to her lover about the nature of their relationship. By systematically attending to and analyzing various language patterns and their functions in the text, students will be able to build up a case about the overall meaning of the poem. Specifically, an examination of line, punctuation, and rhyme scheme reveals that the sonnet consists of two global moves (i.e., observation and conclusion), each organized around an opposition. An exploration of speech function (statement, question, offer, command), mood (declarative, interrogative, imperative), and modality (modal verbs like *may* and *would*) reveals the power relationship between the two central characters in the poem—the speaker (she) and the addressee (her lover). An analysis of the cohesive resources (e.g., pronominal and lexical choices) reveals the dominant motif in the poem—conflict between the speaker's emotional/physical feelings and her intellectual reasoning. An analysis of patterns of verbs (processes) and nouns (participants) reveals that the speaker has a more commanding role, relative to the addressee. An examination of what begins each clause (i.e., grammatical subject) in the poem similarly shows the dominance of the speaker. Through such close reading with systematic, detailed linguistic analysis, students are then in a position to develop a justifiable interpretation that answers three key questions germane to the poem: (a) what is the speaker saying to her lover? (b) how is their relationship depicted? and (c) what sense does the poem communicate about the two lovers?

Teaching Literature in ELA Classrooms: Some Examples

A disciplinary literacy approach to literary reading requires that ELA teachers foreground the unique epistemology, methodology, and goals of literature as a discipline in their instruction, helping students learn to read and think in a manner consistent with how literary experts read, make sense of, interpret, and use the texts in their discipline. In this section, five examples of such instructional practices are shared, each dealing with a different literary genre. Together, they show how ELA teachers design and enact disciplinary literacy instruction in different ways that support the attainment of their specific curriculum goals and learning outcomes.

The first example comes from Smagorinsky and Flanagan (2014), which describes how Ms. Martinez, a 10th-grade ELA teacher with 15 years of teaching experience, teaches literature. Ms. Martinez organizes her literature curriculum into several units, each taking 4–5 weeks and dealing with a developmentally appropriate theme such as loyalty, bullying, coming of age, conflict with authority, personal identity in social context, peer pressure and social groups, the heroic journey, and loss of innocence. For each unit, she includes both literary texts and other reading materials. In a unit on conflict with authority, Ms. Martinez begins by having students read and discuss news stories and internet articles reporting teenagers' conflicts with authority figures such as parents, teachers, coaches, or police. She also has students read and respond to several short stories from the classroom literature anthology, including James Baldwin's *The Man Child*, Willa Cather's *The Sentimentality of William Tavener*, Bordon Deal's *Antaeus*, Daphne du Maurier's *The Old Man*, Simon Ortiz's *Woman Singing*, and Kurt Vonnegut's *Harrison Bergeron*. These readings help the class segue into the unit's major work, George Orwell's *Animal Farm*, a beast fable and satirical allegorical novella that tells the story of a group of farm animals rebelling against their human farmers in order to create a society where the animals can be happy, free, and equal. Students are asked to explore the topic through writing, such as keeping a personal journal or blog about their reading, narrating a personal experience about a conflict with authority, and dramatizing their personal experience narratives as a class performance. The dramatization, accompanied with both a written script and a dramatic storyboard, can be video-recorded and shown on a screen or uploaded to the class website and social media page. Recognizing that writing about conflicts may involve using sentences consisting of clauses with adversative or contrastive relations, Ms. Martinez provides explicit instruction on the language resources that are functional for constructing the semantic relations, including *however, whereas, but, while, although, on the other hand*, and *conversely*. She develops a set of paired clauses that imply contrasts (e.g., "*I wanted to buy a video game console.*" and "*My father denied my request.*") and asks students to connect them into a single sentence using one of the above conjunctive resources (e.g., "*I wanted to buy a video game console; however, my father denied my request.*"). Students are expected to use at least one of these resources in their personal narratives on their conflicts with authority figures.

The second example comes from Langer (2011), which describes a 12th-grade honors English class, where Ms. Wright teaches a unit on Transcendentalism. To start the unit, Ms. Wright has students read and analyze poems by William Ellery Channing and Henry David Thoreau. They keep a journal recording their first impressions as they read. They then discuss the poems, focusing on the philosophical as well as literary features that mark Transcendentalism writing. After discussion, the teacher asks students to read works by Louisa May Alcott and compare them to Channing's poems, paying specific attention to what the author says and how the author says it.

To help students think about similarities and differences across the poems, Ms. Wright has students do some research about the authors, hoping that knowing the authors' lives would help them better understand and appreciate their writing styles (e.g., how each author describes emotions or images). She also encourages students to visit (virtually) some of the places where Transcendentalists once lived and/wrote (e.g., Concord House, Orchard House), hoping they will learn more about the Transcendentalism movement, the authors who were part of the movement, and their works. The information generated from this background research helps students see that Alcott's poems are more structured and use simpler language, whereas Channing's writing is more difficult to understand because he focuses on the intensity of nature and Alcott focuses on the intensity of family relations. As a culminating project for the unit, students write a 5- to 10-page research paper comparing the two literary figures (Alcott and Channing), focusing on things relevant to the authors' professional life/work as well as on the styles of their work. Throughout the unit, students engage in challenging reading and purposeful writing related to the literary work being studied; at the same time, they also receive a range of scaffolds that nurture their ability to read, analyze, reflect on, critique, and converse about literary texts.

The third example is provided by Hicks and Steffel (2012), which describes a high school unit of study on *Of Mice and Men*, a novella written by John Steinbeck that narrates the experiences of two displaced migrant ranch workers moving from place to place in California in search of new job opportunities during the Great Depression in the United States. Before reading the short novel, the teacher asks students to name some literary texts that have been most meaningful to them, hoping that this will remind them of the purpose of literature, which is to share stories that connect people through the ages, across cultures, and around the globe. The teacher also introduces for class discussion certain themes, concepts, or questions that are most germane to the target text (e.g., to what degree are we responsible for one another? What do you do when you feel most lonely? What makes people feel powerful?). After these purpose-setting and prior experience activating sessions, the teacher then introduces the target book but avoids providing too much background information about the author, the time period, or the plot so as to minimize influence on students' interpretation of the text. Next, the teacher reads the first few chapters aloud to the entire class, modeling appropriate connections students can make with the story and pausing regularly to comment on certain aspects of the text (e.g., setting, characterization, voice, tone, language choices). As students begin to read on their own, they are required to keep a response log recording, at regular intervals, their thoughts, feelings, comments, and questions about the text. At the end of the reading or periodically during reading, students pause to discuss the text in small groups. In these discussions, students are encouraged to identify literary devices and elaborate on how they contribute to the overall meaning of the text and the style of writing. They are also guided to notice the author's craft and think about how it helps shape the author's message and facilitates plot development. As an extension, students are encouraged to read another text with a similar theme (e.g., Pam Munoz-Ryan's *Esperanza Rising*) so that they can learn to recognize similarities across the texts among characters, themes, voice, plot, setting, use of symbolism, and other literary elements. At the end of the unit, students complete an assessment task that requires them to discuss how their connections with the story developed throughout the novel and what they have learned about the reality of human nature.

The last two examples concern the teaching of plays by William Shakespeare, whose works are still considered relevant to our time and worthy of our attention today because they reveal timeless truths of humanity. Hammond (2006) describes an 8-week unit on *Romeo and Juliet* that integrates language studies and literature content. One of Shakespeare's most popular plays, *Romeo and Juliet* is a tragedy about two young Italian star-crossed lovers whose deaths ultimately reconcile their feuding families. The unit is designed for first-year students in an Australian high school who have been identified as needing language support for effective participation in academic conversation and academic reading/writing. The goals of the unit are to develop students' understanding and appreciation of the play through analytic and reflective reading and to provide academic language support that enables students to effectively read and respond to the literary work. To achieve these goals, the ELA teacher engages students in a number of tasks across the unit that range from talking about sequences of events and characters in the play to writing about these aspects of the play. There is also a move from everyday ways of talking to more specialist ways of talking about events and characters. The teacher begins the unit by having students view a film of the play and discuss the intricacies of its plot. Next, she conducts a shared reading of the text with students, spotlighting important details in specific scenes and aspects of Shakespearean language. To meet the curriculum requirements, she also has students write a news report about the sequence of events in the play, using eyewitness accounts to learn about the relative nature of point of view. Before completing their own writing, students analyze models of news reports, identifying their rhetorical structures (e.g., summary line, introductory paragraph, elaborating paragraph) and patterns of language features (e.g., use of appropriate tense and punctuation, patterns of reference and conjunction, structure of noun phrases and their role in character description, meanings of new vocabulary words, language choices that construe the author's voice and construct characters' personalities). The teacher also incorporates a range of drama activities designed to engage students affectively with the content of the text and to enable them to move between spoken and written modes of communication. Through these performances, students demonstrate evidence of their reading engagement with the text, their proficiency in writing about the play, their understanding of Shakespearean language, and their ability to use language appropriate for different purposes and contexts.

A more innovative way of teaching Shakespearean plays is described by Harvey, Deuel, and Marlatt (2019), who used digital tools as a way of motivating students to engage with classical texts. To introduce Shakespeare and his comedic play A Midsummer Night's Dream to eighth-grade students, the ELA teacher creates five multimodal literary learning stations by integrating virtual reality, QR codes, videos, and smartphone applications with traditional, print-based texts. Students rotate through these stations in three class periods, spending roughly 30 minutes in each station, where they "undergo virtual tours, explore videos, peruse websites, access scholarly excerpt and articles, and engage with myriad other resources to discover new information" (p. 561). In Station 1, students learn about English theater during the Elizabethan era by reading The Usborne World of Shakespeare (Claybourne & Treays, 2001) and using Oculus Go VR devices to tour the Globe Theatre, where many of Shakespeare's plays were performed. In Station 2, students scan QR codes on their personal phones or classroom tablets to access many different websites to learn about what life looked like in England during the sixteenth century, gaining a better understanding of the historical and cultural contexts around Shakespeare's life and the subject matter illustrated in his writing. In Station 3, students watch and take note on two videos—one on YouTube and the other on a biography website—to learn about Shakespeare's early life, family, education, and marriage. In Station 4, students read four texts about Shakespeare—one graphic story (Stanley, 1998), two printed biographies, and one edited volume (Jowett, Montgomery, Taylor, & Wells, 2005)—to learn about the many plays and poems that Shakespeare wrote and, in the process, gain a better understanding of the genre differences among tragedy, comedy, and historical narrative. In Station 5, students read and discuss a printed or online copy of "Why Shakespeare Still Matters" (https://pursuit.unimelb.edu.au/articles/why-shakespeare-still-matters), an article written by David McInnis, a Shakespearean scholar at the University of Melbourne in Australia, to explore ways in which Shakespeare has continually influenced popular culture. After the completion of five stations, students write a short reflective essay commenting on their experiences with these stations. They then break into small groups to read different scenes with the future goal of acting them out in class. As students read their chosen scenes and prepare for performance, they pursue questions about plot, character development, stage directions, props, and costume design. As a culminating learning experience, students attend a professional live performance of the play in a community playhouse.

Conclusion

Literature is a discursive and interpretive discipline with the potential to give pleasure, provoke imagination, stimulate dialogue, encourage critical thinking, build aesthetic, affective, and cognitive knowledge, and hone logical reasoning (Peels, 2020). Literary texts, as Yagelski (1994) noted, are not simply "great art"; they are also "cultural artifacts that grow out of complex historical, social, political, economic, and cultural circumstances" (p. 34). As such, they open readers up to a world of values, viewpoints, concerns, and experiences that define human reality, inviting ethical and epistemic reasoning about issues and challenges that students have to wrestle with in their own lives (Lee, 2011). Thus, it is vitally important that students develop the capacity and disposition to read and appreciate literature. ELA teachers have a critical role to play in helping students develop both interest and expertise in literary reading. Specifically, they can engage students in communal reading and guided discussion of literature while at the same time providing them with tools for critically examining literature from multiple perspectives and strategies for developing reasoned/original interpretations that are supported by both textual and contextual evidence. This sort of instructional practice will enable students to engage more deeply and productively with complex literary texts from around the world, allowing them to deepen their knowledge and understanding of human experiences, gain new perspectives on the world and cultures, sharpen their intellectual virtues (e.g., open-mindedness, inquisitiveness, empathy, imagination, moral tolerance), and develop language and literacy proficiencies.

Reflection and Application

1 What is the role of literature in the English Language Arts (ELA) curriculum?
2 What are the specific challenges involved in literary reading? How can these challenges be addressed?
3 What does disciplinary literacy mean in relation to literature? What does it mean to be reading like a literary expert?
4 What does a disciplinary literacy approach to literary reading instruction look like in the ELA classroom? In what ways does the approach promote literary literacy?

5 Design a unit of instruction for a specific grade level aimed at developing students' literary expertise. Be sure to identify/describe the disciplinary standards and curriculum goals to be addressed, the textual resources to be utilized, the activities and strategies to be used to promote diverse yet rigorous interpretations of literature, the assessment tools to be employed to monitor and evaluate student progress toward the unit objectives, and a reasonable timeline for implementing the unit.

References

Adams, B., & Fang, Z. (2020). Meeting the demands of close reading performance tasks: Unpacking complex texts with cohesion analysis. *American Reading Forum Yearbook, 39*, 59–70.

Appleman, D. (2015). *Critical encounters in high school English: Teaching literary theory to adolescents* (3rd ed.). New York: Teachers College Press.

Beach, R., Appleman, D., Fecho, B., & Simon, R. (2020). *Teaching literature to adolescents* (4th ed.). New York: Routledge.

Beach, R., Thein, A., & Webb, A. (2015). *Teaching to exceed the English language arts common core state standards: A critical inquiry approach for 6–12 classrooms.* New York: Routledge.

Bernstein, B. (2000). *Pedagogy, symbolic control and identity: Theory, research, and critique* (revised ed). Lanham, MA: Rowman & Littlefield Publishers, Inc.

Bintz, W., & Ciecierski, L. (2021). Crossover literature in the ELA middle grades classroom. *Voices from the Middle, 28*(3), 31–37.

Bloom, H. (1994). *The western canon: The books and school of the ages.* Boston: Harcourt Brace.

Cadiero-Kaplan, K. (2002). Literacy ideologies: Critically engaging the language arts curriculum. *Language Arts, 79*(5), 372–381.

Chapman, S. (2015). *Disciplinary literacy: A study of the cognitive, social, and semiotic practices of disciplinary experts.* Unpublished doctoral dissertation, University of Florida, Gainesville, Florida.

Christie, F., & Dreyfus, S. (2007). Letting the secret out: Successful writing in secondary English. *Australian Journal of Language and Literacy, 30*(3), 235–247.

Christie, F., & Macken-Horarik, M. (2011). Disciplinarity and school subject English. In F. Christie & K. Maton (Eds.), *Disciplinarity: Functional linguistic and sociological perspectives* (pp. 175–196). London: Bloomsbury.

Crain, P. (2000). *The story of A: The alphabetization of America from the New England Primer to the Scarlet Letter.* Redwood City, CA: Stanford University Press.

Eggins, S. (2004). *An introduction to systemic functional linguistics* (2nd ed.). London: Continuum.

Elliott, V. (2021). *Knowledge in English: Canon, curriculum and cultural literacy.* London: Taylor & Francis.

Fang, Z., & Schleppegrell, M. (2008). *Reading in secondary content areas: A language-based pedagogy.* Ann Arbor, MI: University of Michigan Press.

Fang, Z., Sun, Y., Chiu, C., & Trutschel, B. (2014). Inservice teachers' perception of a language-based approach to content area reading. *Australian Journal of Language and Literacy, 37*(1), 55–66.

Goldman, S., Britt, M., Brown, W., Cribb, G., George, M., Greenleaf, C., Lee, C., Shanahan, C., & Project READI (2016). Disciplinary literacies and learning to read for understanding: A conceptual framework for disciplinary literacy. *Educational Psychologist, 51*(2), 219–246.

Goodwin, A., & Jimenez, R. (2020). The science of reading: Supports, critiques, and questions. *Reading Research Quarterly, 55* (S1), S7–S16.

Graesser, A., McNamara, D., & Kulikowich, J. (2011). Coh-Metrix: Providing multilevel analyses of text characteristics. *Educational Researcher, 40*(5), 223–234.

Halliday, M. (1982). Linguistics in teacher education. In R. Carter (Ed.), *Linguistics and the teacher* (pp. 10–15). London: Routledge & Kegan Paul.

Halliday, M., & Matthiessen, C. (2014). *An introduction to functional grammar* (4th ed.). New York: Routledge.

Hamilton, E. (1999). *Mythology: Timeless tales of gods and heroes.* New York: Grand Central Publishing.

Hammond, J. (2006). High challenge, high support: Integrating language and content instruction for diverse learners in an English literature classroom. *Journal of English for Academic Purposes, 5,* 269–283.

Harker, W. (1994). "Plain sense" and "poetic significance": Tenth-grade readers reading two poems. *Poetics, 22,* 199–218.

Harvey, M., Deuel, A., & Marlatt, R. (2019). "To be, or not to be": Modernizing Shakespeare with multimodal learning stations. *Journal of Adolescent and Adult Literacy, 63*(5), 559–568.

Hicks, T., & Steffel, S. (2012). Learning with text in English language arts. In T. Jetton & C. Shanahan (Eds.), *Adolescent literacy in the academic disciplines: General principles and practical strategies* (pp. 120–153). New York: Guilford.

Hillocks, G., & Ludlow, L. (1984). A taxonomy of skills in reading and interpreting fiction. *American Educational Research Journal, 21,* 7–24.

Huisman, R. (2016). Talking about poetry—using the model of language in systemic functional linguistics to talk about poetic texts. *English in Australia, 51*(2), 7–19.

Huisman, R. (2019). The discipline of English Literature from the perspective of SFL register. *Language, Context and Text, 1*(1), 102–120.

Jowett, J., Montgomery, W., Taylor, G., & Wells, S. (Eds.). (2005). *The Oxford Shakespeare: The complete works* (2nd ed.). Oxford, UK: Clarendon.

Langer, J. (2011). *Envisioning knowledge: Building literacy in the academic disciplines.* New York: Teachers College Press.

Lee, C. (1995). A culturally based cognitive apprenticeship: Teaching African American high school students' skills in literary interpretation. *Reading Research Quarterly, 30*(4), 608–631.

Lee, C. (2001). Is October Brown Chinese: A cultural modeling activity system for underachieving students. *American Educational Research Journal, 38*(1), 97–142.

Lee, C. (2011). Education and the study of literature. *Scientific Study of Literature, 1*(1), 49–58.

Lee, C. & Spratley, A. (2010). *Reading in the disciplines: The challenge of adolescent literacy.* New York, NY: Carnegie Corporation of New York.

Lukin, A. (2003). Grammar and the study of poetry. In J. James (Ed.), *Grammar in the language classroom* (pp. 228–246). Singapore: SEAMEO Regional Language Center.

McCormick, K. (1994). *The culture of reading and the teaching of English.* Manchester, UK: Manchester University Press.

National Governors Association Center for Best Practices (NGA) & Council of Chief State School Officers (CCSSO) (2010). *Common core state standards for English language arts & literacy for history/social studies, science, and technical subjects.* Washington, DC: Author.

Peels, R. (2020). How literature delivers knowledge and understanding, illustrated by Hardy's *Tess of the D'Urbervilles* and Wharton's *Summer. British Journal of Aesthetics, 60*(2), 199–222.

Peskin, J. (1998). Constructing meaning when reading poetry: An expert-novice study. *Cognition and Instruction, 16*(3), 235–263.

Purves, A. & Pradl, G. (2003). School subject literature. In J. Flood, D. Lapp, R. Squire, & J. Jensen (Eds.), *Handbook of research on teaching the English language arts* (2nd ed., pp. 848–856). Mahwah, NJ: Erlbaum.

Rainey, E. (2016). Disciplinary literacy in English language arts: Exploring the social and problem-based nature of literary reading and reasoning. *Reading Research Quarterly, 52*(1), 53–71.

Rainey, E., & Moje, E. (2012). Building insider knowledge: Teaching students to read, write, and think in ELA and across the disciplines. *English Education, 45*(1), 71–90.

Reynolds, T., & Rush, L. (2017). Experts and novices reading literature: An analysis of disciplinary literacy in English Language Arts. *Literacy Research and Instruction, 56*(3), 199–216.

Reynolds, T., Rush, L., Lampi, J., & Holschuh, J. (2021). Moving beyond interpretive monism: A disciplinary heuristic to bridge literary theory and literacy theory. *Harvard Educational Review, 91*(3), 382–401.

Rosenblatt, L. (1978). *The reader, the text, the poem: The transactional theory of the literary work.* Carbondale, IL: Southern Illinois University Press.

Sachar, L. (1998). *Holes.* New York: Farrar, Straus & Giroux.

Schnick, T., & Knickelbine, M. (2000). *The Lexile Framework: An introduction for educators.* Durham, NC: MetaMetrics, Inc.

Smagorinsky, P. (2015). Disciplinary literacy in English language arts. *Journal of Adolescent and Adult Literacy, 59*(2), 141–146.

Smagorinsky, P. & Flanagan, J. (2014). Literacy in the English/language arts curriculum. In P. Smagorinsky (Ed.), *Teaching dilemmas & solutions in content-area literacy, Grades 6–12.* Corwin Press.

Snowling, M., Hulme, C., & Nation, K. (2022). *The science of reading: A handbook.* New York: Wiley.

Stanley, D. (1998). *Bard of Avon: The story of William Shakespeare.* New York, NY: HarperCollins.

Warren, J. (2011). "Generic" and "specific" expertise in English: An expert/expert study in poetry interpretation and academic argument. *Cognition and Instruction, 29*(4), 349–374.

Yagelski, R. (1994). Literature and literacy: Rethinking English as a school subject. *English Journal, 83*(3), 30–36.

Zeitz, C. (1994). Expert-novice differences in memory, abstraction, and reasoning in the domain of literature. *Cognition and Instruction, 12*(4), 277–312.

3
Reading History

What is History?

History is a key component of social studies, a term widely used in K-12 education to designate a field of study that combines two or more subjects dealing with human beings and their interrelationships. Subjects that deal with human activities, achievements, and relationships include history, geography, civics, law, economics, political science, sociology, psychology, philosophy, religion, anthropology, art, archaeology, and literature, among others. In K-12 contexts, the umbrella term "social studies" is most often used to include civics, economics, geography, and history, as well as other subjects whose content and aim is predominantly social, in the same way that mathematics is used to include arithmetic, algebra, geometry, trigonometry, and calculus, or science is used to include astronomy, biology, physics, zoology, chemistry, and others. Of these subjects, history is described in a landmark document, *American History in Schools and Colleges* (American Historical Association, 1944), as "the most inclusive and pervasive of the social studies" in that it "partakes of the nature of each of the others when it records activities which fall within their scope" (unpaged). As such, history addresses a wide variety of topics, ranging from government and immigration to international trade and world resources. It contributes eminently to the aim of social studies, which is, according to the National Council for the Social Studies, "to help young people develop the ability to make informed and reasoned decisions for the public good as citizens of a culturally diverse, democratic society in an interdependent world" (https://www.socialstudies.org/about). For these reasons, we focus on the discipline of history in this chapter, recognizing that its study inevitably involves topics that are also germane to other disciplines.

History is the study of the human past. Historians use written documents and other artifacts (e.g., photos, remnants of buildings, paintings, tools) left

DOI: 10.4324/9781003432258-3

behind by people in an effort to construct narratives, explanations, or arguments about what really happened yesterday or centuries ago so that we can have a better understanding of the world (e.g., ourselves, other people, how/when/why change occurred) and make more informed decisions about today's complex questions and dilemmas. The construction of these narratives, explanations, or arguments is not a process of simply cataloguing names, dates, events, and other "facts"; rather, it is a process of "constructing, reconstructing, and interpreting past events, ideas, and institutions from surviving or inferential evidence" (Ravi, 2010, p. 36). It involves careful selection, in-depth analysis, and critical evaluation of existing (old and new) historical records. And because these records are often incomplete and at times contradictory, historians must render judgments regarding the veracity and worth of particular pieces of evidence, make inferences about the relationships among these pieces of evidence, and engage in discipline-legitimated social and intellectual critique in order to proffer any credible historical explanation or argument. History is, therefore, an inherently human construction imbued with personal bias, perspectives, intentions, prejudices, and worldviews.

In this sense, history is, like literature, a very much interpretive subject. It has what British educational sociologist Basil Bernstein (1996, pp. 172–173) called a horizontal knowledge structure, comprising a series of segmented, strongly bounded languages, "each with its own specialized modes of interrogation and specialized criteria . . . with non-comparable principles of description based on different, often opposed, assumptions" (cited in Maton, 2006, p. 47). For example, historians using different interpretive frameworks (e.g., social, cultural, economic, political, thematic) tend to select different historical sources, prioritize different pieces of evidence, and produce coherent accounts that align with their chosen framework. As Goldman et al. (2016, p. 19) explained,

> one historian might explain the American Civil War in terms of differences in the economies of the states that seceded as compared to those that remained in the Union. Another might argue that the Civil War was fought over the inhumanity of slavery, drawing on philosophical arguments and conflicts dating back to the nation's beginnings.

Similarly, a piece of clothing may mean different things to historians with different interpretive frameworks. To a cultural historian, the artifact may provide "evidence of changing fashions and consumer tastes"; but to a social historian, it may be used as "evidence of class differences or production patterns" (https://www.hist.cam.ac.uk/getting-started-reading-primary-sources).

Historians with different critical lenses (e.g., feminist, Marxist, psychoanalytic, semiotics) are also likely to generate different, and often competing, interpretations of past events. Those with a Marxist lens tend to view China's infamous "Cultural Revolution" (1967–1976) as a response to the escalating class struggle between the so-called "revolutionists" (e.g., proletarians) and "counter-revolutionists" (e.g., bourgeois), whereas those with a psychoanalytic lens are more likely to focus on the catastrophes brought about by the historical event, delving into the traumas it inflicted on individuals, groups, and the society as a whole.

Moreover, historical events are often reinterpreted with the availability of new evidence or change of time and context. For example, the declassification of previously secret government documents often reveals new details about events in the past (e.g., the Cuban Missile Crisis, the civil rights movement), giving historians new knowledge and insights that often lead them to reinterpret past events (Connelly, 2023). China's isolationist policy from the sixteenth to the nineteenth centuries used to be described by Western scholars and in Chinese history textbooks as a total disaster because it led to the "century of humiliation", when China was forced to open its borders to foreign powers on unequal terms after the Opium Wars (1839–1842, 1856–1860). However, today, at a time when many people are speculating about the Chinese government's commitment to its open door policy during the Covid-19 pandemic and a brewing new cold war between China and the U.S.-led West, that interpretation is questioned. For example, a team of scholars from the Chinese Academy of History now argues that the isolationist policy of the Ming (1368–1644) and Qing (1636–1912) dynasties was a reasonable self-defense strategy to protect China's territorial and cultural integrity and to ward off aggressive Western colonial forces (Zhou, 2022). Because history is riven by disagreements and controversies, "there is less argument about the 'content' to be taught and greater concern with the development of ways of thinking about and evaluating texts" (Schleppegrell, 2011, p. 199).

Reading and Historical Literacy

History is not an immutable body of facts and events, but a discursive practice built on interpretations. It is a predominantly textual construction, as historical events happened once and disappeared, leaving behind only historical remnants in the form of written texts (e.g., personal diaries, government documents, newspaper reports) and other artifacts (e.g., photos, paintings, oral recordings, videos, artworks, tools) for historians

to read, analyze, and interpret (Bain, 2008). This means that reading/
literacy is central to the conception of history and the social practice
of historians. To be considered literate in history, students must be able
to do much more than comprehend and recall discrete historical figures,
timelines, and events. They need to have sophisticated understanding of
historical time, agency, causality, change, significance, and evaluation
(Coffin, 2006), recognizing that historical knowledge is "contested and
contestable" (Goldman et al., 2016, p. 16). Most importantly, they need
to develop the ability to critically examine the various accounts and interpretations they encounter, comparing/contrasting different accounts,
empathizing with historical figures' lived experiences, weighing the quality of evidence, assessing the rigor of argument, synthesizing across multiple sources, considering the influence of bias, generating evidence-based
claims about the past, and communicating these claims to others in
discipline-legitimated ways. In the words of Nokes (2013, p. 20), historical literacy is

> the ability to construct meaning with multiple genres of print, non-
> print, visual, aural, video, audio, and multimodal historical texts; crit-
> ically evaluate texts within the context of the work historians have
> previously done; use texts as evidence in the development of original
> interpretations of past events; and create multiple types of texts that
> meet disciplinary standards.

This emphasis on the development of historical thinking over the acquisition of historical knowledge is also evident in prominent national standards. The C3 (College, Career, & Civic Life) Framework for Social Studies
State Standards (Swan et al., 2013), for example, identified four dimensions
in which students are expected to develop competence. They are (1) pro-
posing questions and planning inquiries, (2) applying disciplinary concepts
and tools, (3) evaluating sources and using evidence, and (4) communicating
conclusions and taking informed actions. Applied to the discipline of history, these dimensions require students to

- construct compelling and supporting questions that can frame and advance
  historical inquiries
- locate, assess, and use historical sources to answer these questions and develop arguments about the past
- acquire knowledge about significant events, development, individuals, groups,
  documents, places, and ideas to support inquiries
- explain how historical events and developments were shaped by historical
  contexts

- analyze how historical contexts shaped and continue to shape people's perspectives
- detect possible limitations in various kinds of historical evidence
- critique the usefulness of historical sources for a specific historical inquiry
- analyze multiple and complex causes and effects of events in the past
- integrate evidence from multiple relevant historical sources and interpretations into a reasoned argument or plausible explanation about the past
- evaluate historical interpretations for coherence, completeness, the quality of evidence, rigor of reasoning, and authorial perspective
- understand the value-laden, contested, and evolving nature of historical interpretations, and
- apply historical thinking and inquiry process to make decisions and take action on civic matters within and outside school contexts.

These reading/literacy abilities are similarly emphasized in the Common Core State Standards for History/Social Studies (NGA & CCSSO, 2010), as can be seen in the following standards for grades 11–12:

- Cite specific textual evidence to support analysis of primary and secondary sources, connecting insights gained from specific details to an understanding of the text as a whole.
- Determine the central ideas or information of a primary or secondary source, providing an accurate summary that makes clear the relationships among the key ideas and details.
- Evaluate various explanations for actions or events and determine which explanation best accords with textual evidence, acknowledging where the text leaves matters uncertain.
- Determine the meaning of words and phrases as they are used in a text, including analyzing how an author uses and refines the meaning of a key term over the course of a text.
- Analyze in detail how a complex primary source is structured, including how key sentences, paragraphs, and larger portions of the text contribute to the whole.
- Evaluate authors' differing points of view on the same historical event or issue by assessing the authors' claims, reasoning, and evidence.
- Integrate and evaluate multiple sources of information presented in diverse formats and media in order to address a question or solve a problem.
- Evaluate an author's premises, claims, and evidence by corroborating or challenging them with other information.
- Integrate information from diverse sources into a coherent understanding of an idea or event, noting discrepancies among sources.

Types of Historical Materials

In constructing interpretations of the past, historians work with many different kinds of historical materials. These materials vary in terms of media, source, and purpose. They comprise mainly written texts (e.g., government documents, press release, newspaper articles, letters, memoirs, transcripts of oral histories or speeches), but other media are also used regularly, including visual representations (e.g., photographs, drawings, figures, maps, paintings, political cartoons), physical artifacts (e.g., monuments, sculptures, remains of buildings, tools, equipment, clothing), and audio-visual materials (e.g., recordings of speeches and interviews, videos, music, films).

Historical materials can also be classified according to sources. Primary sources are original records or objects created by participants or witnesses at the time (or even well after) historical events occurred. They can include diaries, letters, interviews, autobiographies, oral histories, photographs, music, poems, sales records, property deeds, local phone books, recordings, newspaper articles, government documents, maps, census records, memoirs, and physical artifacts. Two popular places to locate primary sources are the Library of Congress Primary Source Sets and Digital Public Library of America Primary Source Sets. Secondary sources are created based on rigorous analysis, evaluation, and synthesis of information from primary sources. They are essentially commentaries on or discussions of primary sources and can include documents, books, monographs, articles, biographies, and reviews of laws and legislations. Tertiary sources are publications that index, summarize, compile, or digest the information presented in primary and secondary sources. They include textbooks, encyclopedias, manuals, guidebooks, and other reference/indexing materials.

The historical texts that students regularly read and write in school belong to three genres—recording, explaining, and arguing (Coffin, 2006). The recording text retells past events as they unfolded naturally through real time. It typically begins with an orientation that introduces the setting and the main participants and may also foreshadow the problem. This is followed by a sequence of events as they unfolded over time. The story ends with a brief evaluation of the historical significance of the events recorded or the life of the main historical figure. Some recording texts present a chronological recounting of historical events with little or no causal meaning; these texts are called historical recounts (see, for example, Text 3.1). In other recording texts, causal meaning is more salient, though not dominant, in the retelling; these texts are called historical accounts (see, for example, Text 3.2).

Text 3.1

On March 5, 1770, violence erupted. A fight broke out between some Bostonians and soldiers. As British officers tried to calm the crowd, a man shouted, "We did not send for you. We will not have you here. We'll get rid of you, we'll drive you away!"

The angry townspeople surged forward. They began throwing sticks and stones at the soldiers. "Come on, you rascals, you bloody backs, you lobster scoundrels, fire, if you dare," someone in the crowd shouted.

After one soldier was knocked down, the nervous redcoats did fire. They killed five colonists. Among the dead was Crispus Attucks, a dockworker who was part African, part Native American. One Bostonian cried: "Are the inhabitants to be knocked down in the streets? Are they to be murdered . . .?" The colonists called the tragic encounter "the Boston Massacre." (Brinkley et al., 2013, p. 127)

Text 3.2

British officials, faced with a breakdown of law and order, landed two regiments of troops in Boston in 1768. Many of the soldiers were drunken and profane characters. Liberty-loving colonists, resenting the presence of the red-coated "ruffians", taunted the "bloody backs" unmercifully.

A clash was inevitable. On the evening of March 5, 1770, a crowd of some sixty townspeople began taunting and throwing snowballs at a squad of ten redcoats. The Bostonians were still angry over the death of an eleven-year-old boy, shot ten days earlier during a protest against a merchant who had defied the colonial boycott of British goods. Acting apparently without orders, but nervous and provoked by the jeering crowd, the troops opened fire and killed or wounded eleven citizens, an event that became known as the Boston Massacre. One of the first to die was Crispus Attucks, described by contemporaries as a powerfully built runaway "mulatto" and a leader of the mob. Both sides were in some degree to blame, and in the subsequent trial (in which future president John Adams served as defense attorney for the soldiers), only two of the redcoats were found guilty of manslaughter. The soldiers were released after being branded on the hand. (Kennedy, Cohen, & Bailey, 2009, p. 110)

The explaining text explains the causes and/or consequences of past events. Those explaining the reasons or factors that contributed to a particular historical event or outcome are called factorial explanations. Those explaining the consequences or effects of an historical event are called consequential explanations. An explaining text typically begins with identification of an historical phenomenon or outcome, followed by elaboration of a list of causes and/or effects, and ends with summary statements emphasizing or evaluating these factors or consequences. Text 3.3 is a factorial explanation in that it explains the reasons why the trial of the Emmett Till murder case received so much national attention.

Text 3.3

The trial captured the outside world's interest for several reasons. The *Jet* magazine photo of Emmett publicized the gruesome details of the murder, making it more than just another Southern lynching. The nature of the crime itself, a fourteen-year-old boy brutally murdered by two men, made it news, but the reason for the kidnapping and killing – Emmett had allegedly whistled at and made "ugly remarks" to a white woman – turned it into big news. The racial context of the case also contributed to its notoriety; at the same time, Medgar Evers and the NAACP were fighting hard to gain equal rights for Blacks in the South, and Emmett's senseless murder seemed to symbolize the plight of Blacks in the region. Finally, the murder indictment against Milam and Bryant was a landmark event in Mississippi, a state where more than 500 lynchings had occurred since 1880, because, as far as people knew, it was the first time white men had been indicted for killing a Black person. The trial gave many African Americans hope that, finally, equal rights for all citizens, regardless of race, might be on the way. For entrenched Southern segregationists, the trial confirmed the fears that had begun with the Supreme Court's *Brown v. Board of Education* ruling: The white-dominated Southern way of life was in jeopardy. (Crowe, 2003, p. 22)

The arguing text argues the case for or against a particular interpretation of the past. Those arguing for a particular interpretation are called "expositions"; those arguing against a particular interpretation are called "challenge"; and those considering different interpretations before reaching a conclusion or position are called "discussion". An arguing text typically begins by providing a context that identifies the historical issue, followed by articulation of a thesis (or overall position) and presentation of supporting evidence, and concludes by reaffirming the thesis. An example of the arguing text, or exposition, can be found in Text 3.4, where the argument that "Nazi Germany became a genocidal state" is defended with a litany of supporting evidence.

Text 3.4

Nazi Germany became a genocidal state. The goal of annihilation called for participation by every arm of the government. The policy of extermination involved every level of German society and marshaled the entire apparatus of the German bureaucracy. Parish churches and the Interior Ministry supplied the birth records that defined and isolated Jews. The Post Office delivered the notifications of definitions, expropriation, denaturalization, and deportation. The Finance Ministry confiscated

Jewish wealth and property; German industrial and commercial firms fired Jewish workers, officers, and board members, even disenfranchising Jewish stock-holders. The universities refused to admit Jewish students, denied degrees to those already enrolled, and dismissed Jewish faculty. Government transportation bureaus handled the billing arrangements with the railroads for the trains that carried Jews to their death. (Berenbaum, 2006, p. 103)

Each of these genres—recording, explaining, and arguing—enables the historian to think and write about the past in a different way. Most historical texts that students encounter in school typically juxtapose the three genres, with some texts relying heavily on chronological recounting of past events and others foregrounding explanation or argument (Schleppegrell, 2004).

The Challenges of Historical Reading

Perhaps more than any other discipline, history is a literate practice that depends on the use of written texts. The three genres of historical texts discussed above draw on different constellations of lexical and grammatical features that present varying degrees of comprehension and interpretive challenges to students. The recording texts construct the past as story; they are temporally organized, with a focus on concrete events unfolding in real time and involving specific historical figures. These texts tend be objective, truthful records of the past; however, as Martin (2002) pointed out, the selection and arrangement of events, as well as the historical significance attributed to these events, may not be entirely objective. Therefore, while students generally find recording texts more accessible because of their prior experience with stories in the elementary grades, they may not always be aware of the bias and interpretations embedded in these texts. The explaining and arguing texts, on the other hand, construct explanations and debates about the past. They are organized rhetorically around a set of abstract theses and use language that is often metaphorical and evaluative (Coffin, 2006; Schleppegrell, 2004). As such, the explaining and arguing texts are generally more challenging for students to read and interpret than recording texts.

In the elementary school, history is typically constructed as story-like representations of the past, but in middle and high schools, history is more often constructed as abstract interpretations of the past (Coffin, 2006; Martin, 2002). Even when past events are retold as stories in secondary school history, they do not simply record the events as they happened in real time, but usually also include explanations of causal relations among the events and statements regarding their historical significance. Stories are also regularly embedded in the explaining and arguing texts to provide historical back-ground or supporting evidence. There is a gradual shift in the way history is presented in K-12 schooling—from organizing events along a chronological sequence (see, for example, Text 3.1) to including events as part of a larger sequence of explanation or argument (see, for example, Text 3.2) and to ab-stract interpretations of past events with little or no chronological retelling (see Text 3.3 and Text 3.4 for examples), as Figure 3.1 illustrates.

This shift accompanies the shift in the sort of knowledge that students are expected to engage with as they move through K-12 schooling. That is, as students advance in grade level, the knowledge they are expected to learn becomes progressively more abstract and complex. In middle and high schools, students delve further into academic content areas, where the focus of learning is on disciplinary knowledge and habits of mind. The sort of language that students encounter in elementary schooling is no longer adequate for engaging in disciplinary learning, as middle and high school history features a greater degree of generalization and interpreta-tion, which calls for the use of more abstract and evaluative language. This language presents new comprehension and interpretive challenges for ado-lescents, requiring them to expand their language resources and to develop new ways of using language in order to engage productively in discipli-nary learning. To illustrate the sort of challenges that students may face in

chronological retelling of past events

(roughly grades 3–5)

↓

explaining/arguing about the past with some chronological retelling

(roughly grades 6–9)

↓

abstract interpretations of the past with little or no chronological retelling

(roughly grades 10–12 and beyond)

Figure 3.1 Shifts in How History is Represented in K-12 Schooling

reading history, let's turn to Text 3.5, an excerpt from an award-winning social studies trade book for middle school analyzing and interpreting the historically significant trial of two White men in Mississippi who abducted and killed an African-American boy from Chicago named Emmett Till (Crowe, 2003, pp. 15–20).

Text 3.5

It was after 2:00 A.M. when the killers' car, its headlights off, coasted to a stop on the gravel road about fifty feet from the darkened sharecropper's shack. When the car engine shut down, the steady thrum of locusts resumed, filling the humid night air with a pulsing buzz.

Shadows from the persimmon and cedar trees in the yard cloaked two white men as they emerged from the sedan and spoke to a man and a woman in the backseat. When they finished their brief conversation, Roy Bryant and his half brother, J.W. Milam, walked boldly toward the shack with vengeance on their minds. Milam, the bigger of the two, carried a long flashlight in one hand and an Army-issue .45 pistol in the other.

. . .

The kidnapping and murder of Emmett Till and the trial of his killers became one of the biggest news items of 1955. The viewing of his disfigured corpse at Rainer Funeral Home and his funeral at the Roberts Temple of the Church of God in Christ in Chicago attracted more than ten thousand mourners. The grisly open-casket photo of Emmett that appeared in *Jet* magazine horrified and angered hundreds of thousands more. The National Association for the Advancement of Colored People (NAACP), other civil rights organizations, and political leaders expressed outrage at the cold-blooded murder of this boy from Chicago. In an interview, Roy Wilkins, Executive Secretary of the NAACP, labeled the crime a racist act, saying, "It would appear that the state of Mississippi has decided to maintain white supremacy by murdering children." Newspapers across the country, especially those in the Northern states, condemned the killing and the racist attitudes that led to it.

The protests and condemnations from civil rights leaders and Northerners poked an already raw nerve in the South. The white leaders in Southern states like Mississippi that enforced Jim Crow laws, regulations that segregated Blacks from whites, were still stinging from the 1954 Supreme Court decision *Brown v. Board of Education of Topeka*, which declared that racially segregated schools were unconstitutional. In May of 1955, the Supreme Court pushed the issue even further when it ordered that integration of schools must proceed "with all deliberate speed." The two rulings alarmed Southern leaders who feared that the federal government and Northern agitators planned to destroy the Southern way of life. Comments from a speech given by the police commissioner of

Montgomery, Alabama, typify the attitude of many white Southerners regarding forced desegregation of public schools:

> "Since the infamous Supreme Court decision rendered in 1954, we in Montgomery and the South have been put to a severe test by those who seek to destroy our time-honored customs. Not since Reconstruction have our customs been in such jeopardy . . . We can, will and must resist outside forces hell-bent on out destruction . . ."

The text begins by recounting the people and events connected to the murder of Emmett Till. The retelling of what actually happened in that fateful night of Emmett Till's kidnapping and murder is followed by explanations about the consequences of the killing. Embedded in these explanations are brief mentions of relevant historical events as well as quotes from important historical figures. The recounting portion of the text (the first two paragraphs) uses language that is characteristic of storytelling, similar to the way language is used in stories (see Chapter 2), with clauses strung together into sentences through subordination indicating the chronological sequence (e.g., *when, as*) and participants constructed as mostly concrete nouns or short noun phrases (e.g., *the killer's car, Roy Bryant, Rainer Funeral Home, Jet magazine*). With the exception of a few potentially unfamiliar vocabulary words (e.g., *thrum, vengeance*), the two paragraphs should present little comprehension challenge to adolescents.

The third and fourth paragraphs present a greater comprehension challenge in part because they require more extensive and specialized background knowledge about American history. Readers without some background knowledge about the Civil Rights Movement may have trouble understanding the passage. They may not know what *Jim Crow laws* and *Brown v. Board of Education of Topeka* are about; nor may they appreciate the racial tension described in the text. Adding to the challenge is the dense, abstract language that the historian employed to construct his interpretation. The density is achieved via the use of long noun phrases, such as:

- *the kidnapping and murder of Emmett Till*
- *one of the biggest news items of 1955*
- *the grisly open-casket photo of Emmett that appeared in Jet magazine*
- *The protests and condemnations from civil rights leaders and Northerners*
- *the white leaders in Southern states like Mississippi that enforced Jim Crow laws*
- *Jim Crow laws, regulations that segregated Blacks from whites*
- *the 1954 Supreme Court decision Brown v. Board of Education of Topeka*
- *Southern leaders who feared that the federal government and Northern agitators planned to destroy the Southern way of life*

- *comments from a speech given by the police commissioner of Montgomery, Alabama*
- *the attitude of many white Southerners regarding forced desegregation of public schools,* and
- *the infamous Supreme Court decision rendered in 1954.*

Each of these long noun phrases consists of a head (e.g., *photo, decision*), one or more premodifiers (e.g., determiner [*the*], describer [*grisly, 1954*], classifier [*open-casket, Supreme Court*]), and one or more postmodifiers (e.g., prepositional phrase [*of Emmett*], embedded clause [*that appeared in Jet magazine*], appositive [*Brown v. Board of Education of Topeka*]). They pack into the sentence a large quantity of semantic data that can overwhelm the reader's cognitive capacity. Psychological research (e.g., Miller, 1969) has shown that when processing information, people can only hold an average of seven items at a time in their short-term memory before these items dissipate into oblivion. If a sentence contains two long noun phrases (a subject and an object) linked by a verb, with each noun phrase containing at least 4–5 meaningful lexical items, such as the first sentence of the third paragraph, it can create information overload that overwhelms the reader's working memory, especially when s/he has little relevant background knowledge about the historical event.

More significantly, the third and fourth paragraphs of the text are populated with abstract entities that may be challenging for adolescents to grapple with. These include what functional linguist James Martin (1997) referred to as generic abstractions, institutional abstractions, and metaphoric abstractions. Generic abstractions refer to places (e.g., *the South, Southern states, the Northern states, public schools*), groups of people (e.g., *Blacks, whites, Northern agitators, Southerners, civil rights leaders, mourners*), and groups of things (e.g., *news items, attitudes, customs*) that have no perceptual correlates. Institutional abstractions include terms such as *the National Association for the Advancement of Colored People, Jim Crow laws, regulations, civil rights organizations, the Supreme Court, Brown v. Board of Education of Topeka, the federal government,* and *the police commissioner of Montgomery, Alabama.* These are, in the words of Martin (1997, p. 31), "bureaucratic ratchets" that organize people's lives. Metaphoric abstractions are nominalizations that derive from processes (verbs) or qualities (adjectives). They include *the kidnapping and murder* of Emmett Till, *the trial* of his killers, *the viewing* of his disfigured corpse, outrage, the cold-blooded *murder* of this boy from Chicago, white *supremacy*, a racist *act*, the *killing*, the *protests* and *condemnations*, the 1954 Supreme Court *decision* Brown v. Board of Education of Topeka, *integration* of schools, the two *rulings*, the Southern *way* of life, Reconstruction, desegregation, and *destruction.*

The institutional and metaphoric abstractions, together with generic abstractions, help create a world of abstractions in Text 3.5. They participate in historical processes and reasonings in ways that embed the historian's attitudes and naturalize his/her interpretations. These abstractions enable the historian to (a) ascribe agency to laws, regulations, policies, or treaties so that the human actors behind these documents are effaced (e.g., *Jim Crow laws, regulations that segregated . . .*; *Supreme Court decisions Brown v. Board of Education Topeka, which declared . . .*; *the two rulings alarmed . . .*), (b) to bundle together a series of events over a long period time into a package that has ideological connotations (e.g., *Reconstruction*), (c) to ascribe judgment (e.g., *the grisly open-casket photo, a racist act, the cold-blooded murder of this boy from Chicago, the viewing of his disfigured corpse, forced desegregation of public schools*), and (d) to expand information (*the cold-blooded murder of this boy from Chicago, the protests and condemnations from civil rights leaders and Northerners, the racist attitudes that led to it*). Clearly, it is primarily through these nominal structures that the historian was able to infuse his perspectives into the interpretation of the historical event, although other grammatical resources (e.g., *horrified, alarmed, condemned, poked, stinging, pushed, declared, would appear, already raw, must proceed*) also contribute to the evaluation. Readers unaware of how language is used by historians to fashion meaning—or more specifically, represent human agency and authorial perspective and interpretation—are less likely to develop a sophisticated understanding of historical texts.

Another common feature of historical discourse is the way it construes causality and time. In the more commonplace language of everyday life, causality is typically realized between clauses through conjunctive resources such as *because* and *so*. In history, causal meaning is often realized more subtly, in verbs (e.g., *lead to, ensue, make, encourage*), nouns (e.g., *reason, effect, response*), prepositional phrases (e.g., *with, for, through, from, at*), non-finite clauses (e.g., *British officials, faced with a breakdown of law and order, landed two regiments of troops in Boston in 1768.*), or asyndetic constructions—that is, two consecutive sentences without explicit cause–effect signal words (e.g., "*Few Japanese in Hawai'i were imprisoned during World War II. Japanese labor was too important in the islands.*", where the word "because" could have been inserted to link the two sentences) (Coffin, 2006; Fitzgerald, 2014; Martin, 2002). For example, Fitzgerald (2019) reported that over three-fourths of all causal connections used in a sample of middle and high school American history textbooks and historical primary source documents are realized through non-conjunctive elements.

In the case of Text 3.5 above, the sentence—*The white leaders in Southern states . . . were still stinging from the 1954 Supreme Court decision Brown v.*

Board of Education of Topeka, which declared that racially segregated schools were unconstitutional—uses a preposition (*from*) and a verb (*declared*) to imply causality, suggesting that it is the 1954 Supreme Court decision that caused the White leaders in the Southern states to feel pain (like getting stung by a bee) and that made racially segregated schools unconstitutional. In the sentence, *The grisly open-casket photo of Emmett . . . horrified and angered hundreds of thousands more*, the verbs "horrified" and "angered" suggest that it is the display of the grisly photo that caused many people to feel horrified and angry. The verb phrase "led to" in "*Newspapers across the country . . . condemned the killing and the racist attitudes that led to it*" construes not only causality (i.e., racist attitudes caused Emmet Till's killing) but also temporal sequence regarding the order of the events happening in real time (i.e., racist attitudes preceded the killing). In "*political leaders expressed outrage at the cold-blooded murder of this boy from Chicago*", the preposition "*at*" implies cause, meaning that the cold-blooded murder of Emmett Till caused political leaders to be outraged. Such within-clause logical reasoning necessitates the causes and effects of historical events to be constructed as abstract "things" that are realized in nominal expressions. Martin (2002) pointed out that by construing causal relations within the clause rather than between clauses, historians have available to them a much wider array of linguistic resources—nouns, verbs, and prepositions, in addition to conjunctions—to delicately explain how one thing leads to another. In so doing, however, they also make explanations and interpretations less accessible to comprehend and critique for disciplinary outsiders like students.

Other features of the text, such as the use of reference, ellipsis, and appositive, can also cause problems for adolescent readers. In the third paragraph, students need to understand that "*this boy from Chicago*" refers to Emmett Till and that "*hundreds of thousands more*" means "*hundreds of thousands more mourners*". And this sentence from the fourth paragraph—*The white leaders in Southern states like Mississippi that enforced Jim Crow laws, regulations that segregated Blacks from whites, were still stinging from the 1954 Supreme Court decision Brown v. Board of Education of Topeka, which declared that racially segregated schools were unconstitutional.*—is long and complex in part because it uses long noun phrases. Students need to be able to unpack long noun phrases, recognizing, for example, that the appositive phrase, *regulations that segregated Blacks from whites*, is used to define, or provide further information about, Jim Crow laws. They also need to understand that the relative pronoun "*which*" refers to "*the 1954 Supreme Court decision Brown v Board Education of Topeka*". Finally, laws and court decisions are presented here as agentive in bringing about historical changes, thus effacing the human agency behind these documents. This makes it much harder for students to assign responsibility for historical actions and critique historical events.

How do Experts Read Historical Texts?

History privileges analysis and interpretation of historical documents, artifacts, and accounts. This naturally leads it to emphasize reading/writing as its core social practice. What strategies do historians use in their reading practice? To answer this question, researchers (e.g., Wineburg, 1991a, 1998; Shanahan, Shanahan, & Misischia, 2011) have investigated how historians read texts in their discipline. This line of research involves having historians, usually university history professors, read a set of two or more topically related historical texts (e.g., Abraham Lincoln, Battle of Lexington) within and/or outside their own areas of scholarly expertise and verbalize their thinking as they endeavored to make sense of the texts. Based on an analysis of these experts' think-aloud protocols, researchers found that historians recognize that every historical text has a subtext, treating it as both "a rhetorical artifact" and "a human artifact" (Wineburg, 1991b, p. 498). In order to understand the subtext, historians go beyond literal comprehension to try to reconstruct the author's purposes, intentions, and goals and at the same time detect his/her assumptions, beliefs, and worldviews, using strategies (also called protocols or heuristics) such as sourcing, contextualizing, corroborating, close reading, perspective taking, and inferring (Nokes, 2013).

In sourcing, historians note the author's identity, affiliation, and perspective, his/her purpose for creating the document, and his/her intended audience, as well as the venue in which the document was published, thinking about the implications of these pieces of information for interpretation. In contextualizing, historians situate the document in the context of its production, considering how its construction may have been influenced by what was taking place locally, nationally, and even internationally at or around the time of its creation. In corroborating, historians compare multiple historical documents to see if key details across these sources repeat, complement, agree with, or contradict one another so that they can reconcile differences in accounts, determine acceptable facts, and identify credible evidence. In close reading, historians slow down, reread portions of the text, and examine text structure and verbal/visual choices, hoping to understand the nuances or significance of particular words or phrases, detect the author's position or attitude, and determine whether/how the semiotic and rhetorical choices made by the author may have shaped their responses to the text in some way. In perspective taking, also called historical empathy, historians put themselves in the shoes of the historical character, trying to understand the motivation, sequence, and consequences of his/her actions strictly on the basis of historical facts and events, without resorting to their own frames of reference. In inferring, historians make inferences about "historical motives, purposes, causes, or trends" (Nokes, 2013, p. 16); they draw on prior knowledge and use principled imagination (constrained by evidence and reason) to help fill in the gaps when historical documents provide incomplete information or are silent on certain historical details. These strategies help historians discern patterns, fill gaps, weigh evidence, determine credibility, and resolve contradictions as they work through historical documents in an effort to produce evidence-based, reasoned interpretations of the past.

Similar strategies have been reported by other scholars. According to VanSledright (2012, p. 212), for example, when reading history, experts (a) ask significant historical questions, (b) pay attention to who wrote the text and where the text is published, (c) assess the author's perspective, (d) check evidence across multiple sources to facilitate judgments about its quality, (e) judge the reliability of different accounts in relation to addressing a historical question, (f) make judgments within the confines of the historical context in question, (g) exercise historical imagination to fill in evidentiary gaps through a process of mental modeling, (h) build a variety of differing mental incident/thought models, (i) continually refine and revise their understanding and interpretations, and (j) are cognizant of their own biases and limitations in making meaning from historical texts. In the process of using these strategies, historians are actively summarizing and paraphrasing text segments, weighing the meaning and significance of particular language choices that refer to historical events/figures (e.g., *Boston Massacre* vs. *the Incident on King Street*, *invasion* vs. *special military operation*, *pro-democracy demonstrators* vs. *violent mobs*) or indicate the indeterminacy of history, that is, the elusive nature of historical certainty (e.g., *suggest, appear, seem, perhaps, may, likely*), posing relevant questions, making intertextual connections, organizing ideas chronologically and thematically, synthesizing across sources, monitoring their own understanding, making conjectures, challenging the author's claims, formulating their own arguments, searching for evidence, locating additional sources, identifying continuity and change, analyzing causes and consequences, judging the historical significance of events and artifacts, generating historically valid interpretations, and pondering what can be learned from the past to benefit the present (Goldman et al., 2016; Nokes, 2013; Shanahan, Shanahan, & Misischia, 2011). These strategies facilitate the historical reasoning process; they give historians a sense of each document's perspective, focus, and purpose, enabling them to develop original, rigorous interpretations of the past that are evidence-based and valued by their peers.

Developing Historical Literacy Through Reading

Unlike experts whose reading of history is sophisticated and complex, students read history much more superficially, likely due to a lack of deep historical knowledge, extensive experience with historical inquiry and reasoning, and explicit instruction on how to interact with historical texts. Research (e.g., Afflerbach & VanSledright, 2001; Britt & Aglinskas, 2002; Paxton, 2002; Stahl, Hynd, Britton, McNish, & Bosquet, 1996; VanSledright, 2012; Wineburg, 1991b) indicates that adolescent learners

- treat history as consisting of a body of immutable facts about, rather than human interpretations of, the past
- see textbooks as an authoritative and, thus, reliable source of information
- view history reading as a process of extracting facts (or truth) from text for remembering and recall, rather than a process of grappling with the author's intentions or the historical significance of the event or person under study
- focus on discrete pieces of factual information (e.g., time, place, main characters, and sequence of events), rather than the value, bias, and ideology embedded in the text
- consider texts that display bias as untrustworthy and useless
- seldom make comparison and contrast among sources when given multiple documents
- rarely pay attention to linguistic indicators of judgment, emphasis, and certainty
- fail to detect inconsistencies or contradictions within and across texts
- interpret the past from the lens of today (i.e., presentism)
- display little historical empathy, and
- lack disciplinary knowledge and habits of mind to render judgment on sources or produce evidence-based interpretations.

Even academically successful students with a decent amount of historical knowledge have only "a rudimentary sense of how to read a history text" (Wineburg, 1991b, p. 511), as they often seem oblivious to the subtexts in the historical documents they read, focusing on identifying and remembering bits and pieces of "facts" rather than questioning or challenging an interpretation. Results from the 2018 National Assessment of Educational Progress reveal that only 15% of eighth-grade students scored at or above the proficient level on the U.S. History assessment (https://www.nationsreportcard.gov/highlights/ushistory/2018/), confirming that adolescents struggle with attaining historical literacy.

Typical practices of the history/social studies classrooms do not support the development of historical literacy, as they tend to rely only on textbooks and focus on content coverage and basic reading comprehension and summary (Hynd, 1999; Monte-Sano, 2011; Reisman, 2012; Schall-Leckrone, 2017). These practices reinforce the misconception that learning history is about learning facts about past events rather than producing evidence-based interpretations through detailed analysis and critical evaluation. A disciplinary literacy approach to historical literacy can effect changes in the way history has traditionally been taught. The approach foregrounds historical inquiry and historical thinking, providing scaffolded opportunities that engage students in discipline valued practices such as asking historically significant questions, identifying and reading relevant historical sources, analyzing and interpreting historical data, undertaking causal reasoning, grappling with historical issues and problems, synthesizing across sources, and refining/revising interpretation. It makes learning history more than identifying and reciting "facts", aiming, instead, to promote a sophisticated understanding of historical time, agency, and causality and to develop students' capacity to learn to read and think like historians. Several elements of this approach are key to accomplishing the goal of achieving historical literacy. They are (a) using multiple sources, (b) teaching historical reading heuristics (or protocols/strategies), (c) conducting close reading, and (d) writing argument from sources. Each of these elements is described in some detail below. Further resources for promoting historical literacy can be accessed at websites created by the History Education Group at Stanford University (http://sheg.standford. edu/), the Big History Project at the University of Michigan (https:// school.bighistoryproject.com/bhplive), the History Labs at the University of Maryland (http://www.umbc.edu/che/historylabs), and the Annenberg Learner's Reading and Writing in the Disciplines resources (https://www. learner.org/courses/readwrite/disciplinary-literacy/what-is-disciplinary-literacy/1.html).

Using Multiple Sources

Because history is an interpretive discipline grounded in evidence, historians must take information from different sources and try to piece together a multi-dimensional view of history. This sort of interpretive work is very much like detective work or jigsaw puzzles, requiring historians to evaluate witness accounts, find missing pieces, and stitch together seemingly discrete pieces of information into a coherent account and reasonable interpretation of the past. Thus, the number and quality of historical sources will no doubt affect the quality and credibility of interpretation. The more diverse, complete, and reliable sources are, the more well-rounded, accurate, and credible interpretations are likely to be. Just as a teacher's instructional effectiveness cannot be judged by considering a single student's score on one high-stakes test, the significance of an historical event, person, or place cannot be validly judged by examining only a single document. Historians want as many relevant and reliable sources as possible for their interpretive work. Multiple sources are important for historical inquiry, as different sources tend to represent different perspectives and offer somewhat or radically different accounts of the same historical event or person. They give students an opportunity to answer a compelling question using historical thinking skills such as sourcing, contextualization, corroboration, inferring, and close reading.

When selecting sources, it is important to keep in mind the central historical question or issue to be explored and related historical themes (e.g., national identity; politics and power; migration and settlement; science, technology, and society; individuals, groups, and institutions), concepts (e.g., change and continuity, significance, perspectives, sources and evidence; causation and argumentation; empathy and contestability), and period (e.g., The American Revolution [1763–1783] and Civil War and Reconstruction [1861–1877] for American history) to be covered. Different historical questions (e.g., what is the historical significance of the invention of gunpowder? vs. how did Stalin justify the human cost of the *dekulakization* during the Soviet Union's first five-year plan?) call for use of different sets of historical sources. It is also important that sources are not just multiple; they also need to be diverse. Diverse sources are accounts provided by different individuals, groups, and/ or institutions; produced in different contexts, across different time periods, and for different purposes; and representing different viewpoints and interests. They can be primary and secondary/tertiary sources, physical artifacts, audio-visual materials, or even historical fiction. Using diverse sources enables students to have a more accurate and complete picture of the historical details related to the event, person, or location under study. It helps students build their background knowledge, challenge their misconceptions, broaden their horizons, and develop their analytical and critical thinking skills.

For example, in exploring the historically significant question, "Was Abraham Lincoln a White Supremacist?", Wineburg, Martin, and Monte-Sano (2013) recommended a set of five primary source documents—an excerpt from incumbent Illinois Senator Stephen Douglas' address to Lincoln in their first senate campaign debate in Ottawa, Illinois on August 21, 1858; Lincoln's response to Douglas' speech at the Ottawa, Illinois debate; Lincoln's letter to his personal friend Mary Speed on September 27, 1841 about seeing slaves on a riverboat; Lincoln's address on colonization delivered to a group of freed Black men at the White House on August 14, 1862; and words by John Bell Robinson, a White man who lived in Pennsylvania, about race and race relations. Each of these sources was produced at a different time, to a different audience, and for a different purpose. They form a coherent set that can help students gain a more sophisticated understanding of Lincoln's view on race in the context of his time. Through careful analysis of and comparison across these texts, students can better appreciate the role of context in understanding complex historical figures, think more deeply about racialized ideas, recognize the importance of slowing down during reading, reflect critically on their own prior conceptions about Lincoln, and arrive at a reasoned conclusion about Lincoln's racial attitude.

In a world history unit that explores the causes and consequences of the Opium Wars (1839–1842, 1856–1860), teachers can likewise use a set of diverse texts that provide students with multiple perspectives on the historical event. This set can include any number of the following sources:

- two edicts from Emperor Qianlong on the occasion of Lord Macartney's mission to China (September, 1793)
- Chinese official Governor Lin Zexu's letter to Britain's Queen Victoria to protest the Opium Trade (1839)
- *The Treaty of Nanking* (1842)
- an online article describing Opium Wars on the website of Britain's National Army Museum (https://www.nam.ac.uk/explore/opium-war-1839-1842)
- an overview article by the Asian Pacific Foundation of Canada (https://asia-pacificcurriculum.ca/learning-module/opium-wars-china#overview)
- excerpts on the First and Second Opium Wars from a junior high school history textbook in China (Liu, Ding, & Liu, 2013)
- an article from the Office of the Historian (U.S.) website that describes milestones in the history of U.S. foreign relations (https://history.state.gov/milestones/1830-1860/china-1)
- *Letters from China* (Kerr, 1996), a collection of letters ship captain and China trader Robert Bennet Forbes wrote home to Boston during 1838–1840 about his experience in Canton, Macau, and Hong Kong, and
- excerpts from *The Art of Opium Antiques* (Martin & Lakatos, 2007), a book that explores the art and accoutrements associated with opium smoking that reached a pinnacle in 19th-century China and in Chinese communities abroad.

Some of these sources describe the Opium Wars as caused by a trade dispute between British and Chinese governments; some see them as arising from a breach of etiquette in cross-cultural communications between Chinese officials (e.g., Emperor Qianlong) and British officials (e.g., Lord Macartney); and others view the conflicts as an inevitable outcome of Western aggression and imperialism. Some documents are primary sources, and others are secondary or tertiary sources. Some of the secondary or tertiary sources focus on chronicling the events leading up to and following the Opium Wars; some highlight the brutality of Western countries in waging war upon China and their destruction of Chinese civilization; and others place an emphasis on patriotism and national dignity. By reading, analyzing, and discussing these richly different, and sometimes competing, accounts of the same historical event, students gain a more sophisticated understanding of the causes, consequences, and significance of the Opium Wars, as well as the constructed nature of historical knowledge (i.e., history is interpreted differently by different individuals/groups at different time periods in different social, cultural, and political contexts). These understandings will in turn help students make better sense of the current tension between China and the U.S.-led West.

Of course, the number of sources to be used will depend on topic and grade level. Some topics have a lot more sources and different kinds of sources available than do others. And younger students may not be able to effectively handle as many sources as older students. In fact, even adolescent learners have been found to not profit from multiple texts, especially those presenting conflicting opinions, without some specific instruction in how to integrate information across different sources. According to Stahl et al. (1996), for example, high school students rely only on the first two documents they read when asked to compose from multiple sources, and they tend to stay close to the text when writing a factual essay and ignore the information in the texts they read when writing an argumentative essay. For this reason, it may be a good idea to start small when determining the number of sources to be included. For middle school students, 2–3 sources may be sufficient; for high school students, the number can increase to 3–5.

Another factor in source selection is quality. This involves making sure that whatever source is selected has the potential to entice students, stimulate discussion, invite critical thought, and promote the use of protocols/heuristics/strategies that characterize historical reading. More importantly, teachers need to check each source—including its author, its publisher, and the circumstances (e.g., timing, purpose) of its creation/publication—to be sure it is credible and reliable. Authors who do not have the qualifications to write or exercise due diligence to conduct research about the past are likely to produce works of questionable quality. Publishers that have an unflattering history of churning out low-quality products also require extra scrutiny. A case in point is Giorgio Vasari, an art historian who is known for his bias in favor of his native Florentine school of art, his sloppy habit of recording rumors and gossip as "real", and his carelessness in writing. His *Lives of the Most Excellent Painters, Sculptors, and Architects* (Vasari, 1550), though still widely used today in the study of the history of Renaissance art, is considered seriously flawed and in need of verification through modern scientific research.

Merely presenting multiple texts to students does little to encourage them to think critically about these sources (Hynd, 1999). Students need a productive routine that will promote their active engagement with texts. One such routine was described by Reisman (2012). The routine, called document-based lesson (DBL), starts by posing a central historical question to be explored (e.g., *Should Christopher Columbus be honored and revered?*). This is followed by building background knowledge about the topic through teacher lecture (e.g., on the Europeans' quest to find a new path to Asia following the fall of Constantinople to the Ottoman Empire in 1453 that effectively closed the Silk Road to Christian traders). This background knowledge will help students make better sense of and interpret multiple sources. The lesson continues with small group and independent reading of primary, as well as secondary and tertiary, source documents, such as U.S. President Benjamin Harrison's 1892 Proclamation of a new national holiday in honor of Columbus, a revisionist article from *The Nation* by Kirkpatrick Sale (1990) depicting Columbus as a greedy, cruel person who brought disease and destruction to a peace-loving and prosperous people in Native Americans, and an article from *The Atlantic Monthly* by Arthur Schlesinger (1992) that presents a post-revisionist view of Columbus as merely a product of his time and thus neither more cruel nor more courageous than other explorers. The lesson concludes with a class discussion focusing on the central question posed at the beginning of the lesson. This routine has been shown to increase students' historical thinking, their retention of factual knowledge about history, their ability to transfer their historical thinking strategies to contemporary problems, and their general reading comprehension skills (Reisman, 2012).

Teaching Historical Reading Strategies/Protocols/Heuristics

As students interact with multiple sources, they should be encouraged to read like a historian, using the strategies/protocols/heuristics such as inferring, sourcing, contextualizing, corroborating, close reading, and perspective taking. Because adolescents rarely read history texts the way historians do, they need explicit instruction in how/when to use these strategies, as well as why the strategies are important (Nokes, 2013). The instruction can follow a "gradual release of responsibility" model described by Pearson and Gallagher (1983). Specifically, the teacher introduces a strategy (e.g., corroboration), explains what it is (e.g., comparing the accounts of multiple sources against one another) and why it is important (e.g., to help historians figure out what really happened and which source is more reliable), and discusses when to use it (e.g., when synthesizing sources as historical evidence or when evaluating arguments) and how to use it (e.g., considering details across two or more sources to determine points of agreement and/or disagreement). This is followed by the teacher modeling the use of the strategy in a meaningful context (Bereiter & Bird, 1985), thinking aloud the process in which an important detail is identified in one source and then checked against another source. Once students have had the opportunity to observe how the strategy works in disciplinary contexts, they can then work together in small groups to try out the strategy as they engage in reading multiple sources. The teacher provides support as needed during this process using scaffolds such as the worksheets presented in Figures 3.2–3.6. Next, students independently apply the strategy in an assignment that requires them to identify a key detail in one historical document and cross check it with at least one other document. Because the development of historical thinking/reasoning takes time, students need multiple opportunities to practice and apply these strategies across multiple texts; and as they build up their repertoire of strategies, they will use them concurrently when reading multiple sources in pursuit of answers to an historically compelling question.

For example, Nokes, Dole, and Hacker (2007) described an intervention project in which students in one 11th-grade class were explicitly taught how to use sourcing, corroboration, and contextualization in a 15-day unit on the major events and trends in the United States during the 1920s and 1930s, including daily life in the 1920s and 1930s, the Harlem Renaissance, causes and effects of the Great Depression, and foreign affairs of the 1920s and 1930s. On the sixth day of the unit, the teacher began class with a discussion of the Harlem Renaissance, addressing questions such as "What was the Harlem Renaissance?" "What were some of the historical events that had a profound impact on African Americans of the 1920s?" and "What were some of the common themes of the literature of the Harlem Renaissance?". Students were given a packet of poems written during the Harlem Renaissance, as well as a study guide containing two literal questions, two inferential questions, and two opinion questions based on some of the

poems. The teacher reminded students about the heuristic of contextualization, which had been introduced to them in an earlier lesson, and discussed with them how and when to use it and why it was important in
historical reading. The teacher then read one of the poems and modeled

Historical Question Explored_____

Article Title_____Article Author_____

Reason for sourcing	• What is the main idea/claim of this document? • Why did you select this document? • In what way did the document inform, deepen, or challenge your thinking about the question under study?
Author	• Who wrote the document? • What biographical information do you know about the author? • Was the author part of any group (e.g., socioeconomic class, religion, occupation, nationality, political affiliation, gender, ethnic group) that might have influenced his/her viewpoint on the historical event/person?
Publisher	• Who published this document? • What do you know about the publisher (e.g., its political or religious affiliation)?
Purpose	• Why did the author write the document? • Why did the publisher publish the document?
Perspective	• What was the author's point of view on the historical event/person? • How did the author's viewpoint influence the way the document was created?
Place	• Where was the document created? • What are the characteristics of the place (e.g., geography, climate, demography, industry, political/religious leaning) that might have influenced the document's creation?
Audience	• For whom was the document intended? • What were the readers expected to do after reading the document?
Time	• When was the document created? • When was the document published? Why at this time? • What was going on at/around the time that might have influenced the document's creation?
Significance	• Why does the document matter to history or to the question you are pursuing? • What parts of the document are most credible or noteworthy? Why? • What are the limitations of the document?

Figure 3.2 Template for Sourcing
(Source: https://www.youtube.com/watch?v=KuSecMh7BnU)

1. Write a question you want answered or a claim you want to make.

2. Make note of the historical event, process, person, or source being studied.

3. Consider the time and place of the event by
   a. identifying the time and place related to the event, process, person, or source
   b. marking the time on a timeline with a start and an end date (e.g., a person's life span, a regime's time in power, the date of publication)
   c. marking the place where the event took place on a map.

4. Make a list of other historical events that were happening locally/regionally/globally
   a. at the same time as the event being studied, no matter the location
   b. in the same place(s) and at the same time as the event being studied
   c. immediately before this time period
   d. 50 to 100 years before the event.

5. Consider the culture (e.g., attitudes, values, concepts) at the time, including the government and political systems, economic systems, and religious systems.

6. Identify any of the events that might help explain what you are studying.

7. Add any relevant events to your timeline.

8. Write a contextualization paragraph to address the question you want answered or support the claim you want to make by synthesizing the information above.

Figure 3.3 Steps for Teaching Students to Contextualize
Source: https://www.youtube.com/watch?v=oUKhGEhkwLw

contextualization by thinking aloud about the values and attitudes that were implied in the poem. Students then worked in small groups analyzing several other poems. For each poem, they were required to write a general reaction, record what they could infer about the social and political context that surrounded the poem's creation, and summarize the message the poem was trying to convey. After analyzing five of the poems, students responded to this question: How did the historical context of the Harlem Renaissance influence the writers of these poems and the things they wrote about? Each of the subsequent nine strategy lessons followed this same format of having

Source	Author's Point of View	Evidence Supporting the Viewpoint	Your Judgment about the Reliability of the Source
Source 1			
Source 2			
Source 3			

Figure 3.4 Corroborating Chart
Source: Wineburg, Martin, & Monte-Sano (2013)

Details Observed/Noticed	Inference Made
Observation 1	Inference 1
Observation 2	Inference 2
Observation 3	Inference 3

Figure 3.5 Observation–Inference Chart for Both Visual and Verbal Texts
Source: Nokes (2013)

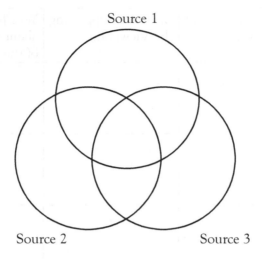

Figure 3.6 Comparing/Contrasting Different Accounts

the teacher discuss heuristics with students, model the use of one or more of these heuristics, and give students an opportunity to practice using the heuristic with multiple texts. The researchers found that students who received explicit strategy instruction with multiple texts scored significantly higher on the content posttest than did their 11th-grade peers in other classes who used textbooks to study the content.

A somewhat different approach to teaching historical reading heuristics was described by Reisman and Wineburg (2008). The approach includes three elements: building background knowledge, designing guiding questions, and modeling conceptualized thinking through expert think alouds. Using contextualization as an example, Reisman and Wineburg argued that contextualized thinking is not likely to occur unless the reader possesses some prior knowledge about the historical event or person under study. Providing students with background knowledge enables them to decipher unfamiliar terms, create accurate mental images, and entertain new interpretations as they read. Background knowledge can be built by watching relevant video clips, taking field trips, listening to teacher lectures, or reading historical fiction. Developing guiding questions is also important as they can help students slow down the reading process and pay attention to important details in the text. Guiding questions are not the type of questions commonly found in history textbooks that requires no more than identifying the bolded terms and copying the surrounding sentences. Rather, they should be designed to "prompt students to read carefully and think deeply about a document's attribution or source, historical context, and use of language" (Reisman & Wineburg, 2008, p. 204). These questions can focus on the author and the text, as well as a particular concept in historical thinking such as historical significance, evidence, continuity and change, cause and effect, historical perspective, and ethical consideration (see Table 3.1 for a list of sample questions). Finally, because historical thinking is invisible, there is a need to make it visible to students. One way to do this is the expert think aloud, that is, having experts report what they are thinking, doing, and feeling when they read. The teacher shows students video clips of think alouds done by historians as they read historical texts. Each think aloud is also accompanied by an outside commentary that identifies the reading strategies demonstrated by the expert historian. The use of think alouds and accompanying commentaries demystifies the processes of historical thinking for students.

Table 3.1 Sample Guiding Questions for Text Exploration

Question Types	Sample Questions
About Author	• Who is the writer? What do you know about the writer (e.g., political view, religious affiliation, life experience, professional credential)?
	• What authority or credential does the writer have? Did the writer conduct the needed research to write about the person/event?
	• What is the writer's attitude toward the topic?
	• What assumptions did the writer make? Are they valid?
	• What beliefs or values did the writer hold? Are they explicit?
About Text	• Who is the intended audience of the text?
	• Why was the text written? What is the writer's purpose?
	• What is the source of the text? Is it reputable? Who is the publisher? What reputation does the publisher have?
	• What is the date of publication? Is it relevant to and appropriate for the inquiry?
	• Did the writer exercise caution when making claims or expressing attitude? How?

(Continued)

Question Types	Sample Questions
	• Whose viewpoint is expressed? What did the writer want us to think?
	• Whose viewpoints are missing, silenced, backgrounded, or discounted?
	• How might alternative perspectives be represented and/or found?
	• How would alternative perspectives impact your understanding of the text?
	• What action might you take on the basis of what you have learned?
About Use of Evidence	• Is there a clear distinction between fact and opinion?
	• Is there evidence to support arguments? How reliable or credible is the evidence? Is there evidence that is excluded, and why?
	• Are there any unsupported points of argument?
	• Did the writer summarize other people's ideas in an angle that connects with his/her specific points of argument?
	• Is the writer's conclusion reasonable in light of the evidence presented?
	• How does the conclusion relate to that of similar research?
About Historical Significance	• Why is this person/event/place/development important?
	• Why should we care about this person/event/place/development?
	• How is this person/event/development connected to us today?
About Historical Perspective	• What was the person (were the people) thinking?
	• What might explain the person/people's action or belief that seems so strange to us today?
	• Why did this person/group not understand what the other person/group was doing or believed in?
	• Why do you think this person (these people) did what s/he (they) did?

Question Types	Sample Questions
About Continuity and Change	• What kind of change did the event bring to the place? • What changed and what stayed the same at this time? • Was the event a turning point in history? How so?
About Cause and Consequence	• Why did the action/event happen? • How did the event or the person make a difference? • What happened to the person/place? Why did it happen? • How has the event changed our lives? • What helped/hindered this person/event from making a difference?
Ethical Dimensions	• How should we remember this person/event/place? • How does the context of the time explain this person's/ these people's actions or beliefs? • What lessons, if any, can we learn from this person/event? • Are we condemned to repeat the past? Or should we learn something from this person/event?

Source: Adapted from https://studylib.net/doc/7066227/historical-thinking-prompts-for-inquiry questions

Britt and Aglinskas (2002) described a computer application that teaches sourcing, contextualization, and corroboration in the context of researching a historical controversy. The app, called the Sourcer's Apprentice, is based on the following design principles: (1) teach through situated problem solving, (2) support expert representations, (3) decompose the task, (4) support transfer, (5) provide explicit instruction, and (6) motivate engagement. It includes a tutorial that provides direct instruction on each of the three strategies. Using the app, students read a set of highly structured and varied documents (excerpts from primary/secondary sources) about a carefully selected historical problem, identify source and document features along with important content, and then use this information to answer questions and write a short essay about the controversy. Each source contains a title page, an author page (detailing author's credentials and possible motives), a document page (explaining the type of document, who published it, when it was written), and a content page (displaying the content of the document). High school students with two-day exposure to the app were found to have made moderate improvement in sourcing, contextualization, and corroboration and wrote essays on the topic that were more integrated, cited more sources, and referenced more information from primary and secondary sources than did their peers who received traditional history instruction with a textbook.

Conducting Close Reading

While there has been a considerable amount of discussion on how to teach the heuristics of sourcing, corroboration, contextualization, inferring, and perspective taking, much less has been written about close reading in history. Close reading aims to develop a deep, precise understanding of a text's message, form, and craft through careful attention to and critical analysis of language and image in the text (Fang & Chapman, 2015). It is a method of academic reading highly recommended in the Common Core State Standards. According to Reisman and Wineburg (2008), "Students can learn a lot about history when they slow down the reading process and attend carefully to source information and language" (p. 203). Close reading is especially important when dealing with challenging academic or disciplinary texts because these texts do not "give up" meaning easily. Primary source documents, for example, often contain unfamiliar vocabulary, arcane syntax, and unconventional spelling. And secondary and tertiary source documents in middle and high schools tend to feature a high degree of generalization and interpretation, using abstract and evaluative language. This language presents new processing demands for adolescent readers. To fully understand the content of these texts, students "need ways to work with the patterns of lexical, grammatical, and organizational choices that constitute the discourse of history" (Schleppegrell & Achugar, 2012, p. 21).

Teachers can support students' close reading of historical texts by showing them how to work through the challenging language of these texts. One way to accomplish this is through functional language analysis, or FLA for short (Fang, 2021a; Fang & Schleppegrell, 2008, 2010; Schleppegrell & Achugar, 2012). FLA draws on a meaning-based theory of language, called systemic functional linguistics (Halliday & Matthiessen, 2014), that offers tools for analyzing how academic/disciplinary texts construe meanings and suggests ways of engaging students in close analysis of those meanings in context. It scaffolds students' understanding through intensive work with a single text or text segment, focusing on the ways different meanings are presented in language patterns. The analysis examines the language of a text from three angles:

1 What is the text about (i.e., experiential meaning)?
2 What is the author's perspective (i.e., interpersonal meaning)? and
3 How is information in the text organized (i.e., textual meaning)?

Each of these angles requires attention to different language patterns. To explore the experiential meaning, students can analyze the meaning of each clause constituent, such as participants (typically realized in nouns), processes (typically realized in verbs), attributes (typically realized in adjectives), and circumstances (typically realized in adverbs and prepositional phrases). To explore the interpersonal meaning, students can analyze word choices—such as hedges (e.g., *possible, may, seems, tend to, hardly*), boosters (e.g., *of course, completely, it is obvious/clear*), adjectives (e.g., *full blame, huge reparations*), adverbs (e.g., *to some extent, significantly*), verbs (*order/force* vs *ask, impose* vs. *put*), and nouns (e.g., *massacre* vs. *incident, the perpetrator* vs. *the person*)—for attitudes, evaluation, and authorial perspective. To explore the textual meaning, students can analyze what begins each clause, how clauses are combined, and how cohesion is created. Table 3.2 presents a more detailed scheme for exploring the meanings of a text through a functional focus on language. Using FLA, students develop a deeper understanding of the information presented in the text; equally important, they gain a better sense of how language works in history to construe time, cause, agency, abstraction, and interpretation—an understanding that should also help them with their writing about the past.

Table 3.2 Guide to Language Analysis of History Texts

Questions to Answer About Text	Relevant Language Focus for Analysis
What historical events are presented?	Identify action verbs
Who are the main participants in these events?	Identify agents and receivers of actions
Who is quoted or cited in the text?	Identify saying verbs and the persons who say
What does the historian comment on in the text?	Identify thinking/feeling verbs and their subjects and objects
Whose opinions or views are presented?	Identify the persons who say or think/feel
What are the views expressed?	Analyze the messages in the saying or thinking/feeling clauses

(Continued)

Questions to Answer About Text	Relevant Language Focus for Analysis
What background information is provided?	Identify relating/linking verbs, passive voice, and nonhuman participants
How is information organized in the text?	Analyze connectors, conjunctions, temporal phrases, and verbs that express cause or movement over time
What is the author's perspective on the historical events or persons?	Analyze nouns, nominalizations, verbs, modal verbs, ergative verbs, adjectives, hedges, and boosters for indications of attitudes and evaluation
How is the text organized?	Identify topic sentence/paragraph, analyze what begins each clause, and examine how clauses are combined to form sentences

Sources: Fang & Schleppegrell (2010) and Schleppegrell & Achugar (2012)

For example, in reading this dense passage from a 10th-grade U.S. history textbook, students are expected to understand the causes and effects of the Panic of 1857. Close reading using FLA can help students develop this understanding.

Text 3.6

Adding to the growing political tension was the short, but sharp, depression of 1857 and 1858. Technology played a part. In August 1857, the failure of an Ohio investment house – the kind of event that had formerly taken weeks to be widely known – was the subject of a news story flashed immediately over telegraph wires to Wall Street and other financial markets. A wave of panic selling ensued, leading to business failures and slowdowns that threw thousands out of work. The major cause of the panic was a sharp, but temporary, downturn in agricultural exports to Britain, and recovery was well under way by early 1859. Because it affected cotton exports less than northern exports, the Panic of 1857 was less harmful to the South than to the North. Southerners took this as proof of the superiority of their economic system to the free-labor system of the North, and some could not resist the chance to gloat. Senator James Henry Hammond of South Carolina drove home the point in his celebrated "King Cotton" speech of March 1858. (Faragher, Buhle, Czitrom, & Armitage, 2007, p. 513)

Specifically, teachers can first assist students to construct a visual, such as Table 3.3, by unpacking each clause into its constituent participants, processes, attributes, circumstances, and connectors. This table shows that the text is mainly about the causes and effects of the Panic of 1857, as most

Table 3.3 Functional Language Analysis of a Sample Text

Clause	Connector	Circumstance	Participant	Process	Participant	Attribute	Circumstance
1			the short, but sharp, depression of 1857 and 1858	adding to	the growing political tension		
2			Technology	played	a part		
3		In August 1857	the failure of an Ohio investment house – the kind of event that had formerly taken weeks to be widely known	was	the subject of a news story flashed immediately over telegraph wires to Wall Street and other financial markets		
4			A wave of panic selling	ensued			
5			[A wave of panic selling]	leading to	business failures and slowdowns that threw thousands out of work		
6			The major cause of the panic	was	a sharp, but temporary, downturn in agricultural exports to Britain		

(Continued)

Clause	Connector	Circumstance	Participant	Process	Participant	Attribute	Circumstance
7	and		recovery	was		well under way	by early 1859
8	Because		it [=the Panic of 1857]	affected	cotton exports		less than northern exports
9			the Panic of 1857	was		less harmful	to the South than to the North
10			Southerners	took	this		as proof of the superiority of their economic system to the free-labor system of the North
11	and		some	could not resist	the chance to gloat		
12			Senator James Henry Hammond of South Carolina	drove home	the point		in his celebrated "King Cotton" speech of March 1858

clauses (7 out of 12) either identify the cause (e.g., *adding to, played, leading to, was, affected*) or attribute the effect (e.g., *ensued, was less harmful to*) of the Panic of 1857. These causes and effects are constructed in dense, abstract noun groups (e.g., *the short, but sharp, depression of 1857 and 1858; the failure of an Ohio investment house—the kind of event that had formerly taken weeks to be widely known; a wave of panic selling; business failures and slowdowns that threw thousands out of work*) and act as grammatical participants in the text. An inspection of what begins each clause shows that the passage is mainly organized around a set of abstract causes and effects, suggesting that the text is an historical explanation with a minimum amount of chronological retelling embedded. An examination of word choices (e.g., *drove home the point, could not resist, gloat, celebrated*) reveals that the text has a sarcastic tone, indicating that the authors likely have a negative (contemptuous) view of the South and its economic system.

As students deconstruct each clause, they tackle the linguistic challenges of the text at the same time. For example, in constructing Table 3.3, students may engage in conversation about the meanings of not only specialized terms that likely require background knowledge building (e.g., *financial markets, free-labor system, King Cotton speech*) but also commonplace words and phrases that are used in atypical ways (e.g., *sharp=steep*, took this as proof=regarded this as proof, *drove home the point=make a point in a very forceful way*). They may reconstruct the first sentence to recover the logical subject (i.e., *the short, but sharp, depression of 1857 and 1858*) and object (i.e., *the growing political tension*) of the sentence. They may track references for pronouns and demonstratives in the text, discovering, for example, that the pronoun "*it*" in clause 8 refers not to "*recovery*" in the preceding sentence but to "*the Panic of 1857*" later in the same sentence and that the pronoun "*this*" in clause 10 refers not to a specific word or phrase in the text, but to the whole idea expressed in clause 9, which is that the South was not as severely affected as the North by the Panic of 1857. They may deconstruct or paraphrase long noun phrases such as "*proof of the superiority of their economic system to the free-labor system of the North*" to better comprehend its meaning. They may also discuss the sequence of events presented in clauses 4, 5, and 6 (*a sharp downturn in agricultural exports to Britain → wave of panic selling → business failures and slowdowns → thousands out of work*), recognizing that in history texts, events are not always presented in a chronological order as they unfolded in real time, causation is often conflated with time, and cause–effect relations are not always signaled explicitly through conjunctions (e.g., *because*) but sometimes more subtly through nouns (*cause*) and verbs (*adding to, played, ensued, leading to, threw, affected*). These discussions help students focus on meanings in the passage while at the same time learning how language works to make causal and temporal meanings in history.

Writing Argument from Sources

Writing, like reading, is central to historians' social practice. Through writing, students deepen their understanding of text. Because an historian's job is to construct interpretations of the past based on multiple sources, it is only logical that students learn to write from sources. In particular, they need to learn how to make a case for a particular claim about, or interpretation of, the past in writing. According to Nokes and de la Paz (2018), writing argument from sources is widely considered "the keystone of historical writing" (p. 551). The task requires that the writer "acknowledges multiple perspectives to deliberately formulate a rational stance" (Nokes & de la Paz, 2018, p. 557) and to explain and argue for/against that stance with text-based evidence. It has been found to enhance content learning and promote historical thinking/reasoning (Gritter, Beers, & Knaus, 2013; Monte-Sano & de la Paz, 2012; Stahl et al., 1996; Wiley & Voss, 1999).

Despite its importance, argumentative writing does not occur often in history/social studies classrooms, where summary writing is more typical (Monte-Sano, 2011). As a result, many students struggle with argumentative writing in history (Coffin, 2006; Gritter, Beers, & Knaus, 2013; Monte-Sano & Miles, 2014): They tend to summarize ideas from multiple sources, rather than purposefully selecting sources and quotes as evidence in support of a specific claim or argument; they lack discipline-specific language resources and literacy strategies to construct historical meanings (e.g., time, causality, evaluation) and present compelling arguments; and they engage in knowledge telling (e.g., haphazard listing of historical "facts") much more than knowledge transformation (i.e., producing well-crafted texts where the thesis is clearly stated, ideas are logically organized, and evidence is selectively used). A major obstacle students face in argumentative writing is their limited repertoire of language resources. As Coffin (2006, p. 77) explained,

> [C]onstructing an arguing genre assumes and subsumes the ability to narrate, abstract from and reason about historical events in the manner of the explaining and recording genres but, in addition, requires the ability to reconfigure the resources of abstracting and reasoning in order to persuade. This requires the use of different interpersonal strategies and new ways of organizing text. Not surprising, this is a challenging shift for many students.

To promote argumentative writing in history, teachers need to present history as an inquiry-oriented subject, engaging students in investigating historically compelling questions and applying historical thinking/reasoning about controversial topics (Hynd, 1999; Monte-Sano & de la Paz, & Felton, 2015). They need to provide ample opportunities for students to examine and discuss multiple sources that reflect multiple perspectives, as well as explicit instruction on how to reason historically with these texts and how to develop valid arguments (i.e., interpretations) based on these texts (Nokes & de la Paz, 2018). They also need to help students develop the language resources needed to construct historical meanings and produce well-crafted discourse that facilitates the development of argument (Christie & Derewianka, 2008; Coffin, 2006; Schleppegrell, 2004).

A pedagogical model that teachers can use to orchestrate these activities in support of argumentative writing is the "genre teaching-learning cycle", adapted from the Sydney School Genre Pedagogy (Rose & Martin, 2012). The model, represented in Figure 3.7, consists of four stages: building knowledge and context, analyzing model text(s), playing with language, and constructing text(s). During the first stage, students explore an historically significant question or controversy that interests them or is important to the curriculum. The exploration involves reading of historical texts from multiple sources, as well as other activities that are authentic to the discipline

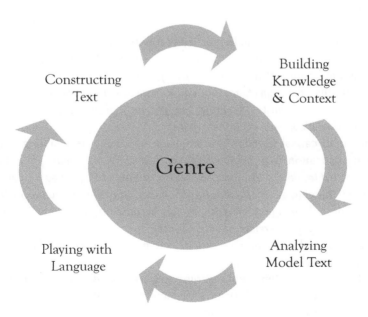

Figure 3.7 Genre Teaching–Learning Cycle
Source: (Fang, 2021a, p. 168)

(e.g., taking field trips, interviewing historical participants, examining physical artifacts, watching relevant videos/films). As students engage with historical texts, they employ the reading strategies/protocols that historians use
(e.g., inferring, sourcing, contextualizing, corroborating, perspective taking)
to help them make sense of the texts. Explicit instruction on how to use
these strategies and why they are important can be conducted when needed.
Reading and discussing multiple sources, together with other disciplinary
activities, helps students develop the content knowledge and language resources they will need to write argument from sources.

In the second stage, model argumentative essays in history are selected for
close reading and detailed analysis. The number of model texts selected for
close reading and analysis will depend on the amount of available time and
the needs of students, as well as the goals of the curriculum. Specifically, the
teacher engages students in in-depth discussion of the writing craft in these
exemplar texts, paying close attention to how experts use language/semiotic
resources and other composing strategies to make historical meanings in
discipline-legitimated ways that help them accomplish the purpose of the
genre. For example, the teacher can, according to Coffin (2006), focus on
how disciplinary experts represent cause–effect relations in history, helping
students learn to

- recognize how causality is linguistically constructed, such as through the use
  of prepositions (e.g., *because of, due to, with, from*), verbs (e.g., *ensue, lead
  to, result in*), conjunctions (e.g., *because*), conjunctive adjunct (e.g., *therefore,
  thus*), nouns (e.g., *effect, reason, cause, consequence*), and non-finite clause
  (*Liberty-loving colonists, <u>resenting the presence of the red-coated "ruffians"</u>,
  taunted the "bloody backs" unmercifully.*)
- understand causal functions of language use, such as enabling and determining causation (e.g., *enable, influence, allow, bring about, promote, affect;
  result in, led to, determine, force, make, is attributed to*), packaging cause as an
  abstract thing (e.g., *effect, reason, influence*), appraising causation (e.g., *the
  <u>main</u> reason, <u>little direct</u> influence, <u>in part</u> because of*), and deducing historical
  significance (e.g., *therefore, show, indicate*)
- organize causal phenomena rhetorically (e.g., *first, second, in addition, another,
  further, moreover*)
- conflate cause and temporal meaning (e.g., *when, after, lead to, ensue, follow*)
- negotiate and debate historical causes and effects, and
- reason about the historical significance of events.

The teacher can also highlight how experts conceptualize and use time in
ways that move beyond personal perception and lived experience, helping

students move from personally oriented representation of time (e.g., *last year, in 1945, then*) to ones that are historically valued (e.g., *the Great Depression, The Cold War, the Middle Ages*), develop different ways of representing historical time, and dismantle the timeline as an organizing device (Coffin, 2006). Equally important, the teacher can show how experts summarize sources in an angle that connects with and bolsters their point of the argument, helping students learn to use precise verbs (e.g., *explain, assert, acknowledge, suggest, admit, concur, argue, declare, implore, caution, encourage, question, emphasize, conclude, repudiate*) to report what others said, deploy hedges (e.g., *likely, perhaps, may, appear to, suggest, somewhat*) to indicate the uncertain nature of historical knowledge, draw on appraisal resources (e.g., adjectives, nominalizations, quotation marks, modality, concession) to infuse judgment and evaluation, select and integrate appropriate quotes as evidence for their argument, and juxtapose explaining and recounting in the development of argument (Fang, 2021b). The teacher can also draw students' attention to how historians efface human agency by presenting historical documents such as policies, laws, and treaties as agentive in bringing about historical changes, as illustrated in these two sentences—*The Economic Growth and Tax Relief Reconciliation Act squeaked through Congress with bipartisan support. It lowered tax rates and included a popular provision resulting in most Americans receiving a check in the mail from the IRS as "reconciliation" for paying too much in taxes.*—where "*The Economic Growth and Tax Relief Reconciliation Act*", rather than President George W. Bush (and his Republican-dominated Congress), is seen as responsible for lowering tax rates and giving most Americans a check.

Next, the teacher designs language-based tasks that highlight key, unfamiliar, or challenging features of historical discourse. For example, to further understanding and promote use of diverse language resources for presenting causal meanings, the teacher can have students search for words, phrases, and clauses in the texts they have read that indicate cause–effect relations. S/he can also have students practice different ways of representing causality by transforming sentences with causal meanings—e.g., changing a sentence where a prepositional phrase or a non-finite clause indicates causality to a sentence where causality is indicated by a conjunction, or vice versa—and then discussing what is gained (e.g., logico-semantic clarity, comprehensibility) or lost (e.g., focus, flow) when moving from within-clause causal reasoning to between-clause causal reasoning. The teacher can have students construct comparison between two source texts using a block structure (i.e., Points 1, 2, and 3 for Thing A—Points 1, 2, and 3 for Thing B) or a point-by-point structure (i.e., Point 1 for Thing A—Point 1 for Thing B, Point 2 for Thing A—Point 2 for Thing B, Point 3 for Thing

A—Point 3 for Thing B), discussing the affordances and challenges associated with each structure. S/he can also design paraphrasing exercises in which students reconstruct a densely packed sentence using their own words or combine two or more loosely strung sentences into one tightly knit sentence. Another exercise the teacher can use is to have students "build noun trains" by expanding a head noun (e.g., *deficits*) into a long noun phrase with pre- and postmodifiers (*spiraling budget deficits that wiped out the surpluses of the Clinton years*). These tasks give students the opportunity to "play" with the specific language features or discourse structures used in the texts they have been reading, furthering their understanding of the structure, logic, meaning, and function of these features/structures and developing their facility in using them in historical writing. In other words, these exercises help students consolidate control over the linguistic resources that are functional and effective for presenting historical content and construing historical reasoning/thinking.

In the final stage, the teacher encourages students to use some of the key or unfamiliar language features discussed earlier as they attempt to write, first collaboratively (with teacher or peers) and then independently, an historical argument from multiple sources. Students are guided through the composing process of generating ideas, developing an outline, gathering information, creating drafts, making revisions, and publishing their work, with an emphasis on revision, where special attention is given to the power of lexis and grammar in shaping, clarifying, and manipulating meaning in ways that serve the writer's purpose and meet disciplinary standards. For struggling writers, especially those with learning disabilities, further scaffolds can be provided for their composing process using the self-regulated strategy development model (SRSD, Harris & Graham, 1996), which explicitly teaches general writing strategies (e.g., planning, drafting, revising) along with procedures for regulating these strategies and the writing process (e.g., goal setting, task analysis, self-monitoring, and self-instructions). The final essays can be evaluated in terms of completeness of rhetorical structures, factual and interpretive accuracy, sourcing of evidence, corroboration of evidence, persuasiveness of evidence, contextualization of evidence, and effectiveness of language choices (Fang, 2021b; Monte-Sano, 2012).

Conclusion

History is not the past but evidence-based interpretations of the past. To construct a rigorous interpretation, historians engage in an inquiry, or problem-solving, process that involves asking an historically significant question; identifying a multitude of relevant historical sources; making sense of these documents through sourcing, contextualizing, corroborating, inferring, close reading, and other strategies; wrestling with issues of causality, connections, significance, perspective, and context; formulating an argument that addresses the historical question posed; weighing and selecting evidence from sources to support the argument; and crafting a coherent essay that makes a compelling case for the argument. Learning history, thus, means more than attaining knowledge about significant historical events, developments, individuals, groups, documents, places, and ideas; it also entails learning ways of generating and inquiring into historically compelling questions, ways of interacting and reasoning with historical sources of many different types, and ways of producing texts that provide credible explanations of and convincing arguments about historical events and developments. Teachers can support students' history learning by engaging them in meaningful historical inquiries; promoting the use of multiple sources; explicitly teaching the strategies/protocols/heuristics historians use in their reading practice; demonstrating how language is used to present information, infuse perspective, and structure discourse in history; and providing scaffolded opportunities for writing arguments from sources. This disciplinary literacy approach is more likely to ensure that students develop historical literacy that enables them to participate fully as informed citizens in a democratic society.

Reflection and Application

1 What is history? What is the role of reading in developing historical literacy?
2 What does disciplinary literacy mean in relation to history? What does it mean to be reading like a historian?
3 What are the specific challenges involved in historical reading? How can these challenges be addressed?
4 What does a disciplinary literacy approach to history reading instruction look like? In what ways does the approach promote historical literacy? And how is it different from the way history was traditionally taught?
5 Design a unit of instruction for a specific grade level aimed at developing students' historical literacy. Be sure to identify/describe the disciplinary standards and curriculum goals to be addressed, the textual resources to be utilized, the activities and strategies to be used to promote historical inquiry and historical thinking/reasoning, the assessment tools to be employed to monitor and evaluate student progress toward the unit objectives, and a reasonable timeline for implementing the unit.

References

Afflerbach, P., & VanSledright, B. (2001). Hath! Doth! What? Middle graders reading innovative history text. *Journal of Adolescent and Adult Literacy, 44*(8), 696–707.

American Historical Association (1944). *American history in schools and colleges.* New York: Macmillan Company.

Bain, R. (November, 2008). What is competent historical thinking in and out of the classroom? Paper presented at *The History Summit II: What promise does history education hold for student learning.* Davis, CA: University of California.

Bernstein, B. (1996). *Pedagogy, symbolic control and identity: Theory, research, critique.* London: Taylor & Francis.

Bereiter, C. & Bird, M. (1985). Use of thinking aloud in identification and teaching of reading comprehension strategies. *Cognition and Instruction, 2*(2), 131–156.

Berenbaum, M. (2006). *The world must know: The history of the Holocaust as told in the United States Holocaust Memorial Museum.* Washington, DC: John Hopkins University Press.

Brinkley, A., Broussard, A., McPherson, J., Ritchie, D., & Appleby, J. (2013). *Discovering our past: A history of the United States—Early years.* New York: McGraw-Hill.

Britt, A., & Aglinskas, C. (2002). Improving students' ability to identify and use source information. *Cognition and Instruction, 20*(4), 485–522.

Christie, F., & Derewianka, B. (2008). *School discourse: Learning to write across the years of schooling.* London: Continuum.

Coffin, C. (2006). *Historical discourse: The language of time, cause, and evaluation.* London: Continuum.

Connelly, M. (2023). *The declassification engine: What history reveals about America's top secrets.* New York: Pantheon.

Crowe, C. (2003). *Getting away with murder: The true story of the Emmett Till case.* New York: Phyllis Fogelman Books.

Fang, Z. (2021a). *Using functional grammar in English literacy teaching and learning.* Beijing: Foreign Language Teaching and Research Press.

Fang, Z. (2021b). *Demystifying academic writing: Genres, moves, skills and strategies.* New York: Routledge.

Fang, Z., & Chapman, S. (2015). Enhancing English learners' access to disciplinary texts through close reading practices. In M. Daniel & M. Kouider (Eds.), *Research and practice that makes a difference in English learners' success* (pp. 3–18). New York: Rowan & Littlefield.

Fang, Z., & Schleppegrell, M. (2008). *Reading in secondary content areas: A language-based pedagogy*. Ann Arbor, MI: University of Michigan Press.

Fang, Z., & Schleppegrell, M. (2010). Disciplinary literacies across content areas: Supporting secondary reading through functional language analysis. *Journal of Adolescent and Adult Literacy, 53*(7), 587–597.

Faragher, J., Buhle, M., Czitrom, D., & Armitage, S. (2007). *Out of many: A history of the American people* (15th ed.). Upper Saddle River, NJ: Prentice Hall.

Fitzgerald, J. (2014). An analysis of causal asyndetic constructions in the United States history textbooks. *Functional Linguistics, 1*(5). https://doi.org/10.1186/2196-419X-1-5

Fitzgerald, J. (2019). Teaching the reasons why: An analysis of causation in history textbooks and historical primary source documents. *Universal Journal of Educational Research, 7*(4), 1027–1036.

Goldman, S., Britt, M., Brown, W., Cribb, G., George, M., Greenleaf, C., Lee, C., Shanahan, C., & Project READI (2016). Disciplinary literacies and learning to read for understanding: A conceptual framework for disciplinary literacy. *Educational Psychologist, 51*(2), 219–246.

Gritter, K., Beers, S., & Knaus, R. (2013). Teacher scaffolding of academic language in an advanced placement U.S. history class. *Journal of Adolescent and Adult Literacy, 56*(5), 409–418.

Halliday, M., & Matthiessen, C. (2014). *An introduction to functional grammar* (4th ed.). New York: Routledge.

Harris, K. R., & Graham, S. (1996). *Making the writing process work: Strategies for composition and self-regulation* (2d ed.). Cambridge: Brookline Books.

Hynd, C. (1999). Teaching students to think critically using multiple texts in history. *Journal of Adolescent and Adult Literacy, 42*(6), 428–436.

Kennedy, D., Cohen, L., & Bailey, T. (2009). *The American pageant: A history of the American people (Vol. I: To 1877)* (14th ed.). Boston, MA: Wadsworth.

Kerr, P. (1996). *Letters from China: The Canton-Boston correspondence of Robert Bennet Forbes, 1838–1840*. Mystic, CT: Mystic Seaport Museum.

Liu, Z., Ding, S., Liu, L. (2013). *Zhongguo li shi* (in Chinese) [Chinese history]. Hunan: Yuele Shuyuan Press.

Martin, J. (1997). Analysing genre: Functional parameters. In F. Christie & J. Martin (Eds.), *Genre and institutions: Social processes in the workplace and school* (pp. 3–39). London: Continuum.

Martin, J. (2002). Writing history: Construing time and value in discourse of the past. In M. Schleppegrell & C. Colombi (Eds.), *Developing advanced literacy in first and second languages: Meaning with power* (pp. 87–118). Mahwah, NJ: Lawrence Erlbaum.

Martin, S., & Lakatos, P. (2007). *The art of opium antiques*. Chiang Mai, Thailand: Silkworm Books.

Maton, K. (2006). On knowledge structures and knower structures. In R. Moore, M. Arnot, J. Beck, & H. Daniels (Eds.), *Knowledge, power and educational reform: Applying the sociology of Basil Bernstein* (pp. 44–59). London: Routledge.

Miller, G. (1969). *The psychology of communication: Seven essays*. Baltimore, MD: Penguin Books.

Monte-Sano, C. (2011). Beyond reading comprehension and summary: Learning to read and write in history by focusing on evidence, perspective, and interpretation. *Curriculum Inquiry, 41*(2), 212–249.

Monte-Sano, C. (2012). What makes a good history essay? Assessing historical aspects of argumentative writing. *Social Education, 76*(6), 294–298.

Monte-Sano, C., & de la Paz, S. (2012). Using writing tasks to elicit adolescents' historical reasoning. *Journal of Literacy Research, 44*(3), 273–299.

Monte-Sano, C., de la Paz, S., & Felton, M. (2015). Teaching argumentative writing and "content" in diverse middle school history classrooms. *Social Education, 79*(4), 194–199.

Monte-Sano, C., & Miles, D. (2014). Toward disciplinary reading and writing in history. In P. Smagorinsky (Ed.), *Teaching dilemmas & solutions in content-area literacy* (pp. 29–56). Thousand Oaks, CA: Corwin.

National Governors Association Center for Best Practices (NGA) & Council of Chief State School Officers (CCSSO) (2010). *Common core state standards for English language arts & literacy for history/social studies, science, and technical subjects*. Washington, DC: Author.

Nokes, J. (2013). *Building students' historical literacies: Learning to read and reason with historical texts and evidence*. New York: Routledge.

Nokes, J., & de la Paz, S. (2018). Writing and argumentation in history education. In S. Metzger & L. Harris (Eds.), *The Wiley international handbook of history teaching and learning* (pp. 551–578). Hoboken, NJ: Wiley.

Nokes, J., Dole, J., & Hacker, D. (2007). Teaching high school students to use heuristics while reading historical texts. *Journal of Educational Psychology, 99*(3), 492–504.

Paxton, R. (2002). The influence of author visibility on high school students solving a historical problem. *Cognition and Instruction, 20*, 197–248.

Pearson, D., & Gallagher, M. (1983). The instruction of reading comprehension. *Contemporary Educational Psychology, 8*(3), 317–344.

Ravi, A. (2010). Disciplinary literacy in the history classroom. In S. McConachie & A. Petrosky (Eds.), *Content matters: A disciplinary literacy approach to improving student learning* (pp. 33–62). San Francisco, CA: Jossey-Bass.

Reisman, A. (2012). The document-based lesson: Bringing disciplinary inquiry into high school history classrooms with adolescent struggling readers. *Journal of Curriculum Studies, 44,* 233–264.

Reisman, A., & Wineburg, S. (2008). Teaching the skill of contextualization in history. *The Social Studies, 99*(5), 202–207.

Rose, D., & Martin, J. (2012). *Learning to write, reading to learn: Genre, knowledge and pedagogy in the Sydney School.* Bristol: Equinox.

Sale, K. (1990, October 22). What Columbus discovered. *The Nation, 251*(13), 444–447.

Schall-Leckrone, L. (2017). Genre pedagogy: A framework to prepare history teachers to teach language. *TESOL Quarterly, 51*(2), 358–382.

Schleppegrell, M. (2011). Supporting disciplinary learning through language analysis: Developing historical literacy. In F. Christie & K. Maton (Eds.), *Disciplinarity: Functional linguistic and sociological perspectives* (pp. 197–216). London: Bloomsbury.

Schleppegrell, M. J. (2004). *The language of schooling: A functional linguistics perspective.* Mahwah, NJ: Erlbaum.

Schleppegrell, M., & Achugar, M. (2012). Learning language and learning history: A functional linguistics approach. *TESOL Journal, 12*(2), 21–27.

Schlesinger, A. (1992). Was America a mistake? Reflections on the long history of efforts to debunk Columbus and his discovery. *The Atlantic Monthly, 270*(3), 16–23.

Shanahan, C., Shanahan, T., & Misischia, C. (2011). Analysis of expert readers in three disciplines: History, mathematics, and chemistry. *Journal of Literacy Research, 43*(4), 393–429.

Stahl, S., Hynd, C., Britton, B., McNish, M., & Bosquet, D. (1996). What happens when students read multiple source documents in history? *Reading Research Quarterly, 31*(4), 430–456.

Swan, K., et al. (2013). *College, career & civic life (C3) framework for social studies state standards.* Silver Spring, MD: National Council for the Social Studies.

VanSledright, B. (2012). Learning with texts in history: Protocols for reading and practical strategies. In T.L. Jetton & C. Shanahan (Eds.), *Adolescent literacy in the academic disciplines: General principles and practical strategies.* New York: Guilford.

Wiley, J., & Voss, J. (1999). Constructing arguments from multiple sources: Tasks that promote understanding and not just memory from text. *Journal of Educational Psychology, 91*(2), 301–311.

Wineburg, S. (1991a). Historical problem solving: A study of the cognitive processes used in the evaluation of documentary and pictorial evidence. *Journal of Educational Psychology, 83*(1), 73–87.

Wineburg, S. (1991b). On the reading of historical texts: Notes on the breach between school and academy. *American Educational Research Journal*, 28(3), 495–519.

Wineburg, S. (1998). Reading Abraham Lincoln: An expert/expert study in the interpretation of historical texts. *Cognitive Science*, 22(3), 319–346.

Wineburg, S., Martin, D., & Monte-Sano, C. (2013). *Reading like a historian: Teaching literacy in middle and high school history classrooms*. New York: Teachers College Press.

Zhou, X. (August 30, 2022). Chinese historians' review of past isolationist policy goes viral, reflecting unease over closed borders, lockdowns, crackdowns. *South China Morning Post*, https://www.scmp.com/news/china/article/3190589/chinese-historians-review-past-isolationist-policy-goes-viral-reflecting

4
Reading Science[1]

Reading and Science Literacy

Science is both a body of knowledge about how things work in the universe and a process for discovering, explaining, cataloguing, generating, communicating, critiquing, and renovating that knowledge. It permeates practically every facet of our daily lives. Becoming scientifically literate is, therefore, essential not only to our personal well-being but also to the prosperity and security of our nation. Science literacy can be understood from a fundamental sense and a derived sense (Norris & Phillips, 2003). The fundamental sense of science literacy refers to the ability to access, comprehend, evaluate, and produce science texts. The derived sense of science literacy concerns knowledge about key concepts, big ideas, important relationships, core practices, and unifying themes in science. Its development is dependent on the fundamental sense of science literacy. In other words, the ability to access, comprehend, critique, and create science texts is fundamental to becoming "knowledgeable, learned and educated in science" (Norris & Phillips, 2003, p. 224).

It is now widely recognized that reading—or more broadly, literacy—is not an adjunct to the practice of science, but an essential component of engaging with science (Fang, 2010; Patterson et al., 2018). In fact, reading is one of the most common activities performed by scientists (Yore, 2004). Scientists spend a considerable amount of time reading journal articles and other sources (books, documents, notes, blogs, webpages, newspapers) to gain new ideas, synthesize information, generate questions for inquiry, evaluate claims, seek explanations, and deepen understanding. They review the work of others to keep abreast of the latest development in the field, scrutinize its conceptual underpinnings, assess its logic of argument and quality of evidence, determine what questions or topics to investigate, make predictions about what to expect from the investigation, and offer evidence-based

DOI: 10.4324/9781003432258-4

explanations or arguments. As Osborne (2002) aptly put it, science without reading is akin to a ship without a sail or a car without an engine.

This privileging of reading in science means that science educators must give prominence to reading in science teaching and learning (Patterson et al., 2018; Wellington & Osborne, 2001). Recent national standards in science education, such as the Next Generation Science Standards (NGSS Lead States, 2013), recognize the centrality of reading and literacy to science education, calling on science teachers to promote language use and support reading/literacy development in service of scientific inquiry, learning, and sense making (Lee, Quinn, & Valdes, 2013). The eight science and engineering practices identified by the NGSS as central to science learning—asking questions and finding problems, developing and using models, planning and carrying out investigations, analyzing and interpreting data, using mathematics and computational thinking, constructing explanation and designing solution, engaging in argument from evidence, and evaluating and communicating information—cannot be effectively undertaken without reading. Similarly, the three dimensions of science learning envisioned by the National Research Council (2012)—practices, crosscutting concepts, and disciplinary core ideas—cannot be effectively attained without substantial engagement with text. The Common Core State Standards (NGA & CCSSO, 2010), likewise, emphasize the essential role of reading in disciplinary learning, noting that students should demonstrate increasing proficiency and sophistication in reading disciplinary texts in order to support knowledge acquisition and communication.

Empirical research (e.g., Cervetti et al., 2012; Fang & Wei, 2010; Romance & Vitale, 2001) has shown that reading enhances content understanding, promotes inquiry and conceptual change, contributes to knowledge building, and cultivates scientific habits of mind. Because the process underlying text comprehension is similar to that required to demonstrate proficiency in science (van den Broek, 2010), knowledge and skills that drive higher reading comprehension (e.g., background knowledge, vocabulary, inference) also drive higher science attainment. In fact, medium to high correlations have been reported between reading comprehension measures and science achievement measures, with students who struggle with reading often performing poorly in science (August et al., 2009; O'Reilly & McNamara, 2007; Reed, Petscher, & Truckenmiller, 2016). On a more macro level, Cromley (2009) analyzed three international data sets from the Programme on International Student Assessment (PISA) and found that the correlation between science scores and reading scores for 15-year-old students was robust (>0.80) and that although this correlation varied among countries, the reading–science relationship was the weakest in countries with low country mean reading scores. Taken together, these findings reinforce the need—as well as support the current push by the science education and literacy education communities—to make reading an integral and more prominent part of the science education curriculum.

The Challenges of Science Reading

Despite the importance of reading to science and science learning, many school children struggle with reading in science, failing to meet the state or national standards in science and literacy. Children from economically disadvantaged or linguistically minoritized backgrounds are disproportionately represented in this struggling population. Those with reading difficulties tend to have serious trouble with the study of science because scientific knowledge is presented and assessed in school largely through written texts. Paralleling their performance on the 2019 National Assessment of Educational Progress (NAEP) reading assessment (see Chapter 1), only 36% of 4th graders, 35% of 8th graders, and 22% of 12th graders scored at or above proficient in the 2019 NAEP science assessment (https://www.nationsreport card.gov/highlights/science/2019/).

The challenge students encounter in science reading is multifaceted. Science texts present technical content that students are just beginning to learn in the science class, contain implicit or abstract logical–semantic relations that can be difficult for students to interpret, infuse authorial points of view in subtle ways, and use language patterns that are dense and complex (Fang, 2006; Fang et al., 2019; Halliday & Martin, 1993). They place considerable processing demands on reading and understanding, requiring readers to have the content knowledge, academic language skills, and literacy strategies that are specific to science.

More specifically, science aims to construct theorized, evidence-based interpretations of the universe so that we can better understand natural phenomena and improve our living conditions (Krajcik & Sutherland, 2010). It produces knowledge that is distilled from our concrete experience with the physical world. Thus, this knowledge tends to be more technical, abstract, systematic, hierarchically organized, and transcendent than the commonsense knowledge with which we live our everyday lives. In the words of British educational sociologist Basil Bernstein (1996, pp. 172–173, cited in Maton, 2006, p. 47), science has a hierarchical knowledge structure, that is, "an explicit, coherent, systematically principled and hierarchical organization of knowledge" that develops through the integration of knowledge at lower (often more concrete) levels and across an expanding range of phenomena. For example, we commonly refer to small gnawing animals with strong incisors and no canine teeth collectively as "rats"; but in science, they belong to a family of mammals called "rodents"—or, technically, "rodentia"—that also includes mice, gundis, squirrels, chipmunks, hamsters, beavers, porcupines, guinea pigs, gophers, degus, and jerboas. And rodentia itself is an order in a hierarchy of classification that also includes magnorder (*boreoeutheria*), superorder (*euarchontoglires*), granorder (*euarchonta*, *glires*), and order (*lagomorpha*, *rodentia*).

School science knowledge is presented in a range of discourse genres that catalogue the social practice of scientists. They include report, description, explanation, exposition, and discussion, among others. Each of these genres draws on a particular constellation of lexical, grammatical, and discursive features that make it the kind of genre it is and distinguishes it from the language patterns that construct everyday texts or texts in other content domains (Fang, 2010, 2012). These linguistic features also reflect the scientific habits of mind that are embodied in the work of scientists. They tend to be more technical, dense, compact, abstract, and metaphoric than the lexico-grammatical features that characterize the ordinary language that constructs the commonsense knowledge and everyday habits of mind (Fang, 2005; Halliday, 2006; Halliday & Martin, 1993). Lexically, science uses specialist terminology to build technical taxonomies (e.g., *mitosis, meiosis, cytokinesis*) and hedging devices (e.g., *can, perhaps, likely, may*) to exercise caution and increase precision. Grammatically, science privileges nominalizations (e.g., *growth, ability, reason, the problem*)—that is, abstract nouns derived from verbs (*grow*), adjectives (*able*), conjunctions (*because*), or clauses (*The traffic came to a standstill.*)—because they enable the author to distill previously presented information, bury agency, create technical terms, and facilitate discursive flow. These nominalizations are often combined with other grammatical elements to form long noun phrases that contain a large sum of semantic data (e.g., *the incredible ability to perform the task under extreme circumstances*). Science also relies heavily on verbs of relational process, or "being" verbs (e.g., *be, have, become, concern, consist of, belong to, deal with, weigh, measure, mean*), to identify, define, classify, explain, characterize, or describe concepts, entities, and relationships. In fact, many clauses in science consist of two long noun phrases linked by a being verb (e.g., *The first law of thermodynamics* **is** *a universal law of nature in which no exceptions have been observed. The natural frequency of vibration for electrons in glass* **matches** *the frequency of ultraviolet light.*). Another grammatical resource privileged in science is the passive voice (e.g., *is released, were created*) because it allows the author to foreground concepts/ideas and background actors. From an organizational point of view, science features a tightly knit, logically sequenced structure that facilitates information flow and argument development.

Consider, for instance, Text 4.1, an excerpt from an 11th grade chemistry textbook (Dingrando, Tallman, Hainen, & Wistrom, 2006, p. 848). The text uses specialist terminology (e.g., *acid rain, acidity, nutrients, aquatic, vegetation, precipitation*) to construct technical knowledge. It also uses a number of nominalizations (e.g., *acidity, removal, loss, resistance, damage, reaction*) for functional reasons. In sentence #1, the process of removing nutrients from the soil is repackaged as "*the removal of essential nutrients from the soil*" so that the focus is on the idea of removing (as a thing) rather than on the process of removing (as an action) or the actor engaging in the process (acid rain). In the same sentence, the quality of being acidic is transformed into the state of being acidic, in effect creating a technical term "*acidity*" that foregrounds the concept. Similarly, "*the loss of nutrients*" repackages "*the removal of essential nutrients*" so that the idea from sentence #1 can continue to be discussed in sentence #2. In sentence #4, "*damage to trees and to outdoor surface*" synthesizes "*leaving trees and plants . . .*" in sentence #2 and "*which can kill or harm aquatic life*" in sentence #3; and "*this reaction*" in sentence #6 distills "*the acid in precipitation reacts with CaCO₃*" in a way that buries the participating agents. Thanks to these nominalizations, the linkages among sentences are tightened, creating a discursive flow that facilitates the presentation of information and the development of argument.

Text 4.1

(1) Acid rain increases the acidity of some types of soil, resulting in the removal of essential nutrients from the soil. (2) The loss of nutrients adversely affects the area's vegetation, leaving trees and other plants with less resistance to disease, insects, and bad weather. (3) Acid rain also increases the acidity of streams, rivers, and lakes, which can kill or harm aquatic life. (4) As Figure 26–8 shows, damage to trees and to outdoor surface can be extensive. (5) The acid in precipitation reacts with $CaCO_3$, the major component of marble and limestone. (6) What products are produced by this reaction?

These nominalizations combine with other grammatical elements to form long, complex noun phrases that pack a large amount of information. They include "*the acidity of some types of soil*", "*the removal of essential nutrients from the soil*", "*trees and other plants with less resistance to disease, insects, and bad weather*", and "*$CaCO_3$, the major component of marble and limestone*". Each of these noun phrases contains a head (i.e., *acidity, removal, trees and other plants, $CaCO_3$*), which is modified by preposition phrase (*of some types of soil,* *of essential nutrients from the soil, with less resistance to . . .*) or appositive (*the major component of marble and limestone*). Each clause typically contains two noun phrases of varying complexities linked by a being or doing verb. The privileging of nominal expressions in science enables scientists to foreground grammatical participants, which encode concepts and ideas, and background processes, which encode happenings and actions. As Halliday and Martin (1993, p. 15) explained,

> Where the everyday "mother tongue" of commonsense knowledge construes reality as a balanced tension between things and processes, the elaborated register of scientific knowledge reconstrues it as an edifice of things. It holds reality still, to be kept under observation and experimented with; and in so doing, interprets it not as changing with time (as the grammar of clauses interprets it) but as persisting—or rather, persistence—through time, which is the mode of being a noun.

Another notable feature of the text is that causation is not constructed using the usual resources of conjunctions or conjunctive adjuncts (e.g., *because, so*). Instead, it is conveyed less explicitly through the use of nonfinite clauses or non-restrictive relative clauses. In sentence #1, the nonfinite clause *"resulting in the removal of essential nutrients from the soil"* presents the effect of *"increases the acidity of some types of soil"* in the main clause. In sentence #2, *"leaving trees and other plants with less resistance to disease, insects, and bad weather"* presents the adverse effect of nutrient loss stated in the main clause. In sentence #3, the non-restrictive relative clause *"which can kill or harm aquatic life"* presents the potential effects of increased acidity of streams, rivers, and lakes.

Finally, the authors of the text appear to be cautious when presenting information and making claims. In some clauses, statements are presented with no uncertainty (e.g., *acid rain increases* . . ., *the loss of nutrients adversely affects* . . .); whereas in others, modal verbs (e.g., *can kill, can be extensive*) are used to moderate claims. The difference in the degree of certainty or probability projected in these clauses is likely a function of the amount of available evidence or the degree of consensus within the scientific community.

Similar language patterns can also be found in other science reading materials. In Text 4.2, an excerpt from a science trade book on the Grand Canyon (Chin, 2017, unpaged), technical terms such as *species, mammals, invertebrates, endemic, topography,* and *landscape* are used. Sentences #1, #3, and #4 each use a being verb (*is, have*) to link noun phrases of varying complexities. They identify *Grand Canyon* as *home to thousands of species,* attribute *this wide variety of life* to *the canyon's topography*, and describe *its rugged landscape and . . . its great depth* as having *a significant effect on climate throughout the canyon*. Sentence #2 characterizes 29 species as "endemic to the canyon", providing additional information that reinforces the message presented in sentence #1. The non-finite clause "*meaning they don't live anywhere else on Earth*" explains what "*endemic to the canyon*" in the main clause means. The beginning of sentence #3, *this wide variety of life*, is a nominalization that refers to "*thousands of species*" in the predicate position of sentence #1. The preposition "*or*" introduces a synonym (*physical structure*) that explains a preceding term (*topography*), thus avoiding the need for a separate sentence (*Topography is a physical structure.*), which may disrupt the flow of information and diffuse the focus of discussion. The beginning of sentence #4, *its rugged landscape and in particular its great depth*, exemplifies, although without an explicit linguistic marker (e.g., *for example*), the concept of topography introduced in the predicate position of sentence #3. These ways of structuring text create a discursive flow that enables the author to effectively present information and develop explanation.

Text 4.2

(1) Grand Canyon is home to thousands of species, including 373 birds, 92 mammals, 1750 plants, and more than 8000 invertebrates. (2) Twenty-nine species are endemic to the canyon, meaning they don't live anywhere else on Earth. (3) This wide variety of life is due to the canyon's topography, or physical structure. (4) Its rugged landscape and in particular its great depth have a significant effect on climate throughout the canyon.

In addition to language, modern science also draws on visual resources such as images, graphs, figures, pictures, tables, diagrams, maps, mathematics symbols, and sonograms to present its knowledge, ideas, and worldviews (Hand, McDermott, & Prain, 2016; Kress et al., 2001), resulting in what Lemke (2002) referred to as "science multimedia genres". These genres arise not only because they are "fit to the internal functional needs of the scientific community", but also because they "play a role in linking that community within the wider social, economic, and political institutions that make their continued existence possible" (Lemke, 2002, p. 28). In fact, today's science has become so heavily dependent on visual representations that it is difficult to imagine a science text without at least some visual elements. In many science texts, whether they are from textbooks, trade books, magazines, academic journals, or web pages, visual elements dominate. The books from which Texts 4.1 and 4.2 are excerpted, for example, contain a large number of visuals (e.g., figures, tables, pictures, illustrations, diagrams, graphs) that participate in communicating scientific meanings.

The increasingly multimodal/multisemiotic nature of today's science texts is due both to the limitations of (nature) language itself and to the invention of new technologies. Lemke (2002) pointed out that while language is a powerful tool for conceptualization and classification, it is not very effective in describing, for example, complex shapes, shades of color, degrees of temperature, or the trajectory of a rocket, for which visual and spatial-motor representations are much better suited. The advent of digital technologies, such as color coding and graphing tools, has enabled writers to manipulate multimodal/multisemiotic resources to meet the communicative needs of science writers. These technologies provide new affordances that significantly expand the meaning-making repertoires of scientists and at the same time facilitate science teaching and learning. For example, a linguistic description of a solid (e.g., *Solid is a state of matter with a definite shape and volume.*) tends to be abstract, but a drawing of a solid affords meaning making at the macroscopic level, and the particle model of a solid affords thinking of matter at the microscopic or nano-level (Yeo & Nielsen, 2020). Similarly, Newton's Laws of Motion can be more effectively taught and learned when verbal definitions or descriptions are combined with visual and material resources such as diagrams, symbolic expressions, numerical calculations, and physical models (Tang, Tighe, & Moje, 2016). Thus, as Prain (2022) has recommended, "[t]o learn to reason in science, students need to develop competence in using and integrating both linguistic and non-linguistic modes, including visual, mathematical, and embodied/actional modes" (pp. 152–153). Developing this competence can be challenging for many students.

How do Experts Read Science Texts?

Because of the nature of their work, scientists employ certain habits of mind in their reading and other social practices. These habits of mind include curiosity, informed skepticism, openness to new ideas, creativity, intellectual honesty, and ethical responsibility (National Research Council, 2012; NGSS Lead States, 2013). They inform the ways scientists read, write, talk, and think in their work. For example, reading in science means more than just the ability to comprehend and recite information in the text; it also involves critically analyzing and evaluating what is read and drawing inferences based on the evidence presented and/or reasonable assumptions. As

Wellington and Osborne (2001) pointed out, "To be capable of reading carefully, critically, and with a healthy skepticism is a vital component of being a scientist" (p. 42). Scientists must accurately assess the validity of knowledge claims, the quality of evidence, the logic of argument, and the coherence of claims in relation to the established body of knowledge in the field in order to produce and renovate knowledge (Yore, 2004).

Studies of expert performance have yielded valuable insights into how scientists read in their professional practice. Bazerman (1985), for example, observed seven research physicists with varied specializations while they were conducting library searches and reading articles in their fields, and interviewed them about their reading processes. He found that the physicists conducted weekly library searches to stay current in the field and were purposeful when selecting materials to read. Specifically, the scientists selected materials for careful reading based on their current or future work and personal knowledge of the field, focusing in particular on the work that was most closely related to their own and that added to or disrupted current knowledge. Once an article had been determined to be of interest, the physicists were just as selective in determining what portions of the article to read. Frequently, they would read only the materials that would provide them with more information about a topic or modify their current understanding of the topic; and they often read the article out of sequence, going backwards or jumping from section to section in order to raise or answer questions. When comprehension challenges arose, the physicists weighed the amount of gain against the amount of effort in tackling the unfamiliar or challenging materials. When encountering information that was unclear due to a lack of knowledge, they read freely and uncritically; however, when reading complicated material in anticipation of using it immediately in their own work, they first read for the gist and then conducted a second or third reading with a more critical stance, a process that involved an evaluation of the article's importance or usefulness. These reading habits and procedures are summarized below by the researcher:

> In this study, we find texts being read piecemeal for specific pieces of information. We see the information being placed within and against personal frameworks of knowledge. We see individual purposes and uses driving and shaping the reading. We see new statements being accepted based on how well they integrate with existing schema of how work should go. We see much reading accepted noncritically, from lack of experience with the work being discussed. (Bazerman, 1985, p. 19)

Shanahan, Shanahan, and Misischia (2011) focused on how chemists (i.e., two chemistry professors, two chemistry teacher educators, and two high school chemistry teachers), as well as historians and mathematicians, interacted with texts in their field. They examined the ways these experts used sourcing, contextualization, and corroboration in their considerations of disciplinary texts. They also examined how text structure and visual elements influenced the ways these experts interacted with the text, the role of interest in their reading, and how they engaged in critiquing and rereading of the text. Through examination of data collected through individual interviews, reading think alouds, and focus group meetings, the researchers found that the chemists had an approach to reading that could be characterized as flexible, pragmatic, and recursive. Specifically, they paid attention to authorship, author affiliation, citations, and publication outlet, using them to determine the quality and credibility of the text and whether they wanted to read it. They also took note of the time period of composition in order to determine the recency and, thus, the worth of the text. However, they did not seem to pay as much attention to corroboration as a way to reveal authorial stance or perspective. Instead, when they made comparisons across texts, their main purpose was to determine the relative value of the texts and to see if differences in experimental results could be attributed to differences in research methods and conditions. They used text structure to help build an understanding of ideas in the text rather than for critique or interpretation. They attended to visual elements (e.g., graphs, charts, diagrams, equations) as much as they did prose, moving back and forth between the two sources of information as they sought to understand and learn from the text.

Building on Shanahan, Shanahan, and Misischia (2011), Chapman (2015) investigated how two scientists—a physics professor and a mechanical engineering professor—read texts in their disciplines. Both participants were asked to think aloud as they read a self-selected but unfamiliar text in their own area of specialization. Data from their think alouds and subsequent discussion of the think alouds, as well as semi-structured interviews, show that both scientists engaged in extensive reading of disciplinary texts and used a variety of strategies to help them make sense of and interpret these texts. The physics professor, Dr. Xavier, read primarily articles in scientific journals, especially those with high impact factors. He found materials of interest mostly by conducting key word searches (by topic or author) on the Science Citation Index and other electronic databases. Most of the materials he read were multimodal texts, where technical, dense prose is interwoven with visual resources and mathematical symbols. Even though author reputation and journal quality impact the value and credibility he attached to an article, it is the reliability of data and quality of evidence that seemed to matter the most in his evaluation of a text. He also considered the time and place of a publication when deciding whether or how to navigate through a text. When reading a book on magnetoresistance in metals, Dr. Xavier used the Table of Contents and the Index to help identify specific sections of interest for further examination. He scanned, or speed read, the pages in the identified sections for "clumps" of potentially important information, often pausing to examine a data plot or an equation. At times, he read aloud certain "clumps" of the text (e.g., where mathematical symbols are defined) as a way of slowing down so that he had enough time to process and digest the information. He regularly drew on his prior knowledge to make predictions about the meaning of a particular mathematical symbol—such as T (tau) and ρ (rho)—as the same symbol can mean different things in different contexts. When getting confused during reading, he asked questions and reread portions of the text to help himself work through the confusion.

Like Dr. Xavier, the mechanical engineering professor, Dr. Jacobs, also read extensively, although the materials he read typically crossed disciplinary boundaries and catered to a variety of audiences (e.g., engineering scholars, practicing engineers, academic agriculturalists, farmers). This need to be knowledgeable about both engineering and at least one other field (e.g., biology, physics, agriculture, chemistry, medicine) has to do with the nature of an engineer's work, which is to design and create things for the betterment of people's everyday life. When reading an agricultural engineering article from a top research journal in his field, Dr. Jacobs previewed the text, skimming through different sections to determine if it was of interest to him. He then returned to the abstract and read it in its entirety, focusing most closely on the final two sentences, where results and conclusion are presented. After reading the abstract, he examined the introduction before moving to the main section about the experiment. During reading, he shifted his focus back and forth between the prose and the visual, gathering information or seeking clarification/confirmation from both simultaneously. In segments that sounded familiar or trustworthy or that were too detailed or challenging, he quickly scanned the material and focused more on the conclusion section, where key information is concisely summarized. In segments that present information of interest or importance, he slowed down, reading the material closely for accuracy and details. Even though he considered the author's reputation, the quality of the publication outlet, and the location where the reported research was conducted when determining the trustworthiness of the text, he relied more heavily on an objective evaluation of its content. He often questioned the methods used and the assumptions, claims, or conclusions made by the authors, flipping back and forth to weigh evidence, evaluate claims, seek clarification, or search for answers.

To summarize, the scientists in the studies described above appear to demonstrate "an extraordinary commitment to the literatures of their fields" (Bazerman, 1985, p. 22), working hard to keep up with the literature and using the literature to inform the work they do. They employ a range of strategies—including recursive reading, rereading, inferring, asking questions, previewing, scanning, skimming, sourcing, selective/purposeful reading, drawing on prior knowledge, detailed reading, evaluating, verifying, and connecting visuals with prose—to help them make sense of and assess the information presented in the texts they read. These strategies constitute the meaning-making repertoire that enables scientists to engage deeply, critically, and productively with texts in their literate practice.

A Blueprint for Improving Science Reading Ability

Science reading comprehension depends on, among other things, readers' background knowledge, language/multimodal proficiency, and use of cognitive strategies. The nature of knowledge encoded in science texts, the complexity of language that presents this knowledge, and the habits of mind needed to process technical content, dense language, multimodal representations, and abstract logical-semantic links make science reading distinct from everyday reading. This difference is the main cause of science reading difficulty for many students (Fang, 2006), requiring teachers to move beyond the traditional foci of reading instruction (i.e., phonological awareness, phonics, fluency, vocabulary, and comprehension strategies) to design instruction that foregrounds and addresses the unique demands of science texts. Science teachers can address the challenges of science reading by helping students (a) build content/conceptual knowledge about science, (b) develop science language proficiency and multimodal competence, and (c) learn to read like a scientist. Each of these components is elaborated below.

Building Science Content Knowledge

Content knowledge is knowledge about a specific and defined subject such as science. It is a subset of background, or prior, knowledge, which refers to all of the world knowledge the reader brings to the task of reading, including episodic (events), declarative (facts), and procedural (how-to) knowledge (Smith et al., 2021). The link between background knowledge and reading comprehension has been a widely recognized aspect of reading comprehension for the past four decades, with research suggesting that knowledge "speeds and strengthens reading comprehension, learning—and thinking" (Willingham, 2006, unpaged). For example, Cabell and Hwang (2020) reported that building knowledge in English language arts instruction can support the development of language and content knowledge, leading to better overall reading comprehension. Cromley, Snyder-Hogan, and Luciw-Dubas (2010) found that compared to narrative texts, science texts place "particularly heavy demands on prior knowledge and inference" (p. 696). This means that building (content) knowledge should be considered foundational to improving students' reading proficiency in general and science reading ability in particular.

Given the robust relationship between background knowledge and science reading comprehension, it is clear that explicitly building knowledge, especially domain-specific content knowledge about science, should be a key piece of science reading instruction. One obvious way of building students' science content knowledge is to engage them in firsthand experiences of doing science (e.g., experiments and observations). Research (e.g., Kontra, Lyons, Fischer, & Beilock, 2022) has shown that students who physically experience science concepts, ideas, procedures, and practices understand them more deeply and, thus, retain them longer in memory. However, not all science concepts, principles, ideas, or processes can be experienced firsthand in school classrooms, due to issues related to resource, expertise, feasibility, or ethics. Thus, a more convenient way of building science content knowledge is through text reading, as "texts are frequent and powerful tools for conveying scientific facts, principles, and explanations" (van den Broek, 2010, p. 456). Students should be provided opportunities to read and discuss many texts on a variety of topics related to nature of science, physical science, life science, earth and space science, and engineering, technology, and applications of science. This variety can be found in science trade books and magazines.

Science trade books and magazines have several distinct advantages over traditional textbooks (Fang, 2010, 2013). First, they provide more contextualized, focused, current, and in-depth coverage of science content. As such, they tend to be more appealing and are the sort of materials that students will actually read. Second, science trade books and magazines are written at different reading levels and on many different topics. As such, they are better able to accommodate the real needs of students with diverse backgrounds, interests, and reading levels. Third, science trade books and magazines portray science as it is practiced in the real world, showing how scientists formulate questions and seek answers to these questions through both firsthand (e.g., hands-on experiments and observations) and secondhand (e.g., reading, writing, diagramming) inquiries. As such, they are generally considered more authentic and motivating than traditional textbooks and widely viewed as a powerful resource for helping students build science content knowledge, develop science inquiry skills, enhance understanding about nature of science, and foster scientific habits of mind.

Not all science trade books are created equal, however. They are of varied qualities. To find quality science trade books, teachers can consult the NSTA Outstanding Science Trade Books for Students K-12, an annual list of about 40 quality science trade books for children and young adults compiled by the National Science Teachers Association (NSTA) in cooperation with Children's Book Council (CBC). Books selected for inclusion in the list are judged by an expert panel to be scientifically accurate, up-to-date, engagingly written, attractively designed, logically organized, and devoid of stereotypes. They are sorted into topical areas, such as archaeology, anthropology, and paleontology; biography; earth and space science; environment and ecology; fiction; life science; physical science; science-related careers; and technology and engineering. They are also identified according to the National Science Content Standards. Additionally, the reading level for each book is identified: P=Primary (K-2), E=Elementary (Grades 3–5), I=Intermediate (Grades 6–8), and A=Advanced (Grades 9–12). These levels are intended as a guide and not meant to limit the potential uses of the books.

Besides the NSTA list, other professional organizations have also created their own lists of quality science trade books. Among them are the AAAS/Subaru SB & F Prize for Excellence in Science Books, created by the American Association for the Advancement of Science, with support from Subaru America Inc., to celebrate outstanding science writing and illustration for children and young adults. The prize is awarded to four categories of books— children's science picture books, middle grade nonfiction science books, popular science for high school readers, and hands-on science/activity books. In addition, the National Council of Teachers of English established the Orbis Pictus Award for Outstanding Nonfiction for Children to recognize books that demonstrate excellence in the writing of nonfiction. Many science books won this award. Although only one award is given each year, up to five titles are recognized as Honor Books.

Finally, two award-winning science magazines, *Kids Discover* (https://kids discover.com/) and *Science News for Students* (https://www.sciencenews forstudents.org/), provide quality reading materials on science topics that school children may also find relevant and engaging. *Kids Discover* publishes high-interest nonfiction materials for children aged 6–14. Each issue focuses on a specific topic in science or social studies. The magazine has published many issues covering life science (e.g., five senses, brain, germs, cells, insects, flower, nutrition), earth science (e.g., climate, weather, oceans, glaciers, rocks, water), and physical and space science (e.g., atoms, energy, astronauts, planets, moon, simple machines). *Science News for Students* is a free online resource for middle and high school students that publishes award-winning journalism on research across the breadth of science, health, and technology fields, showing them how science really works, what scientists do, what goes into conducting first-class research and science projects, and how anyone can get involved doing science.

Teachers can engage students in reading these quality trade books by conducting unit studies, biographical studies, book studies, author studies, genre studies, or read alouds (Fang, 2010). In unit studies, students read and discuss multiple science trade books on an important science topic or idea, aiming to increase understanding of the topic or idea. In biographical studies, students read and discuss biographies of famous scientists to deepen understanding of nature of science (NOS) and develop interest in pursuing science-related careers. In book studies, students form literature circles, reading, analyzing, sharing, and then exchanging a science book of personal interest or disciplinary significance. In author studies, students read and discuss multiple science books written by the same, often accomplished, author, learning how the author's background and life experience shape his/her writing style and creative process. In genre studies, students read and discuss several books belonging to the same genre, aiming to develop a deeper understanding of the social purpose, rhetorical moves, and discursive features of the genre. In read alouds, teachers read a quality science book out loud, demonstrating effective reading strategies and engaging students in discussion about key ideas, important details, and powerful writing crafts in the book. To promote reading, teachers can set up a home science reading program (e.g., Fang et al., 2008), asking students to check out books regularly (e.g., weekly) from the classroom or school library to read at home and complete a short reading response sheet (see Figure 4.1 for samples); they can also hold weekly discussions about these books in class or via an online forum, encouraging students to share with peers (and parents or guardians) what they have learned and what they found exciting about science.

Reading Response to Science Informational Text
Book Title & Author:
Your Name:
• One big idea I have learned from the text
• One key scientific vocabulary word in the text. Explain what the word means in a sentence and/or with an illustration
• One juicy (grammatically complex & challenging) sentence from the text. Try to paraphrase by saying it in your own words
• One question I have after reading the text

Source: adapted from Fang et al. (2008)

Reading Response to Scientist's Biography		
Book Title & Author:		
Your Name:		
Document the use of the inquiry process.	Note information on life locally, nationally, and internationally at the time the scientist lived.	Identify personal traits that you think contribute to the scientist's success. Explain how.
Sense a problem		
Hypothesize		
Experiment		
Evaluate		
Publish		

Source: adapted from Fairweather & Fairweather (2010) and Monhardt (2005)

Figure 4.1 Sample Reading Response Sheets

Developing Science Language Proficiency and Multimodal Competence

Science language is a linguistic register functional for construing scientific knowledge, values, and habits of mind. This language is, as demonstrated earlier, technical, abstract, dense, formal, metaphoric, tightly knit, and complex, epitomizing the sort of academic language that students find foreign and challenging (Fang, 2006, 2021a). Research (e.g., DiCerbo et al., 2014; Uccelli et al., 2015) has suggested that academic language proficiency is a significant predictor of students' reading comprehension and that children from economically disadvantaged or linguistically minoritized backgrounds tend to score lower on academic language measures. This means that proficiency with science language is key to improving science reading comprehension. Despite its importance, science language is rarely an emphasis in science literacy instruction. Efforts to teach science language or, more generally, academic language have typically centered on scientific or academic vocabulary, with much less attention to other aspects of science language, such as dense noun phrases, which are an important and pervasive resource in scientific (and academic) meaning making (Biber & Gray, 2010; Fang, Gresser, Cao, & Zheng, 2021; Fang, Schleppegrell, & Cox, 2006; Halliday & Martin, 1993).

One way to develop students' science language proficiency is to provide explicit instruction about science language in authentic contexts of science reading so that they understand what science language looks like, what it means, what its discursive functions are, and why it is needed in scientific meaning making. Such instruction can be provided during close reading sessions. Close reading, as described in Chapters 2 and 3, is a method of reading texts that involves detailed analysis and thoughtful discussion of how language choices make meaning in ways that realize the purpose of the text and the author's intention (Fang, 2016). A model of close reading that involves systematic analysis and discussion of language patterns in the text is called functional language analysis (FLA) (Fang, 2021b; Fang & Schleppegrell, 2008, 2010), first described in Chapter 3. FLA provides a guiding framework that enables students to explore what a text is about (experiential meaning), how a text is organized (textual meaning), and how the author infuses judgments and points of view (interpersonal meaning) by attending to the lexical, grammatical, and other discursive choices the author made in constructing the text.

Follow-up language-based tasks can be designed to give students the opportunity to practice the linguistic features spotlighted during close reading sessions, further cementing their understanding of and control over these features. Fang (2008, 2010) described a range of such tasks at the levels of word (e.g., morphemic analysis, vocabulary think chart, conception definition word map, word sort), phrase (e.g., noun deconstruction, noun expansion, noun search, definition game), sentence (sentence combining, syntactic anatomy and integration), and discourse (e.g., sentence completion, noticing textual signposts, paraphrasing). Several principles should be observed when designing these tasks: (a) use authentic examples from the texts students are reading and writing, (b) make explicit links between the language feature being introduced and how it works in the text students are reading/writing, (c) explain the linguistic features through examples, not dictionary definitions or lengthy abstract explanations (Fang, 2021b; Myhill et al., 2013).

As noted earlier, scientific meaning is typically made in some combination of words, images, graphs, and mathematics symbols. There is "close and constant integration and cross-contextualization" among various semiotic modalities in science texts (Lemke, 2004, p. 39), making it both normal and necessary to interpret the verbal text in relation to other semiotic formations, and vice versa. According to van den Broek (2010), visual resources are sometimes used to "draw the reader into the text or to lessen the formidability of a dense page of text" and at other times, they are used to "support directly the expansion and modification of the reader's knowledge—often interrupting the processing of the [verbal] text" (p. 455). This means it is also important to consider students' multimodal competence in science reading. As Lemke (2002) stated, "advanced scientific literacy means both using advanced literacy skills specific to scientific activity and making specialized scientific meanings that cannot be made without using some language, in conjunction with other semiotic resources" (p. 42). In other words, developing students' ability to effectively navigate multimodal/multisemiotic textual environments is key to comprehending and understanding science multimedia genres.

Scholars have suggested ways multimodal competence can be fostered in conjunction with science language proficiency. Yeo and Tan (2022) introduced an approach that helps teachers think about how they can engage students in the transformation of multimodal resources at the same time they are socializing students into the language of science. The approach, called Image-to-Writing (I2W), consists of a sequence of tasks that engages students in (a) exploring a phenomenon (e.g., observing, experimenting), (b) creating and transforming images (e.g., drawing, physical models, tabulation, graphs), and (c) transduction of images to writing (e.g., writing verbal definitions, descriptions, or explanations). In a unit on pollination, for example, students first watch a video animation on pollination by a bee and wind. They then sequence a set of images to show the order of events observed from the animation. Next, they write a description for each image in the active voice (e.g., *The bee picks up pollen grain on its body.*), highlighting actors and actions; subsequently, they transform the active voice into the passive voice (e.g., *The pollen grains were transferred from the anther to the stigma.*), where actors (e.g., *bee, wind*) are backgrounded (or buried) and which increases the generalizability of the description of pollination. Finally, students transform the passive voice into a scientific definition through nominalization (e.g., *Pollination is the process whereby pollen grains are transferred from anther to stigma.*).

Lemke (2004) recommended that science educators create partnerships with verbal literacy educators and with visual media educators to promote more explicit attention to teaching students how to read science multimedia genres. More specifically, he encouraged teachers to (a) make greater use of gestural and visual representations and numerical tables and graphs in their instruction, and (b) provide opportunities for students to not only do hands-on science and talk and write science in words, but also draw, tabulate, graph, geometrize, and algebrize science in all possible combinations. He also highlighted the importance of (a) helping students understand the conventions that connect verbal text with visual images, and (b) giving students practice in translating back and forth among verbal accounts, mathematical expressions and calculations, schematic diagrams, abstract graphs, and hands-on actions. Similarly, Tang and Putra (2018) suggested giving students practice in making observations and translating inscriptions from one form to another in the process of conducting experiments and collecting data, such as modeling an experimental procedure and translating the procedure into a flowchart that students can then use to guide their experiment. Prain (2022) advised teachers to guide students to understand science topics "through a process where they visualize, collect, represent, interpret, and model data as a basis for making and refining science claims" (p. 141). In this process, hands-on inquiry, observation, experiment, description, and explanation are "recursively integrated into claim-making" and students are expected to "invent, critique, revise, and refine multimodal representation in response to conceptual challenges" (p. 141).

The process through which meanings are transformed from one semiotic system (e.g., language) to another (e.g., visual) is called resemiotization or transduction. One useful tool for resemiotization is sketchnote. Sketchnote is "a visual thinking form that integrates notes and sketches to explain scientific topics" (Fernandez-Fontecha et al., 2018, p. 7). It is a multimodal complex made up of verbal and visual resources. Using sketchnote, teachers and students can create a visual representation of complex scientific content in their texts. This renders abstract, complex ideas more accessible and digestible, facilitates reading comprehension, and promotes visual thinking and multimodal competence. Similarly, Román, Jones, Basaraba, and Hironaka (2015) showed how science teachers can use graphic organizers strategically to make implicit connections in science texts explicit so that students can visualize the inferences in and the conceptual connections among important text segments. More activities for infusing the use of multimodal representation in science classrooms can be found in Kress et al. (2001), Hand, McDermott, and Prain (2016), and Unsworth et al. (2022).

Learning to Read Like a Scientist

Viewing science reading from a disciplinary literacy lens requires that students learn to read science texts like a scientist. Science texts are not repositories of immutable facts. They communicate scientists' interpretations of the universe through "motivated conjunctions of form and meaning" (Kress, 2003, p. 169). As Lemke (2002) has argued, scientific texts are not just about matters of fact and explanation; they make meaning about "desirability, importance, permissibility, expectedness, and all the other value dimensions" (p. 28). From this perspective, then, science texts are never neutral: they are imbued with authorial intentions, beliefs, attitudes, values, and worldviews. Given the constructed nature of science texts and scientific knowledge, it is important that students adopt a critical stance in science reading, paying close attention to not only what evidence (if any) is used and the quality of the evidence but also how this evidence is presented, linguistically and/or visually, to support a particular explanation or claim.

While it may be argued that not all students will be future scientists, there is still a need for them as citizens to develop this critical reading ability. We are living in the age of science, and no one can live a productive, fulfilling life without at least some interaction with science. Current issues related to science often appear as headlines in newspapers, websites, and other media outlets, from stories of rovers landing on Mars and Hurricane Katrina's destructive power to health news about coronavirus and calls to combat global warming and cyber terrorism. These reports can distort the original source by omitting or backgrounding potentially important details or evidence, casting doubts on scientific findings, twisting logic of argument, diminishing substantive claims, overextrapolating or overgeneralizing research results, foregrounding applications, or taking things out of context. Pescatore (2007), for example, showed how the George W. Bush administration's chief of staff for the White House Council on Environmental Quality edited two draft reports by the Climate Change Science Program and the Subcommittee on Global Change Research in an attempt to produce an air of doubt about findings that most climate experts say are robust—that is, global warming is real and most likely caused by human activities. Similarly, Román and Busch (2016) demonstrated, through detailed linguistic analysis, how the current political and public discourses of climate change, rather than the scientific discourse, has influenced the way pedagogical materials (i.e., school textbooks) discuss the topic of climate change. They reported that similar to the public discourse of doubt about climate change (see, for example, Oreskes and Conway's [2011] *Merchants of Doubt*), middle school science textbooks also frame climate change as uncertain in the scientific community, conveying the message that "climate change is possibly happening, that humans may or may not be causing it, and that we do not need to take immediate mitigating action" (p. 1175). Having the ability to detect inaccuracies, inconsistencies, distortions, or omissions is, therefore, critical to maintaining an informed citizenry and a vibrant democracy. Developing this critical reading ability is especially important in the current sociopolitical climate, where what counts as science, evidence, facts, or news is being debated with intense heat and considerable rancor.

One approach to developing critical reading in science is to read multiple texts on the same topic or the same text from different perspectives. Students should have opportunities to analyze, evaluate, problematize, and transform texts on a regular basis, interrogating the values, points of view, prejudices, and ideologies underpinning the text. Teachers can have students read supplementary texts that cover topics or issues glossed over or avoided in traditional science textbooks. They can also have students read multiple texts on the same topic to gain insights into how different authors present the same topic from different angles and with different interpretations. For example, ivermectin, a drug used to treat parasites in animals, was touted in some media circles as a promising treatment for Covid-19, even though the federal Food and Drug Administration has repeatedly cautioned against its use for Covid-19. Without the ability to think critically about what is presented in the media and what the reporting outlet is, as well as the disposition to check one source against another and weigh the evidence, students may be victimized by misinformation.

When reading a text, students can learn to ask and respond to such questions as: (a) What is the author's background and affiliation? (b) Who/what sponsors the publication? (c) Who/what is or is not represented in the text, and why? (d) What evidence is provided to support a claim or argument? (e) What is the quality of this piece of evidence? (f) How was the evidence produced? (g) Is the evidence sufficiently relevant, credible, and complete? (h) Whose interest is best served by the message of the text? (i) How are various groups/individuals positioned by the text? (j) How do particular content, discourse genres, and mode and methods of inquiry become privileged and acquire power in science? (k) How does such privileging affect access, equity, and learning? and (l) What action might you take on the basis of what you have learned? (Behrman, 2006). For multimodal texts, students can, in addition, discuss why a certain image (e.g., graph, chart, table, diagram, map) is included or excluded, where the image came from, how the image is positioned in relation to verbal text, what is foregrounded or backgrounded in the image, and whether the image repeats, enhances, supplements, extends, or contradicts the message in verbal text.

Teachers can also promote critical reading by encouraging students to make connections between what they read in the text and what they see in their everyday lifeworlds. For example, when reading texts on erosion, the teacher can ask students to examine the erosion that exists on their school grounds (Alvermann & Wilson, 2011). Students can obtain background information about their campus through old photographs, interviews, newspaper clippings, or televised footage. They can analyze these verbal and visual texts to better understand the environment in which they live. They can also create images of their campus before and after erosion, interview various members of the community to elicit their reactions to the state of the campus, and compare/contrast opinions across groups. In short, linking what is read to students' immediate surroundings can deepen their engagement with the text topic and their understanding of the text content while at the same time stimulating their interest in science, promoting their critical thinking, developing their science literacy, encouraging them to make connections between science and their everyday lifeworld, and making a positive impact on their communities.

Another way to foster critical reading ability in science is to promote critical language awareness, that is, to help students become aware of how language choices in science texts—such as nouns (e.g., _some_ scientists, _deforestation_), adjectives (e.g., at an _alarming_ 8.5 percent per decade), verbs (e.g., _hypothesize, claim, conclude, suggest_), modal verbs (_will_ double, _might_ _alter_), adverbs (e.g., have _gradually_ changed, is _somewhat_ problematic, declined _significantly_), and prepositional phrases (e.g., _In the past two million years there have been many major ice ages._)—present knowledge, modulate or boost claims, infuse ideology, embed points of view, construe precision, and facilitate discursive flow (Fang et al., 2019; Román & Busch, 2016;

Zhu & Fang, 2019). During close reading, teachers can highlight a range of lexical, grammatical, and other discursive features that (a) express affect, judgment, or appreciation (e.g., *Influenza A viruses are <u>constantly</u> changing, making it possible on <u>very rare</u> occasions for non-human influenza viruses to change in such a way that they can infect people <u>easily</u> and spread <u>efficiently</u> from person to person.*); (b) convey degrees of certainty, usuality, normality, or likelihood (e.g., *Increased sea levels <u>will</u> cause flooding of low-lying coastal areas. More storms <u>could</u> increase the damage caused to the state.*); and (c) bury agency to promote objectivity and to foreground ideas/concepts and background processes (e.g., *More than one-fourth of the world's coral reefs <u>have been lost</u> to <u>coastal development</u>, <u>pollution</u>, <u>overfishing</u>, <u>warm ocean temperatures</u>, and <u>other stresses</u> that are increasing.*). These analyses help students uncover hidden messages in the text, gain a more nuanced understanding of authorial voice and intention, expand their linguistic repertoires for making meaning in more purposeful and effective ways, sharpen their sensitivity to language, and develop a critical orientation in text reading/writing (Martin & White, 2005). They offer teachers a set of valuable tools for promoting critical engagement with text and should, thus, become an integral part of science reading instruction.

A Heuristic for Teaching Reading in Science

Reading is not just a cognitive activity; it is also a social process because every act of reading takes place in a specific context for a specific purpose. For this reason, Patterson et al. (2018) recommended that reading in science class be done with specific goals defined by the practices of doing science (e.g., developing conceptual understanding, identifying cause–effect relations, constructing explanations, engaging in argument from evidence, understanding how scientists use language to present information and logical reasoning) and that teachers make the goals of reading in science explicit to their students. This section describes a heuristic that science (or reading) teachers can use to help students build science content knowledge, develop science language proficiency and multimodal competence, and promote scientific habits of mind in the process of conducting science inquiries.

The heuristic, captured in Figure 4.2, is called 5Es, or Enquire—Engage—Examine—Exercise—Extend (Fang et al., 2019; Fang, 2020, 2021b). It places inquiry in the center of the instructional cycle, inviting students to **enquire** into a question or issue that is of personal interest and/or disciplinary significance in a unit of study through a variety of activities and tasks that are authentic to the discipline and meaningful to students (e.g., conducting experiments, doing observations, reading texts, taking notes, writing reports).

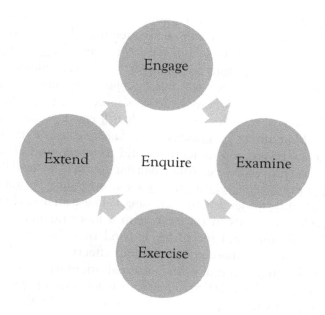

Figure 4.2 5Es Pedagogical Heuristic
Source: Fang (2021b, p. 101)

A key component of these social practices is the use of texts. As students **engage** with texts, they use the strategies scientists use to help them make sense of these texts (e.g., predicting, setting purpose, questioning, skimming, rereading, evaluating, verifying, cross-checking, visualizing, drawing inferences, summarizing, making connections, resemiotizing). Challenging and important portions of these texts are then selected for close reading. During close reading, students **examine** how authors use language (and other semiotic resources) to present information, structure text, infuse points of view, sharpen focus, engage with and position the reader, and express epistemic commitment to knowledge claims. Next, **exercises** are designed to help students cement their understanding of—as well as develop their facility in using—key or unfamiliar features of science language and scientific habits of mind. In the end, students write to **extend**, as well as communicate, their understanding of the focal topic and target genre by using the linguistic/semiotic resources and habits of mind highlighted in the unit.

To illustrate how this heuristic works, the rest of this chapter describes a middle school science unit on humidity and the water cycle in which students **enquire** into important scientific questions (e.g., what is humidity? what is the water cycle? what is the relationship between humidity and the water cycle? how does humidity affect the health of people, animals, and plants?)

through both firsthand (hands-on investigations) and secondhand (reading/writing) experiences. The unit was developed by a team of science and literacy teacher educators at the University of Florida to serve as a model for preservice teachers who were required to plan disciplinary literacy instruction in science (Hershfield & Fang, 2015). It addresses relevant science standards, including science and engineering practices (e.g., asking questions and defining problems, developing and using models, planning and carrying out investigations, using mathematics and computational thinking, engaging in argument from evidence, evaluating and communicating knowledge), disciplinary core ideas (e.g., role of water in the earth's surface processes, weather and climate, global climate change), and crosscutting concepts (e.g., cause and effect, systems and system models, stability and change). It also addresses several literacy standards in the Common Core State Standards, including (a) cite specific textual evidence to support analysis of science and technical texts (RST.6–8.1), (b) determine the central ideas or conclusions of a text (RST.6–8.2), (c) determine the meaning of symbols, key terms, and other domain-specific words and phrases as they are used in specific scientific or technical context (RST.6–8.4), (d) compare and contrast the information gained from experiments, simulations, video, or multimedia sources with that gained from reading a text on the same topic (RST.6–8.9), and (e) read and comprehend science/technical texts in the grades 6–8 text complexity band independently and proficiently (RST.6–8.10). As a whole, the unit was meant to provide preservice teachers with a model for planning science literacy instruction that integrates reading/literacy with science.

To start the unit, the teacher has students in small groups discuss the questions posed in the following scenario:

> You take a short walk outside. It is early in the morning and the temperature is only 80° Fahrenheit. Nonetheless, you are sweating. Why? Now you go into your luxury mobile home. The temperature in the mobile home also reads 80° Fahrenheit, but you suddenly feel cool. Why?

This gets students excited about the unit because it relates the topic (humidity) to their personal experience. It also allows the teacher to assess how much students know about the topic and whether there are misunderstandings about the topic.

After discussion, the teacher asks each group to complete two experiments at their own workstation over the next few days. In the first experiment (see Figure 4.3), students record and graph their findings and discuss what they found. In the second experiment (see Figure 4.4), students observe, record, and explain what happened. In these discussions, students are encouraged to draw on what they have read about the topic in the unit, which helps them think more deeply about what they have observed, engage in evidence-based reasoning, and come up with more sophisticated explanations of the observed phenomena.

Firsthand experiences like these help students develop initial conceptual understanding of humidity and the water cycle and at the same time get them interested in exploring the topic. To further develop their understanding of

Materials
- Two cut-off drink cans
- Room temperature water (one for inside and one for outside)
- Ice
- Thermometer

Procedures
- Step 1: Place room temperature water in both cans. Measure the temperature of the water in both cans. (It should be the same.)
- Step 2: At this point, there should not be any condensation on the outside of the cans. Check this. If there is moisture on the outside of the cans, dry it off and check to be sure it does not reappear.
- Step 3: Add ice to one of the cans while a thermometer is in the can. Carefully watch and record the temperature at which moisture just begins to appear.
- Step 4: Repeat steps 1–3 outside the room
- Step 5: Record your data in a table

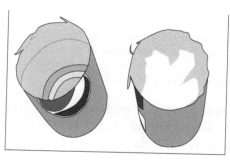 

Reflection
- Why do you think the temperature at which moisture appeared on the outside of the cup was different inside and outside the room? Does this support your initial hypothesis?

Figure 4.3 Science experiment 1

Materials
- A large, clear bowl
- Plastic wrap
- A weight
- A smaller container (example: cut-down yogurt cup)
- A rubber band or piece of string

Procedures
- Place the smaller container in the middle of the large, clear bowl
- Fill the bowl with a little water, being careful not to fill the smaller container inside
- Cover the bowl with plastic wrap, and fasten the plastic wrap around the rim of the bowl with your rubber band or string
- Put a weight on top of the plastic wrap on the center (see picture below)
- Now put your contraption on a windowsill or another place with exposure to the sun

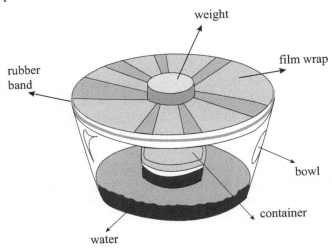

Reflection
- How long does it take for water to evaporate and condense on the plastic wrap? Where does water go after it condenses on the plastic wrap?
- How does this water cycle relate to the way the Earth uses and recycles water?

Figure 4.4 Science experiment 2

Source: https://old.miniscience.com/projects/watercycle/index.html

the key concepts in the unit, the teacher **engages** students in reading related texts on the topic. These texts come from traditional textbooks, trade books, magazines, and websites, varying in text difficulty such that the easier texts help build background knowledge and motivation for the reading of more challenging texts. Some of these texts are used for class read alouds, when the teacher models how to read like a scientist, using the strategies scientists use to read carefully, critically, and with a healthy skepticism. Other texts are for independent reading, when students are expected to ask questions, make connections, take notes, weigh evidence, evaluate statements, and draw inferences as they read. Students also have the opportunity to share their understandings, questions, and wonderings in small groups and/or with the whole class. Through reading and discussing these texts, students increase their content knowledge about humidity and the water cycle and gain exposure to the sort of semiotic resources (language + visuals) that scientists use to construct the content.

A change in relative humidity *can be brought about* in *two primary ways:*

1. by changing the air's water vapor content, and
2. by changing the air temperature.

In Fig. 4.11a, we can see that *an increase in the water vapor content of the air (with no change in air temperature) increases the air's relative humidity. The reason* for *this increase resides in the fact that,* as more water vapor molecules are added to the air, there is *a greater likelihood* that some of the vapor molecules will *stick together and condense. Condensation* takes place in saturated air. *Therefore,* as more and more water vapor molecules are added to the air, the air *gradually* approaches saturation, *and* the relative humidity of the air increases. *Conversely, removing water vapor* from the air decreases *the likelihood of saturation,* which lowers the air's relative humidity. *In summary, with* no change in air temperature, adding water vapor to the air increases the relative humidity; removing water vapor from the air lowers the relative humidity.

These changes in relative humidity are important in determining *the amount of evaporation from vegetation and wet surfaces.* If you water your lawn on a hot afternoon, *when* the relative humidity is low, much of the water will evaporate quickly from the lawn, instead of soaking into the ground. Watering the same lawn in the evening or during the early morning, *when* the relative humidity is higher, will cut down the evaporation and increase *the effectiveness of the watering.*

Figure 4.5 Sample Science Textbook Excerpt for Close Reading
Source: Ahrens (1999, p. 112)

The next step in the 5Es model involves selecting challenging but important text excerpts for close reading. The teacher selects an excerpt from a science textbook (see Figure 4.5), reading it two times, the first for general understanding and the second time with a functional–critical focus on language and image, **examining** how verbal and visual choices present meaning in more or less transparent ways relative to the intended reader of the text.

For example, the teacher discusses the obvious issue of technical vocabulary such as *molecules, saturation, condensation,* and *relative humidity,* as well as general academic vocabulary (e.g., *reside, approach, conversely, determine*). She also draws students' attention to less obvious but equally important text features (italicized in the text), as detailed in Table 4.1. Reading a text closely and critically this way deepens students' understanding of the text content and makes them become more aware of the ways scientists use verbal and visual resources to shape meaning in discipline-legitimated ways.

Table 4.1 Focal Text Features and Teacher Comments During Close Reading

Focal Text Features	Teacher Comments
can be brought about	• Why is passive voice, instead of active voice, used here? • What is the actor that is being buried? • Why is agency backgrounded? • The modal verb *"can"* here denotes possibility, not ability, meaning that it is possible (but not certain) to bring about a change in relative humidity.
two primary ways	• What are some other, primary or minor, ways of bringing about change in relative humidity beyond the two mentioned in the text?
In Figure 4.11a	• Where does the figure/graph come from? Does the author indicate the source? Is the source reliable? • What information is presented in the graph? • Does this information match what is described in the verbal text? • What information from the graph is highlighted or left out in the verbal text? Why?
we	• To whom does this pronoun refer? Does it refer to the author, the reader, the author and the reader, or the scientific community at large? It is likely used here as a way of engaging the reader and invoking a sense of community and shared responsibility between the author and the reader.

Focal Text Features	Teacher Comments
	• In scientific and academic writing, it is becoming more common for the author to embrace a more direct and egalitarian relationship with readers through the use of the first person plural *"we"* in order to engage and persuade them.
an increase in the water vapor content of the air	• This is a long noun phrase with *"increase"* as head, and *"in the water vapor content of the air"* is a prepositional phrase serving as a qualifier specifying the "thing" that increases.
with no change in air temperature	• The use of the preposition *"with"* conflates condition and temporality, meaning "if/when there is no change in air temperature".
an increase vs. increases	• The word *"increase"* is used as both a noun and a verb in the same sentence. When used as a verb—and in this case an ergative verb—it implies causality. That is, the rise in the water vapor content of the air causes the rise in the air's relative humidity.
the air's relative humidity	• This possessive noun phrase can also be reworded using a prepositional phrase, as in "the relative humidity of the air". Normally, the possessive is used when the possessor is animated (e.g., a person or an animal). Here, the possessor *"air"* is not an animated entity, however.
The reason . . . resides in . . .	• The use of *"reason"* (noun) enables the author to express causation within the same clause. The conjunction *"because"* could have been used, but it will require two clauses (main clause + subordinate clause) to express the same logical meaning. • *"Reside in"* is equivalent to the linking verb "is". It identifies the cause of the increase.
this increase	• The phrase (demonstrative + noun) is a nominalization referring to the idea presented in *"increases the air's relative humidity"* in the previous sentence. Its use facilitates the transition from one sentence to the next. This is one way discursive flow is created in scientific writing.
the fact that. . . .	• This is a complement noun clause, with *"the fact"* serving as a nominalization that distills the ideas presented in the two subsequent clauses *"as more water vapor molecules are added to the air, there is a greater likelihood that some of the vapor molecules will stick together and condense"*.

Focal Text Features	Teacher Comments
a greater likelihood	• This is a nominalization that could have been expressed in more everyday language as *"is more likely"*. • What does *"likelihood"* mean? Does it mean 25% chance, 60% chance, 80% chance, or 95% chance?
. . . stick together and condense . . . Condensation takes place . . .	• *"Condensation"* here is a nominalization of "stick together and condense" in the preceding clause. It distills a process (*stick together and condense*) into a technical concept, making it the subject of the ensuing sentence. This is how scientists create technical terminology and engineer information flow at the same time in text construction.
Therefore	• This adverb indicates causality. What comes after the word is the effect, but can the cause be pinpointed? The cause is usually indicated in the sentence(s) or even paragraph(s) preceding it. Exactly which sentence(s) indicate(s) the cause here?
. . . as more and more water vapor molecules are added to the air . . .	• The conjunction *"as"* conflates condition (*if*), temporality (*when*), and causality (*because*) at the same time. This sort of ambiguity benefits disciplinary insiders because they have the requisite background knowledge to resolve it.
. . . the air gradually approaches saturation,	• The adverb *"gradually"* is a hedging device used to increase precision in scientific meaning making. It tells us that saturation is not reached in a jiffy. • Scientific and academic writing generally privileges caution, possibility, and delimited claims over certainty. This stance is achieved through the use of a variety of hedging devices, such as modal verbs (e.g., *could, might*), verbs (e.g., *appear to, suggest, surmise*), nouns (e.g., *assumption, likelihood, possibility*), adverbs (e.g., *approximately, usually, hypothetically, maybe*), adjectives (e.g., *probable, tentative, questionable*), and phrases (e.g., *to our knowledge, in some sense, to a certain extent, according to NASA*).
. . . and the relative humidity of the air increases.	• The conjunction *"and"* implies causality, with the cause being expressed in the preceding clause "*the air gradually approaches saturation*" and the effect in the clause following "*and*".

(Continued)

Focal Text Features	Teacher Comments
conversely	• This adverb indicates that the author is going to present something that is in opposition to what has just been discussed.
Removing the water vapor from the air decreases the likelihood of saturation.	• Agency is buried here via the use of a gerund phrase (*removing the water vapor*) as the subject of the sentence and a nominalization (*the likelihood of saturation*) as the object of the sentence. This is the sort of compact syntax that scientists value. It enables the author to reason logically (in this case, causally) within, rather than between, clauses. • Compact syntax like this elides information and creates ambiguity that sometimes only disciplinary insiders can resolve. What/who removes the water vapor from air? How is the water vapor removed from air? What gets saturated? What is the degree of probability in getting saturated?
, which lowers the air's relative humidity	• This is a non-restrictive relative clause. But what does "*which*" refer to? Does it refer to "*the likelihood of saturation*" or the idea expressed in the entire clause "*removing the water from the air decreases the likelihood of saturation*"? This kind of writing benefits disciplinary insiders but disadvantages students who may not have the requisite background knowledge to make the right inference.
In summary	• This phrase signals that the author is ready to distill what has just been discussed. So pay attention; this is likely where I can find the main idea of the paragraph.
. . . with no change in air temperature . . .	• The prepositional phrase is a metaphoric expression of what would normally be presented in a clause. It buries the logical meaning that would have become transparent if a clause were to be used. Is the logical relationship being expressed here conditional (*if no change in air temperature occurs*), temporal (*when no change in air temperature occurs*), causal (*because no change in air temperature occurs*), or a conflation of all three? • Again, this is how scientists reason logically within, rather than between, clauses. This kind of writing creates ambiguity that benefits disciplinary insiders.

Focal Text Features	Teacher Comments
These changes	• This phrase is a nominalization that refers to the changes in relative humidity described in the preceding paragraph. • Scientists use nominalizations like this one to summarize and distill previously presented information so that they can discuss the idea further.
the amount of evaporation from vegetation and wet surfaces	• This is a long noun phrase with nominalizations (*amount, evaporation*) embedded. It enables scientists to compact information for within-clause logical reasoning. In more everyday language, the same information is usually expressed as "how much water evaporates from vegetation and wet surfaces".
when	• The adverb "*when*" in the last two sentences of the last paragraph is used to introduce a non-restrictive relative clause that provides extra, often non-essential, information about "*a hot afternoon*" and "*the evening* and *the early morning*", respectively. • This is another way scientists create dense sentences and at the same time stay focused on the main idea. Had each adverbial clause been rewritten into an independent clause, the information it presents would have become equal in importance to the information presented in the main clause of the original sentence. This rewording would then result in diffusion of focus and disruption of information flow.
the effectiveness of the watering	• This is a highly abstract noun phrase with two nominalizations (*the effectiveness, the watering*) embedded. The phrase "*the watering*" refers to the process of watering the lawn described in the beginning of the sentence. • The use of nominalizations increases abstraction but at the same time facilitates the construction of compact sentences with the "abstract/long noun phrase (as subject) + verb + abstract/long noun phrase (as object)" structure. This is one main reason students feel turned off when reading science texts. In everyday language, the same amount of information is spread out in more clauses, making it easier to process and comprehend.

Next, the teacher highlights nominalization, one of the most important and pervasive resources used in scientific (and academic) meaning making. Using examples from the close reading excerpt and other texts students have read, the teacher explains how nominalization allows the author to distill/summarize information, bury agency, create technicality, and facilitate discursive flow. She also designs sentence completion **exercises**, such as the example below, to show students how nominalization works.

> As the air cools during the night, the relative humidity increases. Normally, the highest relative humidity occurs in the early morning, during the coolest part of the day. As the air warms during the day, the relative humidity decreases, with the lowest values usually occurring during the warmest part of the afternoon. _____ are important in determining the amount of evaporation from vegetation and wet surfaces. [answer: these changes (in relative humidity)]

Finally, the teacher has students write a text that (a) explains how humidity relates to the water cycle and/or (b) discusses how humidity impacts the health of humans, animals, or plants. They go through the writing process of brainstorming, outlining, drafting, revising, editing, and publishing, with an emphasis on writing from sources, which requires critical analysis and synthesis of ideas across multiple texts, and on revision, where students focus on how verbal and visual choices realize the purpose of their text and present its content. A writing sample, presented in Figure 4.6, is shared with the class and analyzed and critiqued with respect to its content, organization, and style, as well as language choices, so that students understand what is expected of them for the assignment. This task clarifies, enhances, and **extends** students' conceptual understanding while at the same time providing an opportunity for them to apply some of the verbal/visual skills and habits of mind highlighted in the unit.

As a whole, the unit creates experiences that engage students in three-dimensional learning as recommended by the Next Generation Science Standards. It offers students the opportunity to engage in some of the same **practices** that scientists use in scientific inquiry, including asking questions, carrying out investigations, reading relevant sources, analyzing and interpreting data, reasoning with evidence, constructing explanations, and communicating information. It also allows students to see how **crosscutting concepts**, such as cause/effect and pattern, are essential to understanding not only life sciences but also earth science. Equally important, students are able to learn some of the **core ideas** about weather, climate, and the environment by reading and discussing science texts and engaging in discipline-legitimated practices.

Have you ever visited a place that just made you feel hot and sticky the entire time, no matter what you did to cool off? You can thank humidity for that unpleasant feeling.

Humidity is the amount of water vapor in the air. If there is a lot of water vapor in the air, the humidity will be high. The higher the humidity, the wetter it feels outside.

On the weather reports, humidity is usually explained as relative humidity. Relative humidity is the amount of water vapor actually in the air, expressed as a percentage of the maximum amount of water vapor the air can hold at the same temperature. Think of the air at a chilly -10 degrees Celsius (14 degrees Fahrenheit). At that temperature, the air can hold, at most, 2.2 grams of water per cubic meter. So if there are 2.2 grams of water per cubic meter when it's -10 degrees Celsius outside, we're at an uncomfortable 100 percent relative humidity. If there was 1.1 grams of water in the air at -10 degrees Celsius, we're at 50 percent relative humidity.

When humidity is high, the air is so clogged with water vapor that there isn't room for much else. If you sweat when it's humid, it can be hard to cool off because your sweat can't evaporate into the air like it needs to.

Humidity is blamed for all kinds of negative things, including mold in your house (usually the bathroom, where it's wet a lot of the time), as well as malfunctions in regular household electronics. Moisture from humid air settles, or condenses, on electronics. This can interrupt the electric current, causing a loss of power. Computers and television sets can lose power like this if not protected from the effects of humidity. Living with humidity is easier with the aid of a dehumidifier, which sucks moisture out of the air.

High humidity is also associated with hurricanes. Air with high moisture content is necessary for a hurricane to develop. U.S. states such as Texas and Louisiana, which border the very warm Gulf of Mexico, have humid climates. This results in tons of rainfall, lots of flooding and the occasional hurricane.

Figure 4.6 Sample Student Writing on Humidity and the Water Cycle
Source: http://www.nationalgeographic.org/encyclopedia/humidity/

Conclusion

Science requires "both material and semiotic practices" (Halliday, 1998, p. 228). It involves conjecture, rhetoric, and argument, as well as the empirical work of observation and experiment in natural and laboratory settings. Contrary to popular misconceptions, the empirical work is not the bedrock upon which science is built, but rather a subsidiary activity used to support the discursive practice of generating and justifying knowledge claims about how the universe works (Osborne, 2002). This means that reading plays a pivotal role in science learning. It helps students identify questions or problems for inquiry, gain information on the topic and process of inquiry, consolidate understanding of core concepts and ideas, evaluate competing explanations of scientific phenomena, enhance understanding of epistemology of science, develop scientific habits of mind, and learn the language (and other semiotic resources) for communicating scientific understanding (Goldman et al., 2016). Thus, a vital part of becoming scientifically literate entails learning to access, comprehend, evaluate, and produce science texts in discipline-legitimated ways. In particular, students need to develop the ability to read these texts carefully, deeply, proficiently, critically, and with a healthy skepticism. Science teachers can support such learning by regularly engaging students in reading and discussion of texts on science-related topics and at the same time conducting close reading sessions that explicitly teach students how to read like a scientist and draw their attention to how verbal and visual choices fashion meaning in genre-specific, discipline-legitimated ways. In other words, a disciplinary literacy approach that emphasizes the building of science content knowledge, the development of science language skills and multimodal competence, and the cultivation of scientific habits of mind in the context of authentic science inquiries is more likely to succeed in improving students' science reading ability and raising their science literacy achievement.

Reflection and Application

1. What does disciplinary literacy mean in relation to science? What is the role of reading in science learning?
2. What does it mean to be reading like a scientist? Why is it important for the average citizen to read science texts carefully, critically, and with an informed skepticism?
3. What are the specific challenges involved in science reading? How can these challenges be addressed?
4. What does a disciplinary literacy approach to science reading instruction look like? In what ways does the approach promote science literacy?

5. Design a unit of instruction for a specific grade level aimed at developing students' science literacy. Be sure to identify/describe the disciplinary standards and curriculum goals to be addressed, the textual resources to be utilized, the activities and strategies to be used to promote the reading and writing of science multimedia genres, the assessment tools to be employed to monitor and evaluate student progress toward the unit objectives, and a reasonable timeline for implementing the unit.

Note

1 This chapter is a revised, expanded version of Fang and Colosimo (2023).

References

Ahrens, C. (1999). *Meteorology today: An introduction to weather, climate, and the environment* (6th ed.). New York: Brooks Cole.

Alvermann, D., & Wilson, A. (2011). Comprehension strategy instruction for multimodal texts in science. *Theory into Practice, 50*(2), 116–124.

August, D., Branum-Martin, L., Cardenas-Hagan, E., & Francis, D. (2009). The impact of an instructional intervention on the science and language learning of middle grade English language learners. *Journal of Research on Educational Effectiveness, 2*(4), 354–376.

Bazerman, C. (1985). Physicists reading physics: Schema-laden purposes and purpose-laden schema. *Written Communication, 2*(1), 3–23.

Behrman, E. (2006). Teaching about language, power, and text: A review of classroom practices that support critical literacy. *Journal of Adolescent and Adult Literacy, 49,* 490–498.

Bernstein, B. (1996). *Pedagogy, symbolic control and identity: Theory, research, critique.* London: Taylor & Francis.

Biber, D., & Gray, B. (2010). Challenging stereotypes about academic writing: Complexity, elaboration, explicitness. *Journal of English for Academic Purposes, 9*(1), 2–20.

Cabell, S., & Hwang, H. (2020). Building content knowledge to boost comprehension in the primary grades. *Reading Research Quarterly, 55*(S1), S99–S107.

Cervetti, G., Barber, J., Dorph, R., Pearson, D., & Goldschmidt, P. (2012). The impact of an integrated approach to science and literacy in elementary school classrooms. *Journal of Research in Science Teaching, 49*(5), 631–658.

Chapman, S. (2015). *Disciplinary literacy: A study of the cognitive, social, and semiotic practices of disciplinary experts.* Unpublished doctoral dissertation, University of Florida, Gainesville, Florida.

Chin, J. (2017). *Grand Canyon*. New York: Roaring Book Press.

Cromley, J. (2009). Reading achievement and science proficiency: International comparisons from the Programme on International Student Assessment. *Reading Psychology*, 30(2), 89–118.

Cromley, J., Snyder-Hogan, L., & Luciw-Dubas, U. (2010). Reading comprehension of scientific text: A domain-specific test of the direct and inferential mediation model of reading comprehension. *Journal of Educational Psychology*, 102(3), 687–700.

DiCerbo, P., Anstrom, K., Baker, L., & Rivera, C. (2014). A review of the literature on teaching academic English to English language learners. *Review of Educational Research*, 84(3), 446–482.

Dingrando, L., Tallman, K., Hainen, N., & Wistrom, C. (2006). *Chemistry: Matter and change*. Columbus, OH: Glencoe/McGraw-Hill.

Fairweather, E., & Fairweather, T. (2010). A method for understanding their method: Discovering scientific inquiry through biographies of famous scientists. *Science Scope*, 33(9), 23–30.

Fang, Z. (2005). Science literacy: A systemic functional linguistics perspective. *Science Education*, 89(2), 335–347.

Fang, Z. (2006). The language demands of science reading in middle school. *International Journal of Science Education*, 28(5), 491–520.

Fang, Z. (2008). Going beyond the Fab Five: Helping students cope with the unique linguistic challenges of expository reading in intermediate grades. *Journal of Adolescent and Adult Literacy*, 51(6), 476–487.

Fang, Z. (2010). *Language and literacy in inquiry-based science classrooms, grades 3–8*. Thousand Oaks, CA: Corwin and Arlington, VA: NSTA Press.

Fang, Z. (2012). The challenges of reading disciplinary texts. In T. Jetton & C. Shanahan (Eds.), *Adolescent literacy in the academic disciplines: General principles and practical strategies* (pp. 34–68). New York: Guilford.

Fang, Z. (2013). Disciplinary literacy in science: Developing science literacy through trade books. *Journal of Adolescent and Adult Literacy*, 57(4), 274–278.

Fang, Z. (2016). Teaching close reading with complex texts across content areas. *Research in the Teaching of English*, 51(1), 106–116.

Fang, Z. (2020). Toward a linguistically informed, responsive, and embedded pedagogy in secondary literacy instruction. *Journal of World Languages*, 6(1–2), 70–91.

Fang, Z. (2021a). *Demystifying academic writing: Genres, moves, skills, and strategies*. New York: Routledge.

Fang, Z. (2021b). *Using functional grammar in English literacy teaching and learning*. Beijing: Foreign Language Teaching and Research Press.

Fang, Z., Adams, B., Gresser, V., & Li, C. (2019). Developing critical literacy through an SFL-informed pedagogical heuristic. *English Teaching: Practice & Critique*, *18*(1), 4–17.

Fang, Z., & Colosimo, N. (2023). Promoting science literacy through reading: A disciplinary literacy approach. In E. Ortlieb, B. Kane, & E. Cheek (Eds.), *Unpacking disciplinary literacies: Research, theory, and practice* (pp. 55–86). New York: Guilford.

Fang, Z., Gresser, V., Cao, P., & Zheng, J. (2021). Nominal complexities in school children's informational writing. *Journal of English for Academic Purposes*, *50*, https://doi.org/10.1016/j.jeap.2021.100958

Fang, Z., Lamme, L., Pringle, R., Patrick, J., Sanders, J., Zmach, C., Charbonnet, S., & Henkel, M. (2008). Integrating reading into middle school science: What we did, found, and learned. *International Journal of Science Education*, *30*(15), 2067–2089.

Fang, Z., & Schleppegrell, M. (2008). *Reading in secondary content areas: A language-based pedagogy*. Ann Arbor, MI: The University of Michigan Press.

Fang, Z., & Schleppegrell, M. J. (2010). Disciplinary literacies across content areas: Supporting secondary reading through functional language analysis. *Journal of Adolescent and Adult Literacy*, *53*(7), 587–597.

Fang, Z., Schleppegrell, M., & Cox, B. (2006). Understanding the language demands of schooling: Nouns in academic registers. *Journal of Literacy Research*, *38*(3), 247–273.

Fang, Z., & Wei, Y. (2010). Improving middle school students' science literacy through reading infusion. *Journal of Educational Research*, *103*(4), 262–273.

Fernandez-Fontecha, A., O'Halloran, K., Tan, S., & Wignell, P. (2018). A multimodal approach to visual thinking: The scientific sketchnote. *Visual Communication*, *18*(1), 5–29.

Goldman, S., Britt, M., Brown, W., Cribb, G., George, M., Greenleaf, C., Lee, C., Shanahan, C., & Project READI (2016). Disciplinary literacies and learning to read for understanding: A conceptual framework for disciplinary literacy. *Educational Psychologist*, *51*(2), 219–246.

Halliday, M. (1998). Things and relations: Regrammaticising experience as technical knowledge. In J. Martin & R. Veel (Eds.), *Reading science: Perspectives on discourses of science* (pp. 185–235). London: Routledge.

Halliday, M. (2006). *The language of science* (edited by J. Webster). London: Continuum.

Halliday, M., & Martin, J. (1993). *Writing science: Literacy and discursive power*. Pittsburgh, PA: University of Pittsburgh Press.

Hand, B., McDermott, M., & Prain, V. (2016). *Using multimodal representations to support learning in the science classroom*. London: Springer.

Hershfield, S., & Fang, Z. (2015). *Humidity and the water cycle*. A science unit developed for Project ADePT Summer Institute, University of Florida, Gainesville, Florida.

Kontra, C., Lyons, D., Fischer, S., & Beilock, S. (2022). Physical experience enhances science learning. *Psychological Science, 26*(6), 737–749.

Krajcik, J. S., & Sutherland, L. M. (2010). Supporting students in developing literacy in science. *Science, 328*(5977), 456–459.

Kress, G. (2003). *Literacy in the new media age*. London: Routledge.

Kress, G., Jewitt, C., Ogborn, J., & Tsatsarelis, C. (2001). *Multimodal teaching and learning: The rhetorics of the science classroom*. London: Continuum.

Lee, O., Quinn, H., & Valdes, G. (2013). Science and language for English language learners in relation to next generation science standards and with implications for common core state standards for English language arts and mathematics. *Educational Researcher, 42*(4), 223–233.

Lemke, J. (2002). Multimedia semiotics: Genres for science education and science literacy. In M. Schleppegrell & C. Colombi (Eds.), *Developing advanced literacy in first and second languages* (pp. 21–44). Mahwah, NJ: Erlbaum.

Lemke, J. (2004). The literacies of science. In E. W. Saul (Ed.), *Crossing borders in literacy and science instruction: Perspectives on theory and practice (pp. 33–47)*. Newark, DE: International Reading Association, and Arlington, VA: NSTA Press.

Martin, J., & White, P. (2005), *The language of evaluation: Appraisal in English*. New York: Palgrave.

Maton, K. (2006). On knowledge structures and knower structures. In R. Moore, M. Arnot, J. Beck, & H. Daniels (Eds.), *Knowledge, power and educational reform: Applying the sociology of Basil Bernstein* (pp. 44–59). London: Routledge.

Monhardt, R. (2005). Reading and writing nonfiction with children: Using biographies to learn about science and scientists. *Science and Children, 28*(6), 16–19.

Myhill, D., Jones, S., Watson, A., & Lines, H. (2013). Playful explicitness with grammar: A pedagogy for writing. *Literacy, 47*(2), 103–111.

National Governors Association (NGA) Center for Best Practices & Council of Chief State School Officers (CCSSO) (2010). *Common core state standards for English language arts & literacy in history/social studies, science, and technical subjects*. Washington, DC: Author.

National Research Council (2012). *A framework for K-12 science education: Practices, crosscutting concepts, and core ideas*. Washington, DC: The National Academies Press.

NGSS Lead States (2013). *Next generation science standards: For states, by states*. Washington, DC: National Academies Press.

Norris, S., & Phillips, L. (2003). How literacy in its fundamental sense is central to scientific literacy. *Science Education, 87*(2), 224–240.

O'Reilly, T., & McNamara, D. (2007). The impact of science knowledge, reading skill, and reading strategy knowledge on more traditional "high stakes" measures of high school students' science achievement. *American Educational Research Journal, 44*(1), 161–196.

Oreskes, N., & Conway, E. (2011). *Merchants of doubt: How a handful of scientists obscured the truth on issues from tobacco smoke to global warming.* New York: Bloomsbury.

Osborne, J. (2002). Science without literacy: A ship without a sail? *Cambridge Journal of Education, 32*(2), 203–218.

Patterson, A., Román, D., Friend, M., Osborne, J., & Donovan, B. (2018). Reading for meaning: The foundational knowledge every teacher of science should have. *International Journal of Science Education, 40*(3), 291–307.

Pescatore, C. (2007). Current events as empowering literacy: For English and social studies teachers. *Journal of Adolescent and Adult Literacy, 51*(4), 326–339.

Prain, V. (2022). Teachers' language-based knowledge to support students' science learning. In L. Seah, R. Silver, & M. Baildon (Eds.), *The role of language in content pedagogy: A framework for teachers' knowledge* (pp. 137–158). Singapore: Springer.

Reed, D., Petscher, Y., & Truckenmiller, A. (2016). The contribution of general reading ability to science achievement. *Reading Research Quarterly, 52*(2), 253–266.

Román, D., & Busch, K. (2016). Textbooks of doubt: Using systemic functional analysis to explore the framing of climate change in middle-school science textbooks. *Environmental Education Research, 22*(8), 1158–1180.

Román, D., Jones, F., Basaraba, D., & Hironaka, S. (2015). Helping students bridge inferences in science texts using graphic organizers. *Journal of Adolescent & Adult Literacy, 60*(2), 121–130.

Romance, N., & Vitale, M. (2001). Implementing an in-depth expanded science model in elementary schools: Multi-year findings, research issues, and policy implications. *International Journal of Science Education, 23*(4), 373–404.

Shanahan, C., Shanahan, T., & Misischia, C. (2011). Analysis of expert readers in three disciplines: History, mathematics, and chemistry. *Journal of Literacy Research, 43*(4), 393–429.

Smith, R., Snow, P., Serry, T., & Hammond, L. (2021). The role of background knowledge in reading comprehension: A critical review. *Reading Psychology, 42*(3), 214–240.

Tang, K., & Putra, G. (2018). Infusing literacy into an inquiry instructional model to support students' construction of scientific explanations. In K. Tang & K. Danielsson (Eds.), *Global development in literacy research for science education* (pp. 281–300). Singapore: Springer.

Tang, K., Tighe, S., & Moje, E. (2016). Literacy in the science classroom. In P. Smagorinsky (Ed.), *Teaching dilemmas & solutions in content-area literacy, grades 6–12* (pp. 57–79). Thousand Oaks, CA: Corwin.

Uccelli, P., Galloway, E., Barr, C., Meneses, A., & Dobbs, C. (2015). Beyond vocabulary: Exploring cross-disciplinary academic-language proficiency and its association with reading comprehension. *Reading Research Quarterly, 40,* 337–356.

Unsworth, L., Tytler, R., Fenwick, L., Humphrey, S., Chandler, P., Herrington, M., & Pham, L. (2022). *Multimodal literacy in school science: Transdisciplinary perspectives on theory, research and pedagogy.* London: Routledge.

van den Broek, P. (2010). Using texts in science education: Cognitive processes and knowledge representation. *Science, 328*(5977), 453–456.

Wellington, J., & Osborne, J. (2001), *Language and literacy in science education.* Philadelphia, PA: Open University Press.

Willingham, D. (Spring, 2006). How knowledge helps. *American Educator, 30*(1), https://www.aft.org/periodical/american-educator/spring-2006/how-knowledge-helps

Yeo, J., & Nielsen, W. (2020). Multimodal science teaching and learning. *Learning: Research and Practice, 6*(1), 1–4.

Yeo, J., & Tan, K. (2022). From image-to-writing: A teacher's PCK in supporting primary school students in making sense of the specialized language of science. In L. Seah, R. Silver, & M. Baildon (Eds.), *The role of language in content pedagogy: A framework for teachers' knowledge* (pp. 115–136). Singapore: Springer.

Yore, L. (2004). Why do future scientists need to study the language arts? In W. Saul (Ed.), *Crossing borders in literacy and science instruction* (pp. 71–94). Newark, DE: International Reading Association.

Zhu, S., & Fang, Z. (2019). Has the prose quality of science textbook improved over the past decade? A linguistic perspective. *Journal of World Languages, 5*(2), 113–131.

5
Reading Mathematics

What is Mathematics?

Mathematics is defined in the Merriam-Webster Dictionary as "the science of numbers and their operations, interrelations, combinations, generalizations, and abstractions and of space configurations and their structure, measurement, transformations, and generalizations". Simply put, mathematics is the study of quantity, space and shape, order, change and relationship, and uncertainty involving objects such as numbers, points, and lines (Ojose, 2011). The job of mathematicians is to "seek out patterns, formulate new conjectures, and establish truth by rigorous deduction from appropriately chosen axioms and definitions" (https://www.tntech.edu/cas/math/what-is-mathe matics.php).

Mathematics has several characteristics (Fang, Chapman, Kellogg, & Commeret, 2023), an understanding of which can help teachers design activities that are authentic to mathematics practice and promote mathematical thinking and reasoning (Hoffmann & Even, 2018). First, mathematics is both theoretical (pure) and practical (applied). Some mathematicians focus on exploring the possible relationships among abstractions (e.g., strings of numbers, geometric figures, sets of equations) that have no obvious perceptual correlates in the real world. Other mathematicians devote their attention to solving problems that originate in the world of human experience. Although the works of theoretical and applied mathematicians may seem unrelated, they often influence each other in ways that ultimately lead to advances in both. In fact, the line between theoretical and practical can be difficult to draw because sometimes what was once considered theoretical could later become practical. For example, calculus was once considered incredibly theoretical and deemed to have little practical value. Today, it has widespread use in science, engineering, and economics, among others. This means that mathematics is, in the words of Hoffmann and Even (2018), "not

DOI: 10.4324/9781003432258-5

just a theoretical science disconnected from the physical world, but rather a tool for solving real life problems" across many disciplines (p. 104).

Second, mathematics is not an island unto itself; it is a discipline interconnected with other disciplines. The development of mathematics is informed by advances in other disciplines such as physics, philosophy, art, and even religion; at the same time, it is also widely used to help solve problems in other disciplines such as biology, astronomy, engineering, economics, linguistics, law, psychology, statistics, and architecture. The interconnectedness of mathematics with other disciplines makes it widely applicable to many disciplines and facilitates its intrusion into almost all spheres of the human life. As Hoffmann and Even (2018) observed, mathematics is "wide and varied" and "rich in connections" (p. 102). For example, mathematics is a tool used by physicists to answer questions in their discipline; conversely, physics can be a source of inspiration for mathematicians, who use theoretical concepts from physics, such as general relativity and quantum theory, to help them develop new tools. This relationship is aptly summarized in the landmark document *Everybody Counts: A Report to the Nation on the Future of Mathematics Education* (National Academies, 1989): "Science provides mathematics with interesting problems to investigate, and mathematics provides science with powerful tools to use in analyzing data" (p. 35).

Third, mathematics is less dynamic than other disciplines in that it advances slowly, with each major advancement typically taking decades to achieve and often involving significant ideas. Compared to fast developing disciplines such as biology and engineering, new breakthroughs in mathematics are much slower and more limited. Moreover, unlike experts in other disciplines, mathematicians form a more organic community, sharing common assumptions, standards, approaches, and patterns of behavior (Bernstein, 2000). They usually have fewer ideas but try longer and harder to solve or prove them; and the ones that get solved are often significant. Thus, unlike texts in other disciplines, a text in the field of mathematics may remain relevant for a very long period of time. Because of this, knowledge in mathematics is commonly considered "more secured than knowledge in the sciences and the humanities" (Weber & Mejia-Ramos, 2013a, p. 93). This partially explains why the guiding document for mathematics teaching and learning, *Principles and Standards for School Mathematics* (NCTM, 2000), has not been updated for over two decades, whereas similar documents in other disciplines, such as science and social studies, are updated more frequently.

Fourth, mathematics demands rigor. Rigor is manifested in the way mathematicians present information, develop argument, and explain proofs.

Mathematics is not about running simulations or creating computer models; rather, it is about proving mathematical models using the tools of mathematics discourse (e.g., words, symbols, image, technology), a task that demands precision, logic, and clarity. These traits are important because in mathematics a small error in one step can ruin the rest of the steps, rendering the entire work devoid of scientific value. Thus, to ensure rigor, mathematicians pay careful attention to logic and language use in their writing. They are typically very careful in their wording and rely heavily on axioms, definitions, theorems, and proofs when reasoning with the deductive structure of mathematics. They spend a considerable amount of time writing and revising their work to make sure that the final paper is completely rigorous in logic. Because mathematics theories are often profound and not obvious, the main job of mathematicians is to make the theories and related explanations accessible and easy to follow for the reader; at the same time, they also make careful language choices to ensure accuracy, precision, and rigor in their writing.

Fifth, mathematics is multisemiotic and multimodal. As indicated earlier, mathematics is a science of patterns and relationships among abstract entities. These patterns and relationships are constructed using the "mathematics register" (Halliday, 1978), a type of multisemiotic and multimodal discourse that is functional and effective for mathematical meaning-making and through which mathematical knowledge, ideas, procedures, and processes are presented and critiqued. As discussed in Chapter 4, language is a powerful tool for conceptualization and classification, but it is not particularly effective for giving precise and useful descriptions of natural phenomena in which matters of degree are important (e.g., exact shape of a mountain range or a cloud, the exact movement of a fly through space); for these phenomena, visual and symbolic representations seem better suited (Lemke, 2003). This explains why mathematicians draw on not just verbal resources (i.e., natural language) but also mathematical symbols (e.g., Σ, $f(\chi)$, π, η, μ, β) and images (e.g., graphs, diagrams) to communicate meaning. Each of these semiotic resources works in close partnership with the other two to create mathematics knowledge. O'Halloran (2011, pp. 219–220) described the functions of the three meaning-making semiotic resources in mathematics this way:

> Mathematical language . . . plays an important contextualizing function with regards to introducing and explaining mathematical knowledge. Typical uses include the explanation of new theory and concepts, introduction of problems, instructions regarding the procedures involved in solving the problems and the discussion of results . . . Mathematical symbolism, on the other hand, is the semiotic resource

through which mathematical problems are solved. Having derived from natural language and material actions (e.g., measuring, counting and dividing), modern mathematical symbolism retains some linguistic selections. However, the grammar of mathematical symbolism is organized in such a way that the relations between the mathematical participants can be rearranged and simplified so that the symbolism becomes a specialized tool for logical reasoning . . . Indeed mathematical symbolism is a tool carefully designed to aid logical reasoning through the precise encoding of mathematical participants and processes in a format which facilitates their re-arrangement. Mathematical images (graphs, geometric diagrams) provide a semantic link between the linguistic description of the problem and the symbolic solution. That is, mathematical images provide an intuitive overview of the relations between mathematical participants which are viewed as parts of the whole. From here, the symbolism is used to derive the solution to problem using its specialized grammar and mathematical laws, axioms and pre-established results.

Because of these inter-semiotic relations, texts in mathematics feature various combinations of linguistic, symbolic, and visual resources. This discursive property augurs the need for students to develop facility in resemioticization so that they can effectively traverse the protean "semantic circuit" (O'Halloran, 2011) among the three building blocks of mathematical knowledge in their mathematical learning.

Reading and Mathematical Literacy

What does it mean to be literate in mathematics? The National Council of Teachers of Mathematics (2000) defined mathematical literacy as the ability to (a) understand mathematical entities, processes, and operations, (b) use efficient and accurate methods for computing, and (c) participate in mathematical processes. According to the Organization for Economic Cooperation and Development (2002), mathematical literacy refers to the ability to reason mathematically and to use mathematical concepts, tools, and procedures to describe, explain, and predict phenomena. It is the overarching literacy that encompasses numeracy (i.e., the ability to make sense of number and data related to a problem or situation), quantitative literacy (i.e., the ability to handle quantity, change and relations, and uncertainty), and spatial literacy (i.e., the ability to understand objects in the three-dimensional world in which we live). de Lange (2006) extended this definition of mathematical literacy to include mathematical thinking and reasoning (e.g., distinguishing among various mathematical statements, understanding breadth and limitations of mathematical concepts), mathematical argumentation (e.g., knowing how proofs differ from other forms of mathematical reasoning, following and assessing chains of arguments), mathematical communication (e.g., explaining how a problem is solved, understanding the work of others), modeling (e.g., translating reality into mathematical forms, interpreting mathematical models in context, reflecting on the modeling process), problem posing and solving (e.g., posing, formulating, defining, and solving problems), and representation and interpretation (e.g., using language and operation symbols formally and technically, differentiating and interpreting various forms of object representations and mathematical situations).

These abilities are similarly emphasized in the Common Core State Standards (NGA & CCSSO, 2010), which equates being mathematically literate to being proficient in both mathematical content and mathematical practice. Mathematical content is grade-level specific and includes counting and cardinality, operations and algebraic thinking, number and operations in base ten, fractions, measurement and data, geometry, ratio and proportional relationships, the number system, expressions and equations, functions, and statistics and probability. Mathematical practice, on the other hand, applies to all grade levels and includes the following eight components: (a) make sense of problems and persevere in solving them, (b) reason abstractly and quantitatively, (c) construct viable arguments and critique the reasoning of others, (d) model with mathematics, (e) use appropriate tools strategically, (f) attend to precision, (g) look for and make use of structure, and (h) look for and express regularity in repeated reasoning.

The knowledge, abilities, skills, practices, or habits of mind described in the above definitions cannot be effectively engaged with and developed without the ability to read, interpret, and create a variety of mathematical texts. For example, to develop or communicate conceptual understanding or argument/reasoning in mathematics, students need to be able to read, comprehend, and use the often dense and abstract language of mathematics. They also need to be able to read and understand mathematical expressions (e.g., formulas and equations) so that they "know what steps to perform, how to perform them, how to record and make sense of intermediate results, and how to review a series of computations for accuracy" (Siebert & Draper, 2012, p. 182). Additionally, students of geometry need to know "how to interpret symbolic notation in a diagram such as markings for angles, how to identify relevant parts within a diagram's configuration, and how to purposefully add auxiliary lines that would aid in proving geometric properties" (Gonzalez, 2021, p. 88). Thus, issues with reading may affect students' understanding of verbal descriptions, interpretation of visual elements (e.g., graphs, symbols), evaluation of mathematical proofs, construction of mathematical explanations or arguments, and chance of success in solving mathematics problems.

Research has suggested that reading comprehension and mathematics achievement are positively related. According to Grimm (2008), for example, students with higher reading achievement tend to demonstrate greater conceptual understanding of mathematics and greater competence in the application of mathematics knowledge. This relationship is particularly robust in the area of problem solving. In word problems, for instance, students need to be able to read the problem, identify what information is given, determine which pieces of information are relevant, and understand what the problem asks them to do. Difficulties with reading, such as confusion between *"of"* and *"off"* when solving a percentage problem (e.g., *5% of the retail price* vs. *5% off the retail price*) or inability to unpack dense noun phrases and identify references (e.g., *A line through the center of a circle that is perpendicular to a chord bisects the chord and its arcs.*), can lead students to the wrong solution or even give up trying. In mathematical modeling problems, students must translate real-world situations into mathematical models. And because real-world situations are typically presented in verbal form, the translation process will be impeded if students have poor comprehension skills. Capraro and Joffrion (2006) reported that middle school students struggled with translating English language (describing problem situation) into mathematical symbols (forming an algebraic expression/equation), or vice versa, because they lacked vocabulary knowledge, which is a measure of procedural skills for computing with numbers and variables, and comprehension skills, which is a measure of conceptual understanding of algebra. Fostering reading comprehension has been shown to promote modeling competence, increase interest in modeling, and establish connections between symbolic thinking and problems in the real world (Glenberg et al., 2012; Krawitz et al., 2022).

In short, reading is key to learning and doing mathematics. Learning mathematics is not just about learning to perform operations with numbers and symbols; it also involves learning to consume and produce texts that communicate mathematical concepts, ideas, processes, and reasoning in discipline-legitimated ways. The degree to which students understand what is read impacts the quality and outcome of their engagement in such mathematical activities as "solving word problems, constructing two- and three-dimensional objects, computing, calculating, designing and interpreting graphs, responding to open-ended and multiple-answer questions, and expressing mathematical relationships between concepts or situations"

(Adams & Lowery, 2007, p. 162). And the practices that mathematicians use in doing mathematics—such as asking questions in a given mathematical context, exploring and experimenting with the context, finding ways to mathematically model or represent the context, looking for structure or pattern in order to generate conjectures, consulting others or the research literature, making connections with prior knowledge, seeking proofs or disproofs of conjectures, and writing a finished exposition of the proof in a rigorous but accessible style (Bass, 2011)—are, to varying degrees, all dependent on the ability to read, understand, and create relevant texts in the discipline. For these reasons, reading is often seen as another important dimension of mathematical literacy that students are expected to develop in school (Borasi & Siegel, 2000; Siebert & Draper, 2012). As Adams (2003, p. 794) eloquently stated,

> The words, symbols, and numerals that give the discipline [of mathematics] its substance, framework, and power are the same words, symbols, and numerals that students must use to communicate ideas, perform procedures, explain processes, and solve problems. Hence a knower of mathematics is a doer of mathematics, and a doer of mathematics is a reader of mathematics.

The Challenges of Mathematics Reading

Mathematics is a challenging school subject for many students (Schoenfeld, 2022). Results from the 2019 National Assessment of Educational Progress show that only 34% of eighth-grade students and 24% of twelfth-grade students performed at or above the proficient level on the mathematics assessment (https://www.nationsreportcard.gov/mathematics/). The percentage is much lower for historically marginalized groups including Blacks (14% for 8th grade and 8% for 12th grade), Hispanics (20% for 8th grade and 11% for 12th grade), and English language learners (5% for 8th grade and 3% for 12th grade). For many students, their lack of reading proficiency is a major contributor to the challenges they face in learning and doing mathematics. School mathematics learning and teaching involves mediating the complex relationships among linguistic, symbolic, and visual forms of representing mathematical statements, explanation, and argument. The degree to which students understand the mathematical information presented in the text will determine the level of their success in solving the mathematical problem. An understanding of the challenges mathematics texts present is, therefore, crucial to supporting students' mathematical learning (Martiniello, 2008; Moschkovich, 2010; Schleppegrell, 2007).

The challenge of mathematics stems in part from its multisemiotic/multimodal discourse. To illustrate, let's take a close look at an excerpt from an academic article in a top mathematics research journal (see Figure 5.1). The excerpt uses specialist terminology (e.g., *monotonicity theorem, regularity assumptions, the Prandtl-Batchelor equation, constant, functions*) to construe specialized knowledge; long noun phrases with technical vocabulary (e.g., *the most important of the new versions of the monotonicity theorem (Theorem 1.3), a very simple type in which . . . and zero in the other*) to pack a large sum of semantic data; linking verbs (e.g., *The most important of the new versions . . . does not have any "monotonicity" left. Rather, it is a uniform bound on the monotonicity . . .*) to define concepts, identify relationships, or attribute qualities; nominalizations (e.g., *assumptions, existence, regularity, distributions*) to distill information, create semi-technical terms, or facilitate text structuring; and adverbs (e.g., *rather, hence, then*) and other word choices with precise mathematics meaning (e.g., *suppose, such that*) to engage in rigorous logical reasoning; as well as an array of mathematics symbols, formulas, and equations that encode mathematics concepts, processes, operations, and relationships. This combination of technical, dense language with abstract symbols

---

The most important of the new versions of the monotonicity theorem (Theorem 1.3) does not have any "monotonicity" left. Rather, it is a uniform bound on the monotonicity functional Φ, defined below. We show by example that Theorem 1.3 cannot be improved without further regularity assumptions. The example is of a very simple type in which Δu is a nonzero constant in one of the phases and zero in the other. The example shows that there was a significant technical barrier to proving monotonicity theorems and hence existence and regularity theorems in the case of the Prandtl-Batchelor equation.

. . .

THEOREM 1.3. *Suppose the $u_{\pm}$ are nonnegative, continuous functions on the unit ball B_1. Suppose that $\Delta u_{\pm} \geq -1$ in the sense of distributions and $u_{+}(X)u_{-}(X) = 0$ for all $X \in B_1$. Then there is a dimensional constant C such that*

$$\Phi(r) \leq C\left(1 + \int_{B_1} \frac{|\nabla u_{+}(X)|^2}{|X|^{n-2}}\, dX + \int_{B_1} \frac{|\nabla u_{-}(X)|^2}{|X|^{n-2}}\, dX\right)^2, \ 0 < r \leq 1.$$

Figure 5.1 Monotonicity Theorem

Source: Caffarelli, Jerison, and Kenig (2002, pp. 369–370)

and equations renders mathematics reading exceptionally challenging, demanding careful attention and constant logical inferences.

Secondary school mathematics textbooks, as disciplinary mathematics recontextualized for pedagogical purposes, contain many of the same discursive features found in disciplinary mathematics. These pedagogical resources are typically made up of chunks of text labeled as hypothesis, theorem, proof, example, exercise, review, and so on. Three such chunks of text are presented below. They come from a middle school algebra textbook (Figure 5.2), a high school geometry textbook (Figure 5.3), and a high school precalculus textbook (Figure 5.4).

Technical Vocabulary

One apparent challenge in reading mathematics texts is technical words and phrases. Mathematics is a highly technical discipline requiring the use

---

Factoring a number or a polynomial is the process of finding those numbers or polynomials whose product is the given number or polynomial. A **perfect square trinomial** is the square of a binomial, whereas the **difference of two perfect squares** is the product of binomials that are the sum and difference of the same two. A **prime polynomial,** like a prime number, has only two factors, 1 and itself. To factor a polynomial completely:

1. Factor out the greatest common monomial factor if it is greater than 1.

2. Write any factor of the form $a^2 - b^2$ as $(a + b)(a - b)$.

3. Write any factor of the form $ax^2 + bx + c$ as the product of two binomial factors if possible.

4. Write the given polynomial as the product of these factors.

Figure 5.2 Special Products and Factors
Source: Gantert (2007, p. 464)

Theorem 12.3   Two line segments are divided proportionally if and only if the ratio of the length of a part of one segment to the length of the whole is equal to the ratio of the corresponding lengths of the other segment.

Figure 5.3 Proportion Involving Line Segments
Source: Gantert (2008, p. 483)

> <u>Example 10</u> **Using Trigonometric Functions to Solve Real-World Scenarios**
>
> Suppose the function $y = 5\tan\left(\dfrac{\pi}{4}t\right)$ marks the distance in the movement of a light beam from the top of a police car across a wall where t is the time in seconds and y is the distance in feet from a point on the wall directly across from the police car.
>
> **a.** Find and interpret the stretching factor and period.
> **b.** Graph on the interval [0, 5].
> **c.** Evaluate $f(1)$ and discuss the function's value at that input.

Figure 5.4 Trigonometric Functions
Source: Abramson (2017, p. 537)

of terms that are uniquely mathematical as well as everyday words that assume technical meanings. Words that are solely mathematical are usually of the Latin or Greek origin (e.g., *apothem, cosine, quotient, vector, polynomial, diameter, integer, isosceles*), and they rarely cause confusion for students, even though they can still be difficult. Examples of technical phrases in mathematics include *right angle, degree of freedom, multiplicative inverse, prime factor, least square means,* and *ordered pairs.* A variety of such technical words and phrases are used in the three sample mathematics texts, including *polynomial, perfect square trinomial, prime polynomial, prime number, line segment, greatest common monomial factor, stretching factor and period, interval, ratio,* and *trigonometric functions.* These words and phrases are central to the construction of specialized knowledge in the fields of algebra, geometry, and precalculus.

One of the challenges in learning technical vocabulary and phrases such as these is to understand hierarchies of relationships among the terms. For example, *square, rectangle, rhombus,* and *trapezoid* are all quadrilaterals with different properties: rectangle or square is a parallelogram, but trapezoid is not a parallelogram; a square is always a rhombus or a rectangle, but a rhombus or a rectangle is not a square. The complex relationships among these terms can be stated as follows: A quadrilateral becomes a trapezoid when there is only one pair of parallel sides, but a parallelogram when there are two pairs of parallel sides; a parallelogram becomes a rectangle when its four angles are all right angles, but a rhombus when its four sides are of equal length; a parallelogram becomes a square when all sides are equal and all angles are right angles. Understanding the properties associated with each of these technical terms is, thus, important to understanding logical reasoning in mathematics, as students are sometimes required to write the converse, the inverse, or the contrapositive of the *if–then* statements (e.g., *If a quadrilateral is a rhombus, then it is a parallelogram. If a quadrilateral is a parallelogram, then it is a rhombus.*) and to judge whether the conditionals are true or false.

The use of everyday lexis with precise, technical meanings also presents a challenge to the reader. Words such as *face, solid, power, absolute, times, order, acute,* and *volume* belong to this category. Additionally, conditional constructions such as *if . . . then, if . . . find . . ., if and only if . . ., when . . ., given . . ., let . . ., suppose . . .,* and *assume . . .* play an important role in construing logic and precision in word problems and in developing theorems and proofs. These words and grammatical constructions can cause confusion because students have to distinguish between their meaning in mathematics and their meaning in non-mathematical contexts. There are also nuances among some of the conditional words that students may not be adequately aware of. For example, "*let*" is usually used in a definition for the purpose of doing an exercise such as proof, especially when no earlier context is given, as in "<u>Let</u> *n* be an integer". "*Assume*", on the other hand, is circumstantial. It is used to introduce a hypothesis in a statement that elaborates on a previous statement, as in "<u>Let</u> *n* be an integer . . . <u>Assume</u> that *n* is even . . .". It is also used to indicate an axiom or acceptance of some statement without proof, to go through a proof by exhaustion (that is, a proof by cases), or to begin a proof by contradiction. In the three texts in Figures 5.2, 5.3, and 5.4, ordinary words like *factor, product, function, value, period, segment, input, if and only if, suppose,* and *find* have precise meanings in mathematics.

Semi-Technical Terms

In addition to technical vocabulary, mathematics also uses many semi-technical terms, which are created through nominalization. Nominalization is an indispensable tool for mathematical meaning-making. It helps create abstract "things", or virtual entities, that can then be elaborated or quantified, reified as mathematical concepts, or put into new relationships with other mathematical entities/concepts (Veel, 1999). For example, when mathematical operations such as *add* and *divide* are turned into *addition* and *division*, they become topical areas of study in mathematics that mean much more than the concrete operations of adding and dividing. Veel (1999) distinguishes between "operational facility" and "conceptual understanding", noting that it is possible for a student to be able to divide but still not fully understand the concept of division. In fact, the development from knowing how to add and divide (as in elementary mathematics) to understanding the concepts of addition and division (as in secondary mathematics) is a giant step that involves induction and abstraction.

Similarly, adjectives such as *long, wide,* and *high* can, when nominalized, become mathematical concepts of *length, width,* and *height,* which are key to the discussion of volume in relation to three-dimensional geometric shapes. These concepts capture more than the properties encoded in the adjectival forms and can be further quantified (e.g., *a width of 50 ft, one-fourth of the height of a square prism*). And when a verb such as *measure* is nominalized, the virtual entity *measure* can then be qualified (e.g., *the measure of each angle of a regular polygon*) or entered into relationships with other concepts or virtual entities (e.g., *The sum of the measures of the interior angles of a polygon equals the product of 180° and two less than the number of sides*).

Nominalization is a salient feature of mathematical discourse, as can be observed in the three sample mathematics texts in Figures 5.2, 5.3, and 5.4. The text in Figure 5.2 uses nominalizations such as *the square* (deriving from the process of squaring), *the difference* (deriving from the process of subtracting), *the sum* (deriving from the process of adding), *factor* (deriving from the process of factoring), and *the product* (deriving from the process of finding those numbers or polynomials). The text in Figure 5.3 uses "length" and "ratio", both nominalizations that derive from, respectively, the adjective "long", which denotes quality, and the verb "dividing" or "multiplying", which denotes operation. The text in Figure 5.4 also uses nominalizations (e.g., *the distance, the movement*) that become virtual entities participating in the construction of the word problem.

These ways of using language help create an abstract textual world with semi-technical entities and virtual objects working in conjunction with technical vocabulary to construct specialist knowledge in mathematics. Students who are used to the commonsense reality construed through everyday language will need experience and guidance when interacting with mathematics texts.

Long Noun Phrases

Technical vocabulary and semi-technical lexis do not exist in isolation in mathematics texts. They interact with each other and with other grammatical elements to construct meaning. Like other academic or disciplinary texts, mathematics texts are "rhetorical in nature, addressing and attempting to persuade a reader" (Morgan, 1998, p. 9). It is, therefore, necessary to look beyond the level of vocabulary and at the overall grammatical patterns in the text (Schleppegrell, 2007). While the challenges of technical vocabulary and semi-technical lexis may be obvious to students, the challenges associated with the grammatical patternings that these terms bring with them are often more difficult to recognize. Mathematics texts in English have a tendency to exploit long noun phrases and linking verbs (e.g., *be, have, equal, mean*). These grammatical resources facilitate the construction of mathematical definitions, theorems, propositions, lemmas, corollaries, proofs, scholiums, problems, and so forth, as they enable mathematicians to pack a large number of technical and semi-technical concepts (e.g., *the degree of a polynomial with one variable, the value of the greatest exponent of the variable that appears in any term; the absolute value of a real number, the distance between the origin and the point representing the real number*) and then relate them to each other or to other mathematical concepts through the use of linking verbs (e.g., *The degree of a polynomial with one variable is the value of the greatest exponent of the variable that appears in any term. The absolute value of a real number is the distance between the origin and the point representing the real number.*)

Long noun phrases populate the three mathematics texts in Figures 5.2, 5.3, and 5.4. Samples of these noun phrases follow:

- *the process of finding those numbers or polynomials whose product is the given number or polynomial*
- *the difference of two perfect squares*
- *the product of binomials that are the sum and difference of the same two*
- *any factor of the form $a^2 - b^2$*
- *any factor of the form $ax^2 + bx + c$*
- *the product of two binomial factors*
- *the product of these factors*
- *the distance in the movement of a light beam from the top of a police car across a wall where t is the time in seconds and y is the distance in feet from a point on the wall directly across from the police car*
- *the ratio of the length of a part of one segment to the length of the whole*
- *the ratio of the corresponding lengths of the other segment.*

Long noun phrases such as these increase the informational density of the texts. In addition, they often encode (implicitly) mathematical processes and reasoning that must be unpacked in order for them to be fully understood. For example, several mathematical operations are embedded in the long noun phrase, *the sum of the angle measures divided by the number of angles in the polygon.* These operations include, in sequence, (a) counting (count the number of angles in the polygon), (b) measuring (measure the degree of each angle in the polygon), (c) adding (add up the degree measures of the angles), and (d) dividing (divide the result from step c by the result from step a). The statement—_A cylinder with a height of 5ft and a volume of 100ft_ has _about 89% of the surface area of a square prism with the same height and volume._—contains two long noun phrases (underlined) linked by a verb (_has_). Each noun phrase contains a series of prepositional phrases that pack a large sum of information about a cylinder or a prism. Examples like these show the highly technical and dense character of mathematics texts and why they can be extraordinarily challenging for students to read, comprehend, and problem solve.

Symbolism and Image

Another challenge in reading mathematics texts is that mathematical symbolism and images (visual displays) are often juxtaposed with language in the construction of mathematical meaning. Sometimes, when mathematical symbolism and images are not explicitly included in the linguistic text, it is necessary to translate the language (e.g., _the volume of a cylinder equals the area of a base times the height of the cylinder_) into mathematical symbolism (e.g., $V = \pi r^2 h$, where r is the radius of the cylinder base and h is the cylinder height) and/or visual display (see Figure 5.5) in order for students to truly understand the information presented and then solve the problem posed. This translation, or resemioticization, presents a great challenge for many

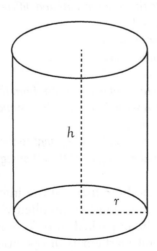

Figure 5.5 Cylinder

students. For example, the statement "the product of 180 degree and two less than the number of sides" is often misinterpreted as "$180 \times (2 - x)$" or "$180 \times 2 - x$", instead of "$180 \times (x - 2)$", where x represents the number of sides, because many students simply move linearly from left to right in their translation.

Like mathematical language, mathematical symbolism too can leave many mathematical processes implicit, requiring the reader to unpack and perform the mathematical operations and reasoning buried in the symbols and equations. For example, the quadratic equation, $y = ax^2 + bx + c$, encodes several arithmetic and algebraic operations such as addition and multiplication. Students need to know the relevant theorems, corollaries, axioms, and propositions subsumed in these operations in order to make sense of the text. O'Halloran (2000) has likened the structure of equations like this one to the structure of a linguistic clause, showing how mathematical symbols are combined to form operations and equations in the same way that words are combined to form phrases and clauses. From this perspective, $y = ax^2 + bx + c$ can be conceived of as a linguistic clause, where y, a, x, b, and c (called *atoms*) are combined into x^2, ax^2, and bx (called *expressions*), which are further combined into an *equation*. With each combination in the hierarchical ordering, the reader is taken further away from the everyday construal of meaning. Here, the terms *atom*, *expression*, and *equation* in mathematical symbolism are analogous to *word*, *phrase*, and *clause*, respectively, in language. Deconstructing the "grammar" of mathematical symbolism in this way shows that reading mathematics texts often involves "long chains of reasoning that provide little or no indication of the results, definitions, axioms, operational properties or laws that have been used" (O'Halloran, 2000, p. 377).

Mathematical symbolism presents other reading challenges as well (Rubenstein & Thompson, 2001, p. 268). For example, the same symbol may have different meanings in different contexts (e.g., a small dash may mean *minus*, *opposite*, or *negative*; the symbol m represents a pronumeral in algebra but meter in measurement). Another challenge is that the placement or ordering of symbols may or may not affect the meaning (e.g., $34 \neq 43$, $xy = yx$; $2n \neq 2^n$). Additional sources of confusion for students include (1) the same concept may be represented by different symbols (e.g., $100 \div 25$, $25\sqrt{100}$, $100/25$), (2) the same formula with different letters is used in different contexts (e.g., $a^2 + b^2 = c^2$ is used in Pythagorean theorem, but $x^2 + y^2 = r^2$ is the formula for a circle centered at the origin), and (3) the same function can be represented in different forms, e.g., $y = mx + b$, $y - y_1 = m(x - x_1)$, and $x/a + y/b = 1$ are all forms of linear functions.

Understanding language and symbolism does not always ensure comprehension of mathematics texts. Students must also be able to read and interpret tables, graphs, and diagrams, recognizing how order, position, relative size, and orientation may alter the meaning being constructed (O'Halloran, 2005). For example, to truly understand the theorem in Figure 5.3, students must be able to construct and interpret a visual display such as the one presented in Figure 5.6. The visual display renders the technical and dense language concrete, enabling the construction of mathematical equations (e.g., DC = AC/2, DC/AC = ½; EC = BC/2, EC/BC = ½; DE = AB/2, DE/AB = ½) that capture the mathematical processes and reasoning construed in language. In short, full comprehension of mathematics texts often depends on simultaneous engagement with all three meaning-making resources of nature language, mathematical symbolism, and visual display.

Summary

The foregoing discussion highlights some of the key discursive features of school mathematics texts that constitute what is often referred to as "the mathematics register" (Halliday, 1978) and the potential challenges these features present to reading comprehension, problem solving, and learning. In mathematics texts, the three meaning-making semiotic resources—language, mathematics symbolism, and visual display—interact in synergistic

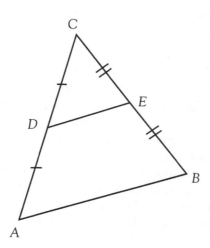

Figure 5.6 Visual Display of Proportion Involving Line Segments
Source: Gantert (2008, p. 480)

ways to construct mathematical knowledge, processes, and reasoning. And to be successful in reading, doing, and learning mathematics, students must develop the inter-semiotic competence that will enables them to shift proficiently among language (that introduces theoretical concepts or a problem), image (that visualizes the relations among mathematical participants), and mathematical symbolism (that captures the relations among the participants and encodes the processes for solving the problem).

How do Experts Read Mathematics Texts?

Compared to science or history, studies of mathematicians' reading practices are more limited. As Weber and Mejia-Ramos (2013a) observed, "research on the reading and nature of mathematics text is sparse" (p. 90). This limited amount of work focuses almost exclusively on the mathematical practice of proof validation and was conducted primarily by mathematics education scholars rather than literacy education scholars. Weber (2008) conducted one of the earliest studies on how mathematicians read purported mathematical proofs and made judgments about the proofs' validity. Using think alouds and retrospective interviews, he found that mathematicians used different modes of reasoning in proof validation, including formal reasoning and the construction of rigorous proofs, informal deductive reasoning, and example-based reasoning. He also reported that mathematicians first examined larger chunks of logical structure (i.e., zoom-out strategy) before reading each line of argument more closely (i.e., zoom-in strategy). That is, in proof validation, mathematicians first determined the structure of the argument, primarily by explicitly checking which assumptions were being used in the argument. If they found the structure of the proof, or methodological moves (e.g., proof by contradiction, direct proof), to be acceptable, they would then check each line of the argument.

This finding was contradicted by Inglis and Alcock (2012), who conducted an eye-tracking study comparing the proof validation behavior of research-active mathematicians with that of first-year undergraduate students. They found that (a) both mathematicians and undergraduate students used the zoom-in strategy (line-by-line close reading), (b) the former used the zoom-in strategy more often than the latter, and (c) neither engaged in the zoom-out strategy. Specifically, in reading mathematical proofs, the mathematicians focused on the logical details of an argument, shifting their attention back and forth between consecutive lines of purported proofs and devoting more effort to inferring implicit between-line warrants. They did not examine the overall logical structure of the proof.

However, a more fine-grained analysis of Inglis and Alcock's data by Weber and Mejia-Ramos (2013b) revealed that when engaging in proof validation tasks, the mathematicians did frequently use an initial skimming strategy (zooming out) before reading individual parts of the proof more carefully (zooming in).

Focusing specifically on how proofs were used to learn and understand mathematics, Wilkerson-Jerde and Wilensky (2011) analyzed the reasoning of eight mathematicians and two mathematics graduate students as they read and made sense of an unfamiliar but accessible mathematical proof in geometric topology with the goal of teaching it to a colleague. Analysis of think-aloud protocols and retrospective interviews indicated that the experts (a) used mathematical resources such as definitions, symbolic structures, and examples to deconstruct mathematical ideas into their fragment components so that each of these components can be isolated, identified, and explored, and (b) recombined these fragments in novel ways to test the definitions and theorems presented in the proof. These findings suggest that simultaneous deconstruction, connection, and coordination of mathematical resources is an important feature of proof reading among mathematicians.

While mathematics education researchers focused on reading behavior when validating proofs, literacy education researchers have focused on how mathematicians read mathematics texts in general for comprehension. For example, Shanahan, Shanahan, and Misischia (2011) studied how mathematicians (i.e., two mathematics professors, two mathematics teacher educators, and two high school mathematics teachers), as well as historians and chemists, interacted with texts in their discipline. Specifically, they examined the ways experts used sourcing, contextualization, and corroboration in their considerations of disciplinary texts. They also examined how text structure and graphic elements influenced the ways experts interacted with the text, the role of interest in their reading, and how they engaged in critiquing the text. By analyzing the data collected from individual interviews, reading think alouds, and focus group meetings, the researchers found that the mathematicians paid little attention to the author of the document (i.e., sourcing) and the time period of publication (i.e., contextualization); however, they used corroboration (i.e., checking one source against another) as a reading strategy to help them verify information and make sense of text. The mathematicians used text structure to help them determine where problems and solutions were located. They placed a strong emphasis on accuracy (but not much on credibility), weighing nearly every word and evaluating each piece of information to ensure understanding. They treated both equations and prose equally and as inseparable, interpreting them in a unified manner.

Some of these findings have been disputed. Weber and Mejia-Ramos (2013a) argued that mathematicians do pay attention to sourcing. They cited as evidence results from two of their own studies. In an experiment conducted by Inglis and Mejia-Ramos (2009), 190 mathematicians were asked to read a mathematical argument and rate it for its level of perceived persuasiveness. Half of the mathematicians were informed that the author was a famous mathematician and the other half were not provided an author. The group who had an awareness of the author rated the argument more than 17 points higher than the other group. In another study (Weber & Mejia-Ramos, 2011), mathematicians stated that they believed a proof to be trustworthy and correct if it appears in a reputable journal. This finding is corroborated by results from the survey data involving 118 mathematicians, where a large majority stated that if a proof was published in a respected academic journal, they felt highly confident that the proof is correct and frequently felt unnecessary to check for accuracy (Mejia-Ramos & Weber, 2014).

Fang and Chapman (2020) examined in greater depth the strategies one mathematician used when reading to comprehend an unfamiliar text in his area of specialization, that is, an article from *Annals of Mathematics* that describes, explains, validates, and applies some new monotonicity theorems. The mathematician, named Kang, was instructed to verbalize his thought processes while reading the article to inform his own research. The think-aloud session was videotaped and later reviewed by Kang and the researchers, when they discussed critical points or questions about his observed reading behaviors. Kang was also interviewed about his literate practices in mathematics. Qualitative analysis of three data sources (reading think alouds, discussion of reading think alouds, and interviews) showed that Kang engaged in extensive reading and employed an array of strategies to help him make sense of what he was reading.

Specifically, Kang read widely and voluminously the work of other scholars (e.g., books, articles, webpages, YouTube lectures) in order to stay current in the field, seek answers to the unknowns, gain new insights to existing problems, and increase motivation for his own work. During reading, Kang read back and forth to clarify confusion, to make inferences and predictions, and to ensure understanding. He said that when he read something he did not quite understand, he did not panic; instead, he read on to seek additional information so as to clarify or substantiate his hunches. Often times, what he read in later sections helped him better visualize and understand what he had read earlier in the text.

Another strategy Kang used while reading is close reading, a habit of mind fostered during his training as a mathematician. Kang read slowly, paying close attention to every detail in the text. He did not hurry to get through the text; instead, he made sure that he understood what he was reading before moving on. He noted that reading fast did not help him understand the text. He acknowledged that some people did skim articles to get the information they wanted to see, but such practice, according to him, runs the risk of being biased because they might already be implicitly agreeing with the author without evaluating or verifying what is said in the text.

During reading, Kang also regularly summarized and paraphrased what he saw in the text, both to clarify his own understanding and to deepen his thinking. The strategies helped him cope with the challenges of mathematical reading. They slowed down his reading, giving him time to process what was being read, clarify his thinking, make connections with what he had just read, and predict what was coming next. Because mathematical texts are often dense, technical, abstract, and formal, periodically distilling and rephrasing what was read in his own words seemed to be a particularly useful strategy for improving comprehension, retention, and learning.

A related strategy Kang used is that he constantly monitored his own understanding of text during reading. As he assessed his understanding of text, he made decisions regarding how much of what he knew and did not know affected his understanding and what coping strategies he could draw upon to help him tackle the comprehension challenges. Part of the monitoring process involves asking questions, some rhetorical in nature, about what he was reading in the text. As Kang read, he posed questions and wonderings to himself and then tried to answer them through logical reasoning, rewording, rereading, reading ahead, verifying, or making inferences. These strategies helped him clarify, confirm, and assess his understanding, as well as sustain active, continuous engagement with the text.

Another reading behavior that Kang demonstrated while reading is constant evaluation and verification of the information in the text. Sometimes, he evaluated the text by verifying the accuracy of calculation. Other times, he evaluated the logic of argument. Because formulas and equations contain important information that is integral, or even central, to the meanings being made in the text, Kang paid close attention to the symbols and visuals in the text, working diligently to understand formulas and equations and to verify their accuracy and logic, as well as their coherence with respect to the explanations offered in the prose.

Kang also checked the creditability of sources during reading. This information helped him decide whether he needed to verify everything he saw on the page. He noted that if the author was someone he knew who had a very good reputation, then he tended to believe what s/he did was right without attempting to verify it. For authors he had not heard of, he would search their public records online. If the record was mediocre, he was less inclined to believe what they did was right and would take time to verify it. Sometimes, he used impact factor to gauge the quality of the journal or to check how many quality papers the author had published in the past.

Additionally, Kang evaluated the quality and significance of the content in the article he read. He indicated that he was picky about what he read, meaning that he usually just read books or articles that are of high quality and contain significant ideas because he felt he could truly learn something from these pieces. He was very excited about reading high-quality books or articles but easily became bored when reading low-quality pieces. He noted that the article he was reading was written by scholars he respected and the subject of the article was very important to him. Because of this, he was motivated to read and hoped to understand everything in the article and to learn good mathematics from it. For other articles, he would just pick up the information he needed for his research without delving too deeply into it.

Kang also evaluated what he read in terms of rhetorical style. Although he admitted that he did not read a mathematics article to enjoy how good the writing style is because he did not think that was the right place to do it, he did indicate that poor writing made an article challenging for readers to understand. When he encountered a well-written article, he savored the reading experience and was eager to learn from it.

A strategy Kang frequently used in his reading is drawing on his prior knowledge and intuition to help him comprehend and evaluate what he read. He relied on prior knowledge to help him grapple with the unknown and make sense of what he was reading. Kang noted that his past experience and intuition would tell him that certain ways would not work when approaching a problem. This saved him time and made him more efficient in reading and in problem solving. The more senior he became, the more experience he accumulated, and the more efficient he became in reading, learning, and problem solving. According to Kang, building prior knowledge and intuition entailed a considerable amount of learning from wide reading and through trial and error. With every reading or attempt at problem solving, he gained valuable knowledge about a certain hunch, hypothesis, method, approach, or theory.

These past experiences and knowledge served as an important reference for Kang as he wrestled with complex ideas in the text or considered ways of working through problems in research.

An intriguing strategy that Kang employed to cope with the challenges of mathematics reading is storying, that is, using a storyline with made-up characters to engage in logical reasoning and to make sense of the prose and formulas/equations in the text. For example, when Kang was reading a formula in the stimulus text, he verbalized his thoughts this way:

> These two guys are going to fight; how do they fight? I said this is where the CP . . . K greater than U plus or minus square over X minus 2 with the X. BK is a portion of them. This is so exciting . . . This is like reading a novel; so these two functions, they are fighting like two soldiers for territory. If this one is large, they are both large. This one is controlled by this.

The use of a war metaphor involving soldiers from two opposing camps fighting for territorial control is significant because it helped him transform what he saw on page—verbal (prose) or visual (equation)—into something more concrete, familiar, and personal, enabling him to better grapple with technical concepts, unpack abstract relationships, follow logical reasoning, and understand the text.

During reading, Kang annotated both on the margins of the text and in separate blank sheets of paper to jot down his thoughts or to verify calculation. Writing, scribbling, drawing, and calculating slowed him down, giving him time to ponder, visualize, digest, and evaluate important or potentially challenging information in the text. Kang valued this slow-down process of annotating because it helped clarify his thinking and improve his understanding. The written notes and diagrams helped him visualize what he was reading, enabling him to come up with a situation model that assisted with his text comprehension and problem solving. He indicated that although different people have different styles, his style was "very visual", such that when he read into a part of mathematics, he might have that picture in his mind. Visualizing helped him make sense of not only logic but more importantly, mathematical theories and principles. Similar to visualization, imagination is also "very important" to mathematics sense making. According to Kang, many mathematicians develop a visual imagination of the things that are going on in the text. He acknowledged that even though mathematics is a very logical subject, when it comes to research, a considerable amount of visual imagination is needed.

To summarize, reading is an integral part of mathematicians' social practice. Mathematics scholars engage in wide reading and use a variety of strategies to help them make sense of the texts they are reading. These strategies include rereading, zooming in (i.e., close reading), zooming out (skimming), deconstructing, coordinating, sourcing, corroborating, monitoring, questioning, evaluating, verifying, summarizing, paraphrasing, storying, drawing on prior knowledge and experience, connecting visual with prose, annotating, visualizing, and imagining. They constitute the meaning-making repertoire that mathematicians use in their literate practice.

Promoting Reading in Mathematics Teaching and Learning

Mathematics teachers play an important role in developing students' mathematical literacy. To maximize their impact on students' learning of mathematics, teachers need to have deep knowledge about the domain of mathematics, the essence and worth of mathematics as a discipline, big ideas of mathematics related to grade-level curricular goals, the challenges students are likely to encounter in learning those ideas, and effective ways of teaching and assessing those ideas (Hoffmann & Even, 2018; NCTM, 2000). Because reading is central to learning and doing mathematics, mathematics teachers need to recognize the literacy demands of their subject and explicitly teach students how to read, interpret, and write mathematics texts on a regular basis (Borasi & Siegel, 2000; Chandler-Olcott, Doerr, Hinchman, & Masingila, 2015). Given the multisemiotic and multimodal nature of mathematics texts, it is essential that students develop the capacity to make sense of, as well as use, the three meaning-making resources in mathematics (i.e., natural language, mathematics symbolism, and visual display), each of which has its own conventions and poses specific challenges. Teachers can support this development work by creating opportunities for students to read and discuss mathematics texts, conducting explicit instruction on the mathematics register, and promoting multiple representations of mathematical ideas and communication of mathematical thinking and reasoning.

Creating Opportunities to Read and Discuss Mathematics Texts

Traditionally, reading is seldom, if ever, an explicit focus in mathematics teaching and learning. This needs to change if students are to become truly mathematically literate. Teachers can promote mathematics reading by creating opportunities for students to regularly read and explore mathematics texts. School mathematics textbooks provide rich information about mathematics theories, concepts, principles, procedures, processes, and problems that students are expected to learn or solve. Each unit of instruction should include activities that require students to read, wrestle with, and interpret texts that define, describe, explain, prove, or discuss relevant mathematics concepts, ideas, and operations. Reading and discussing mathematics texts on a regular basis can help students build conceptual and procedural knowledge and at the same time instill in them the understanding that reading is integral to learning and doing mathematics.

Teachers can scaffold students' interaction with mathematics texts by designing tasks and visual aids that prompt them to access their prior knowledge, set a purpose for reading, develop an interest in reading, recognize the overall text structure, become metacognitive about their meaning-making process, and assess their understanding (Draper, 2002; Thompson et al., 2008). For example, prior to reading, teachers can ask students to preview the text by skimming the title, (sub)headings, and visual displays to gain a general sense of what the text is about and develop questions that engage their reading and sustain their attention. After reading, students can complete a Frayer model (see Figure 5.7) by providing a definition, characteristics, examples, non-examples, and a visual representation for a key concept or vocabulary word in the text. They can also summarize what has been read, evaluate the content of the text, or apply the ideas in the text to new situations.

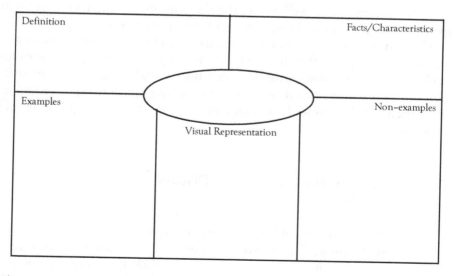

Figure 5.7 A Frayer Model

Teachers can also create an anticipation guide, which is a series of true or false statements about the topic or concept under study, and have students determine, before reading, which statement is true and which statement is false based on their current knowledge. After reading, students return to the statements, review the responses they made before reading, decide whether they have changed their mind regarding these statements, and cite evidence from the text to support their final decision. The true/false statements for the anticipation guide are usually small in number (5–8), focusing on key concepts, important details, challenging ideas, or potential misconceptions. They can involve a rewording of the information presented in the text, require students to detect and interpret the rules or conventions not explicitly or fully explained in specific examples of worked problems, relate to a common misconception students may have, or encourage students to think about new applications for the rules, principles, or procedures used in text examples. Anticipation guides can help teachers identify students' misconceptions and engineer productive discussion of mathematical content. They provide a valuable tool for "fostering a culture of reasoning and justification, creating habits of mind that motivate students to consider essential content ideas, develop meaningful and precise language, and deepen conceptual understanding" (Adams, Pegg, & Case, 2015, p. 504).

Another way to support students' reading of mathematics texts is to encourage them to use the comprehension strategies that experts employ during reading, including predicting, zooming out, zooming in, rereading, summarizing, paraphrasing, questioning, evaluating, storying, annotating, visualizing, and imagining. Teachers can model these strategies during read alouds and have students practice them through reciprocal teaching. In read alouds, the teacher selects a text excerpt (e.g., description of a key concept, explanation of a proof, a word problem) and reads it out loud to class. During reading, the teacher makes his/her thinking and reasoning overt, showing how s/he strives to make sense of the text by, for example, slowing down the reading to allow time for thinking and troubleshooting, underlining parts of the text to highlight key or puzzling pieces of information, formulating conjectures, making predictions, taking notes to summarize or make connections, asking questions about particular language/visual choices or operation procedures to monitor understanding, rereading portions of the text to clarify or seek understanding, rephrasing dense or technical expressions to glean meaning, drawing diagrams to visualize text information, verifying the accuracy of calculation, evaluating the rigor of an explanation or the logic of an argument, and making connections to prior knowledge or other texts.

In reciprocal teaching (Oczuks, 2003; Palincsar & Brown, 1984), students work in small groups of 4–5, reading a common selection together and stopping intermittently to discuss what has been read. Each member of the group is assigned a role and is responsible for performing the role during group discussion. Possible roles include summarizer (who highlights the key ideas presented thus far in the text), questioner (who asks a question about an unclear, confusing, or uncertain part of the text), clarifier (who attempts to answer the question just posed), evaluator (who verifies the accuracy of calculation in the text), translator (who translates verbal information in the text into a mathematical expression and/or a visual display), storyteller (who tells a made-up story using the information provided in the text for its plot and characters), detective (who identifies a rule or an assumption not fully explained in a mathematical operation), and forecaster (who offers predictions about what the next part of the text will be about). The selection of roles will depend on the genre of the text to be read (e.g., a concept definition vs. a geometry proof vs. an algebra word problem). Some of these roles may be more appropriate for some types of texts than others. Students can switch roles or assume new roles throughout the reading (or across reading sessions) so that they have the opportunity to try out different strategies.

When reading word problems, teachers can have students work through a mathematics problem-solving heuristic (MPSH) chart (see Table 5.1) by answering the seven questions proposed by Huang and Normandia (in Fang & Schleppegrell, 2008, pp. 66–67). These questions do not have to be answered in a strictly linear order, as students can always go back to previous question(s) before proceeding further down the list. The first two questions are reading intensive, requiring students to read and comprehend the text. Here, teachers can assist students by drawing their attention to the ways requests to solve problems are made in word problems. For example, a word problem may request information by asking

- *how many/how much/how far/what*, as in *How many pens did he have at first? How much more water is needed to fill the tub and the tank completely? How far is the bus when it passes Town A?* and *What is the radius of the circle that passes through X, Y, and Z?*, which suggests that the answer will involve a quantity
- *which/where*, as in *Where is the circumcenter of a right triangle?* and *Which two of the triangles below must be congruent?*, which suggests that a choice is to be made between two or more answers, or
- *why*, as in *Is it possible for there to be points E and F on side BC of △ABC such that BE=EF=FC and ∠BAE=∠EAF= ∠FAC? Why or why not?*, which suggests a rationale is to be articulated but may also involve the mathematical process of computing or proving.

Table 5.1 Mathematics Problem-Solving Heuristic (MPSH) Chart

Word Problem:	
1. What is the problem to be solved?	
2. What relevant information is provided in the text?	
3. Which mathematical concepts are indicated or signaled in the information?	
4. What are the mathematical principles needed for solving the given problem?	
5. What procedures do I follow to use those principles in solving the problem?	
6. What is the solution that results from these procedures?	
7. How can I justify the solution? (Does the solution make sense?)	

Questions asked with these *wh-* words can sometimes be quite complex (e.g., *For what value(s) of k is x–2 a factor of $x^3 + 2ks^2 + k^2 x + k–4$? What fraction of the day did he spend on working on the project?*), such that students may have trouble recognizing what they are being asked to do. Sometimes, problems use commands that explicitly direct students to do something to solve the problem (e.g., <u>Prove</u> *that the sum of the lengths of the diagonals of a quadrilateral is greater than half the perimeter of the quadrilateral.* <u>Compute</u> *the positive integer x such that $4x^3 – 41x^2 + 10x = 1989$.* <u>Show</u> *that it is impossible for any 5-pointed star like ABCDEFGHIJ on right to have AB>BC, CD>DE, EF>FG, GH>HI, and IJ>JA.* <u>Solve</u> *the following inequalities.* <u>Find</u> *the area of trapezoid ABCD shown on right.* <u>Factor</u> *abc-ab-bc-ca+a+b+c-1*).

After identifying the task to be performed, students need to recognize key information provided in the problem. This often involves careful reading and detailed analysis of language through which the information is presented, a task that many students find forbidding and will need to be scaffolded by teachers (see next section). Caution needs to be exercised here about over-reliance on "key words" as a way to determine a particular operation to be taken (e.g., "in all" signals addition and "left" signals subtraction) because the approach can often be unreliable. Answering questions 3–6 in the MPSH chart depends on students' knowledge of mathematics, but whether they are able to retrieve and apply relevant mathematics schema depends heavily on the extent to which they have comprehended the text. To answer the last question, students need to bring together the information presented in the text and the mathematics schema they have accessed.

Besides textbook reading, students can also read stories about mathematics topics and biographies of mathematicians. Stories are part of the fabric and life of all human experiences (Gabriel, 2000). They help us make sense of ourselves and of the world around us and share that understanding with others (Newkirk, 2014; Wells, 1986). As such, stories are a powerful tool for learning, problem solving, and sense making in disciplinary learning. They help us turn dense ideas and abstract symbols into concrete scenarios consistent with how we typically perceive, live, and interpret our lives. For this reason, Borasi, Sheedy, and Siegel (1990) have suggested that reading and writing mathematical stories should be seen as an important learning event in mathematics classrooms, rather than just an "enrichment" activity. They explored the educational potential of mathematics stories for "familiarizing students not only with the final product but also with the whole process involved in solving a mathematical problem" (p. 181). They highlighted aspects of a story about a protagonist and his wife trying to find an ideal location in New York City for their future apartment that provided (a) a familiar context for understanding non-Euclidean geometry, (b) authentic problems for which the reader has not previously been taught a method of solution, (c) a real reason for solving the problems, and (d) the potential for alternative solutions, none of which seems possible when working with preset problems. They noted that the protagonist's report of and reflection on his thought processes while trying to define, explore, evaluate, and redefine solutions dovetailed with the emotions connected with genuine problem solving in mathematics—confusion, frustration, elation, and disappointment.

Another way to bring stories into mathematics classrooms is through the reading and discussion of mathematics trade books, including stories, such as *Sir Cumference and the Dragon of Pi* (Neuschwander & Weber, 2019), and biographies of mathematicians, such as *Significant Figures: The Lives and Work of Great Mathematicians* (Stewart, 2017). These books tell stories (with characters, questions or problems, and solutions) about a mathematics topic that students tend to see as abstract and detached from their personal lives. They can stimulate students' interest, hold their attention, and engage them in deeper learning. They have been found effective for teaching about the nature of mathematics, important mathematics concepts, the process of mathematics inquiries, the impact of mathematics discoveries, and personal and professional attributes that contribute to the success of mathematicians (e.g., Capraro & Capraro, 2006; Gunbas, 2015). Borasi,

Sheedy, and Siegel (1990) cautioned, however, that "reading mathematical stories is unlikely to have an impact on students unless it is embedded in a learning context which values the thinking process over the attainment of right answers" (p. 182).

Teaching the Mathematics Register

The activities described above give teachers a structure with which to support students' mathematics reading and learning. They work to create "a student-centered, constructivist classroom" (Draper, 2002, p. 525), providing students with the practice they need to develop as strategic readers and independent learners. Additional support can be provided through an explicit and functional focus on the mathematics register, the official language of mathematics, during mathematics instruction (Schleppegrell, 2007; Wilkinson, 2018). As discussed earlier, mathematics language is highly technical, dense, and abstract, presenting a serious challenge to students, especially English language learners (ELLs) and struggling readers, in their mathematics reading and learning (Avalos, Medina, & Secada, 2015; Beal & Galan, 2015; Lager, 2006; Martiniello, 2008; Walkington et al., 2018). A focus on mathematics language entails learning not just a set of new vocabulary words that encapsulates technical mathematics concepts (e.g., *radicals, polynomials, tangents, functions, reciprocals, slope*) but also new styles of meaning and modes of argument involving both verbal and visual resources. According to Burton and Morgan (2000), who analyzed 53 published mathematics research papers and interview data involving 70 mathematics scholars, mathematicians foreground impersonality through the use of passive voice, assert authority through the use of boosters (e.g., *it is obvious that, clearly*) and the indeterminate use of first person plural pronoun (*we*), moderate claims through the use of hedges (e.g., *could, possibly*), engage and persuade readers through a narrative style that uses interactive personal pronouns (*we* or *I*) and timeless present tense, indicate membership within the mathematics community through co-authorship and references to the work of other mathematicians, claim status for and value of their work through demarcation of territory and of knowledge, project different images of the nature of mathematical activity (e.g., pure vs. applied), present the source of new mathematics knowledge as primarily from within the system of mathematics itself (i.e., mathematical objects rather than humans), and occasionally indicate the human processes of doing mathematics through expressions of opinions or feelings, conjectures, questions, or explanations for decision. Understanding the linguistic (and other semiotic) tools mathematicians use to construe technical content of the discipline, present their disciplinary identities to the world, and represent the nature of mathematics and mathematical activity is an important dimension of mathematics literacy that students should be expected to develop. As Johnson et al. (2011) have advocated, "Apprentices of mathematics must learn the language of math, the syntax and grammar of proof, and learn how to read the classic texts, which use more mathematical language than current textbooks" (p. 105). Explicit teaching of the language of mathematics has been found to improve students' understanding of mathematics content (Espinas & Fuchs, 2022; Zagata, Payne, & Arsenault, 2021).

One oft-recommended strategy for helping students cope with the challenges of mathematics reading, particularly in relation to word problems, is linguistic simplification. Some examples of linguistic simplification are presented in Table 5.2, where the more abstract and dense language of Version A is modified into the less complex and more concrete language of Version B. The effects of the modification on students' mathematics performance have been found to be largely positive but small and only occasionally statistically significant (see Clinton, Basaraba, & Walkington, 2018 for a systematic review). For example, Abedi and Lord (2001) modified the language of 69 released mathematics items from the 1992 National Assessment of Educational Progress (NAEP) to make meaning more accessible to students. For each item, they kept the mathematics task, mathematics vocabulary, and the visual display, but changed potentially challenging non-mathematics vocabulary and linguistic structures by

- replacing unfamiliar or infrequently used words/phrases with familiar, common, or concrete ones (e.g., *travel at a uniform speed → travel at the same speed*)
- switching from passive verb forms to active verb forms (e.g., *if a marble is taken from the bag → if you take a marble from the bag*)
- shortening long noun phrases (e.g., *the pattern of the puppy's weight gain → the pattern above*)
- replacing conditionals with separate sentences or changing the order of conditional and main clauses (e.g., *If two batteries in the sample were found to be dead → he found two broken skateboards in the sample*)
- changing complexly-worded questions into more straightforwardly-worded questions (e.g., *Which of the following is the best approximation of the number of apples in the basket? → About how many apples are in the basket?*)
- removing or recasting relative clauses (e.g., *the total number of newspapers that Lee delivers in 5 days → how many newspapers does Lee deliver in 5 days?*) and
- making abstract or impersonal presentations more concrete (e.g., *25 purchases were made at a fast food company → The McDonald's sold 25 burgers*).

Table 5.2 Examples of Linguistic Simplification

Version A	Version B
Jim has ¾ of a yard of string that he wishes to divide into pieces, each 1/8 of a yard long. How many pieces will he have?	Jim divides ¾ yard of string into pieces. Each piece is 1/8 yard long. How many pieces of string will he have?
Find the balance of an account with $1200 and an interest rate of 5% compounded annually for 7 years.	Ms. Brown has an account with Bank of America. The account has $1200 in it. The money earns a 5% interest. The interest is compounded every year. How much money will Ms. Brown have in her bank account by the end of seventh year?

The researchers reported that when 1174 eighth graders from 11 schools in the Greater Los Angeles area were given the original and simplified versions of the same math test, most chose the simplified version and performed slightly better on it than they did on the original version. Students in low-level and average math classes, students from low socioeconomic backgrounds, and English language learners benefited more from the revisions than, respectively, those in high level mathematics and algebra classes, those from middle and high socioeconomic backgrounds, and those who are proficient speakers of English. Comparable findings were reported by Huang (2019), who administered two versions of the same math test—an original version and a linguistically simplified version—to 254 seventh- and eighth-grade students in five southern California schools. The researcher reported that both English language learners (ELLs) and non-ELLs scored slightly higher on the modified version than on the original version and that the gain is, surprisingly, greater for non-ELLs than for ELLs, although no statistically significant differences were found in both comparisons.

These findings raise caution about the recommendation for linguistic simplification. Linguistic simplification carries with it the risk of compromising precision, clarity, or logic, all of which are of paramount importance to mathematics (Schleppegrell, 2007). It is possible that while the task of simplifying language makes words and sentences more accessible to students, it may sometimes result in text that is less clear, less precise, less coherent, and, thus, more difficult to comprehend. It is also likely that not all potentially challenging linguistic features are identified for modification because the difficulties of a text lie in the interaction between the text and the reader. In the following set of problems used in Huang (2019), for example, the modified version takes out the sentence in the original version that provides the context for the problem (i.e., Ms. *Thierry and 3 friends ate at a restaurant.*), which is important to problem solving in mathematics (Martiniello, 2008). It deletes a conjunctive phrase, *in addition*, that signals the relationship between the bill and the tip, implying the $67 does not include the $13 tip. It also fails to simplify the last sentence, which may be challenging for students to understand. Thus, even though the modified version is shorter than the original version, it is likely more ambiguous and thus more difficult to comprehend because the context of the problem is lost and the relationship between bill and tip is buried.

> Original: Ms. *Thierry and 3 friends ate dinner at a restaurant. The bill was $67. In addition, they left a $13 tip. Approximately what percent of the total bill did they leave as a tip?*
>
> Modified: *A restaurant bill is $67. The tip is $13. Approximately what percent of the bill is the tip?*

Additionally, students' English language proficiency and mathematics knowledge may moderate the effects of linguistic simplification. Huang (2019) suggested that the ELLs in her study did not benefit much from linguistic simplification because their English proficiency level was so low that further simplification might be needed. She also reported that students in schools with more rigorous mathematics instruction appeared not to benefit much from linguistic simplification. Relatedly, Barbu and Beal (2010) reported that students performed more poorly on math word problems that are both linguistically and mathematically challenging than on word problems that are just linguistically challenging.

Given the potential risks associated with linguistic simplification, it may be wise to focus attention on helping students learn to control the mathematics register. After all, learning the mathematics register is the sine qua non of learning mathematics (Chapman, 2003). The mathematics register is challenging due to its use of technical, dense, and abstract language in conjunction with mathematics symbols and visual representations. Students do not typically come to school well equipped with knowledge of the mathematics register; they learn it in the process of doing mathematics in school. Teachers can support this learning through oral explanation of mathematics content (Pimm, 1987; Veel, 1999). Specifically, they can use a classroom discourse framework developed by Herbel-Eisenmann (2002) that engages students in multiple ways of talking about concepts and ideas in mathematics texts. The framework recognizes the multimodal/multisemiotic nature of the mathematics register and draws on students' everyday language as a resource to learn the more technical language of mathematics. It introduces the notion of "bridging" to help students move among three types of language that roughly parallel the three strands of language in literacy development discussed in Chapter 1 and elaborated in Fang (2012)—from contextualized language through bridging language to mathematical language, and vice versa—as they talk about mathematical ideas/concepts using both student contributions and multiple representations. Contextualized language, or everyday language, is language that is dependent on specific, recurring contexts. It cannot usually be understood without reference to the immediate physical context in which communication takes place. Bridging language, or instructional language, is language generated by students and teachers in discussion about specific mathematical objects or representations without contextual references. It bridges contextualized language and mathematical language. Mathematical language refers to discipline-legitimated language recognized by the mathematics community. It is part of the mathematics register. Continual and frequent shifts in classroom discourse among these three more or less mathematical kinds of language makes mathematics concepts/ideas more accessible to students and facilitates their construction of mathematical meanings and disciplinary understanding. These shifts are, according to Chapman (1993), necessary to learning mathematics in school classrooms. The particular language choices the teacher makes in these shifts enable students to draw on their everyday language and funds of knowledge, connect with real-world contexts, and use learning in other subjects to facilitate engagement with challenging new concepts or ideas that involves reading and working with the mathematics register (Gonzalez, 2021).

To facilitate these classroom talks in mathematically meaningful ways, teachers can adopt the six discourse moves that Herbel-Eisenmann, Steele, and Cirillo (2013) have identified as particularly effective in engaging students and promoting understanding. They are waiting (wait time), inviting student participation, revoicing, asking students to revoice, probing a student's thinking, and creating opportunities to engage with another student's reasoning. Wait time, a period of uninterrupted silence between the time when a question is asked and the time when the question is answered, is critical to productive and powerful discourse. It gives students time to process teacher questions, think about their own responses, and make sense of others' actions. Research by noted science educator Mary Budd Rowe (1974) shows that teachers typically wait 0.7–1.5 seconds before speaking after they have asked a question; however, when teachers utilize wait times of 3 seconds or more, there are demonstrated increases in student creativity and learning.

"Inviting student participation" encourages all students to take risks and be active participants in meaning making and problem solving. It is used to solicit multiple solution processes or strategies for the same answer or to determine how students arrived at their answers. Revoicing occurs when the teacher repeats, rephrases, explains, or comments on what a student has just said. It gives the teacher an opportunity to model the use of mathematics language to define/explain/conjecture/argue mathematically, clarify students' contributions, correct possible misconceptions, and stimulate interactions among students. In the following discussion about linear functions shared by Chapman (1993, p. 38), the teacher rewords, comments, and elaborates on students' responses, modeling a more mathematical way of talking about linear functions. For example, Arthur's answer, which is essentially correct, is put into a more "proper" sentence structure. Stuart's answer is repeated and his term "the same" is clarified as "the same amount" as the teacher probes the thinking/reasoning behind the answer.

Teacher: So far we've had functions we could call linear. What were the distinguishing features of our linear functions? Arthur?
Arthur: A straight line.
Teacher: They formed a straight line. What else can you tell me about linear functions in terms of the tables of values? Stuart?
Stuart: It always went up by the same.
Teacher: It always went up by the same. So how did you think that, how did you know that it always went up by the same amount?

Similarly, "asking students to revoice" gives them an opportunity to clarify, elaborate on, visualize, add, or modify information to their initial contribution. "Probing a student's thinking" encourages students to make explicit their thinking and reasoning behind the solution, strategy, or question they have contributed. "Creating opportunities to engage with another student's reasoning" allows the teacher to invite students to add to or revise another student's explanation or conjecture, try out a problem-solving strategy proposed by a particular student, or evaluate a solution contributed by one of their peers.

Explicit attention to mathematics language can also be achieved through functional language analysis (Fang & Schleppegrell, 2008, 2010) (see also Chapters 3 and 4). Teachers can spotlight unique features of mathematical language during reading of mathematics texts, showing students how to unpack the meanings in dense noun phrases, identify relationships that are constructed in verbs and conjunctions, and detect meanings that might have been left implicit in the formulation of statement or problem

(O'Halloran, 2000; Schleppegrell, 2007). For example, when reading this word problem in algebra—*Is there a greater difference between the number of flowers planted in a park in March and April or in April and May?*—the teacher can draw students' attention to the compact, yet somewhat confusing, nature of the question, due to the use of ellipsis and the incorrect use of "*between . . . or . . .*", letting them know that the expected comparison is between A and B, with A being the difference between the number of flowers planted in March and the number of flowers planted in April and B being the difference between the number of flowers planted in April and the number of flowers planted in May. And when reading this sentence in a test item—*You can find the number that when added to 7 equals 56.*—the teacher can tell students that "*when added to 7*" is a subordinate (conditional) clause that interrupts the main clause "*You can find the number that equals 56.*" but specifies the condition under which the number equals 56. A comma should have been inserted before and after the subordinate clause to make meaning clearer, as in "*You can find the number that, when added to 7, equals 56.*" Alternatively, the subordinate/conditional clause can be placed at the end of the sentence, as in "*You can find the number that equals 56 when added to 7.*" The full form of the subordinate clause is "when it (the number) is added to 7".

Similarly, when reading this tangent-chord theorem—*The measure of an angle formed by a chord and a tangent line to a circle is equal to that of the inscribed angle on the other side of the chord.*—the teacher can, besides defining and diagrammatically illustrating technical terms such as "tangent line" and "inscribed circles", show students how the two long noun phrases in the statement are constructed (see Table 5.3), explaining that the key piece of information in either phrase is its head "*the measure*" and "*that*", respectively, with the latter ("*that*") acting as a substitute for the former ("*the measure*") to avoid verbatim repetition. Such discussion can enhance students' interpretation of both visual representation (see Figure 5.8) and symbolic representation ($\angle$BAD $\cong \angle$BCA), resulting in better overall understanding of the theorem. It also enhances students' awareness of the ways language is used in mathematics meaning making.

When reading the following problem from an intermediate algebra textbook (see Text 5.1), the teacher can draw students' attention to the words "let", "when", and "if", telling them that although the three words, as well as words like "assume", "suppose", or "pretend", all construe the conditional in some way, there are subtle differences among them. The word "let" is generally used to assign a mathematical value to a symbol so that a condition for the purpose of an exercise can be set up. The word "assume" is used to reason

Table 5.3 Explaining the structure of mathematical language

the measure	*of an angle*	*formed by a chord and a tangent line to a circle*
This is the head of the noun phrase.	This is a prepositional phrase qualifying the head ("the measure").	This is a non-finite clause that modifies "an angle". It specifies how the angle is constructed. Its full form is "the angle is formed by a chord and a tangent line to a circle".
that	*of the inscribed angle*	*on the other side of the chord*
This is the head of the noun phrase. It is used in place of "the measure" to avoid repetition.	This is a prepositional phrase qualifying the head ("that").	This is a prepositional phrase specifying where the inscribed angle can be located.

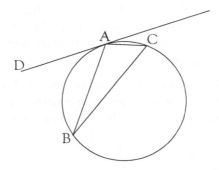

Figure 5.8 Visual Representation of the Tangent–Chord Theorem

based on a conditional proposition or to prove implications. The word "suppose" or "pretend" assumes the truth value of a statement or proposition and is used to set up a hypothetical situation. The word "if" can be used to write a converse, inverse, and contrapositive to the conditional. And while "if" is used to introduce a possible or unreal condition, "when" is used to refer to a condition that we are certain of. Another area of attention could be the technical terminology such as *positive constant, quotient, remainder, coefficient,* and *roots,* as well as symbols such as $f(x)$, which represents the value of the function, and $(x-a)q_1(x)$, which denotes a series of computational operations. The word "respectively" is also worthy of attention. It clarifies the order of the two items mentioned in a previous statement, allowing the reader to identify $q_1(x)$ as the quotient and r_1 as the remainder. In short, discussion of language choices in mathematics texts reveals how mathematics knowledge and reasoning are constructed through language and other semiotic choices (e.g., symbols, images), helping students develop more explicit, precise, and nuanced understanding of the nature and role of language (and other semiotic resources) in mathematics meaning making.

Text 5.1

Let $f(x)$ be a polynomial and a be a positive constant. Let $f(x)=(x-a)q_1(x) + r_1$, so that $q_1(x)$ and r_1 are the quotient and remainder, respectively, when $f(x)$ is divided by $x-a$. If r_1 is positive and the coefficients of $q_1(x)$ are all nonnegative, explain why $f(x)$ has no roots that are greater than a. (Rusczyk & Crawford, 2013, p. 214)

Communicating Mathematics Through Writing

Not only do students need to participate orally in mathematics sense making and problem solving, they also need to write to describe reasoned conjectures, explain solution process, present arguments about theorems, and keep ongoing records of learning (Morgan, 1998; Moschkovich, 1999; Pugalee, 2005; Thompson et al., 2008). These writing activities, to be completed in conjunction with reading, help students organize ideas, clarify thinking, deepen conceptual understanding, develop fluency with the mathematics register, become metacognitive about learning, and ultimately improve competence in mathematics reading and problem solving. The writing product also gives teachers a window into students' thought processes and understandings, providing useful information that can inform subsequent lesson planning. According to Burton and Morgan (2000), addressing mathematical writing explicitly in the classroom can "make successful participation in mathematical practices more accessible for all students" (p. 450).

For these reasons, NCTM (2000) considers writing "an essential part of mathematics and mathematics education" (p. 60), recommending that students be provided with ample opportunities to write about mathematics concepts, processes, problems, and experiences in the classroom. Zagata, Payne, and Arsenault (2021) identified four main types and purposes of writing that students can do in the mathematics classroom. These are (a) exploratory writing, which helps students explore and make sense of a given problem of their own ideas, (b) informative or explanatory writing, which describes or explains a mathematics concept or a process, (c) argumentative writing, which constructs or critiques a mathematics argument or proof, and (d) creative writing, which is to provide space for students to demonstrate original ideas and flexible thinking about mathematics. In all these types of writing, clarity and accessibility are highly valued. In this connection, it is worth bearing in mind Burton and Morgan's (2000) observation that "clarity is not absolute; it is relative to the context and, in particular, to the expectations and prior knowledge of readers" (p. 434).

More specifically, teachers can ask students to write formal definitions of key concepts in mathematics. Definitions, a type of informative writing, are essential to mathematics; they contribute to the creation of new mathematical objects, characterization of these objects, and description of relationships among these objects. A new definition can be the start of a lengthy investigation into new mathematical questions and discoveries. Mathematics textbooks are populated with definitions, and students often struggle to comprehend them because these definitions are typically constructed in highly compact, dense syntax featuring precision, rigor, formality, and hierarchy, as can be seen in the two examples below, where the concepts being defined are highlighted in bold:

- An expression or function with more than one variable is **a multivariable polynomial** if it is a sum of terms such that each term is a product of a constant and a nonnegative integer power of each variable. (Rusczyk & Crawford, 2013, p. 261)
- **A convex polygon** is a polygon such that no line containing a side of the polygon contains a point in the interior of the polygon. (Jurgensen, Brown & Jurgensen, 2004, p. 101)

An academic, or formal, definition is usually "a concise, logical statement that identifies the characteristics of the concept being defined and reveals its relationships to other concepts in the same class" and typically consists of "the target term to be defined, a linking verb, the class to which the term belongs, and an embedded clause that expands on the concept by providing further details about what it does, looks like, or is made of" (Fang, 2021, pp. 65–66). Producing a formal definition of a disciplinary concept requires linguistic resources different from those needed for an informal definition. In mathematics, a definition usually calls for the use of precise lexicon (e.g., technical vocabulary) and dense syntax (e.g., long noun phrases with prepositional phrases and embedded clauses), as well as conditional and resultative clauses that qualify statements (e.g., *if . . ., when . . ., such that . . .*). The ability to write a formal definition is positively correlated with reading scores on standardized tests (Gini, Benelli, & Belacchi, 2004; Snow et al., 1989). Galloway and Uccelli (2015) found that middle school students still have difficulties producing definitions that meet academic expectations due to a lack of the linguistic resources needed for the task. They advocated the use of "language-conscious instruction, or instruction that supports writers to attend to a range of language choices as they learn to convey their meanings" in disciplinary learning contexts (p. 821). In other words, teachers can draw students' attention to features of mathematics language during the reading and discussion of mathematics texts, design exercises to deepen students' understanding of the forms and functions of these features, and encourage students to use the features when writing definitions (and other genres). Burton and Morgan (2000) believed that promoting critical awareness, through (functional) analysis of text, of how language fashions and influences meaning is an important avenue to improving students' written communication in mathematics, including writing definitions. They elaborated,

> [K]nowledge of the forms of language that are highly valued within mathematical discourses and of the effects that may be achieved by various linguistic choices would not just help writers to conform to conventional expectations but would also empower them to make informed choices to break the conventions in order to achieve deliberate effects, including to demonstrate creativity and to express their own personalities through their writing. (p. 431)

When writing a definition, students need to recognize that one mathematical concept can be defined in multiple ways (e.g., a rectangle could be defined as "parallelogram with one right angle" or "a quadrilateral with four right angles"), with each definition containing a different set of attributes and assumptions (Thompson & Rubenstein, 2014). Before writing a definition, students should have the opportunity to study several technical mathematics definitions. For each definition, they can start by reading the definition several times, trying to identify what "things" (e.g., concepts, attributes, conditions) the definition is talking about, how these "things" are structured syntactically, and what lexical and grammatical resources are used to present these "things" and package them into a sentence. Once students understand how definitions are constructed and equipped with the linguistic resources to construct them, they can practice writing sample definitions by first jotting down the defining properties and necessary conditions related to the target concept and thinking about ways to compact and package them into a grammatically correct sentence structure. They then share in small groups, discussing whether their definitions make sense and are complete, noncircular, precise, succinct, and clear, as well as how they can be improved. Writing definitions helps students develop the habit to think concisely, precisely, logically, and clearly. It can also help them better comprehend definitions in mathematics texts specifically and in academic texts generally.

Teachers can also have students write explanations that describe and justify the process they went through in arriving at the solution for a problem they have been working on, encouraging them to use the tools mathematicians employ in their meaning making—including words, symbols, diagrams, physical models, and technology—to present and defend their ideas. Too often, students care more about finding the correct answer to a problem than reflecting on the process they took to get to the answer, with the consequence that they often have trouble applying what they think they know to new but similar problems. Students can use a three-column chart (see Figure 5.9 for a sample) that describes the steps they took to solve a problem and the reason or logic underlying their decision for each step of the process. The chart provides students with a platform to make their thinking and reasoning visible, helping them monitor their own problem-solving process and compare it with those of their peers. It also makes it easier for the teacher to review students' work, helping him/her identify what students knew and did well, what went wrong, and where/why breakdowns occurred.

Alternatively, students can write in an essay form when describing how they solved a problem and justifying why their method is correct. Some useful linguistic resources for describing the problem-solving process include sequencing devices (e.g., *first, second, third, to begin with, next, also, another step, the next step, a further step, prior to, previously, after, when, until, at the same time, follow, later, in the following steps, subsequently, finally*), reasoning devices (e.g., *since, because, therefore, so, hence, accordingly, thus, it follows that, such that, we see that, then*), conditional devices (*provided that, assuming, if, given, suppose, when, let, where x stands for . . .*), proving devices (e.g., *show, find, demonstrate, prove, explain why, indicate*), reminding devices (e.g., *notice, note that, recall*), and referring devices (e.g., *using the formula above, see the equation below, this tells us that . . .*). Students should be encouraged to maximize their use of the mathematics register in their writing; however, the expectation needs to take into account students' ability level if it is going to foster the development of mathematics knowledge.

Finally, students should be encouraged to write their own problems, particularly word problems (Thompson et al., 2008). Picot and Schneider (2021) identified four common types of word problems in mathematics textbooks that students can attempt to write: process, content, narrative, and affective. The process problem requires students to explain the process they encounter when solving the problem and to reflect on why they used the steps

Mathematical Operations	Verbal Description of Steps	Justification for Steps

Figure 5.9 Explanation Chart

or the specific strategy to solve the problem. The content problem requires students to define a mathematics concept, compare/contrast mathematics concepts, or explain relationships among concepts/ideas in mathematics. The narrative problem requires students to demonstrate an understanding of mathematics concepts aligned to imaginary or real-world application. The affective problem requires students to write a response expressing their feelings or opinion about a specific mathematics concept or topic. According to Picot and Schneider (2021), teachers typically use these types of word problems "as a formative assessment measure", "as a vehicle for teaching and uncovering skills/strategies", "as a discourse method for communicating mathematically", and "as a tool for the facilitation of real-world mathematics" (p. 61).

To write a problem, students must know the structure of the problem, understand the mathematics concepts and principles behind the problem, and have the appropriate linguistic, symbolic, and visual resources to instantiate the problem. Writing their own problems gives students an opportunity to connect what they are learning to their lived experiences, use the mathematics register in meaningful contexts, and demonstrate their conceptual understanding. Teachers can then analyze students' writing to identify their strengths and weaknesses and use the information to guide lesson planning. For example, when students express, in writing, the information presented in the following diagram (Figure 5.10), which compares the number of lost dogs and cats in an animal shelter that has lost numerous dogs and cats over a decade of service (MacGregor, 2002), as "6 *times as many dogs as cats*", "6 *times more dogs than cats*", "6 *times as many dogs than cats*", "*dogs are 6 times* as the cats", "6 times the number of dogs compared to cats", "5 times as many dogs than cats", "5 more dogs than cats", "the number of dogs are 6 times as the cats", "there is a greater amount of dogs to cats", "the numbers of dogs are more than the number of cats", "there is a greater amount of dogs to cats", "the amount of dogs is 6 times greater than the amount of cats", "there is 6 times more dogs than cats", "there are 5 dogs more than there is a cat", or "there are 6 times as many dogs compared to cats", the teacher will discover that the issue for students is not merely a matter of conceptual understanding but, more importantly, a matter of written communication. That is, students have trouble using mathematics language to express precisely the information presented in the diagram, which is "there are 5 times more lost dogs than lost cats" or "there are 6 times as many lost dogs as lost cats". There are a few questions that students should be encouraged to consider when writing their own problems. These include: (1) Are the words used correct and precise? (2) Are the mathematical symbols used correctly? (3) Are the visual displays (e.g., tables, diagrams) clearly labeled? (4) Are all the variables defined clearly and described adequately? (5) Is the sentence structure clear and grammatically sound? (6) Are the assumptions underlying the formulas stated? and (7) Is the problem clearly articulated?

Finally, given the centrality of stories to human experience and learning in general (Gabriel, 2000; Wells, 1986) and to mathematics meaning making in particular (Fang & Chapman, 2020), it seems that students should also be encouraged to write stories as a way of making sense of mathematics concepts, ideas, and procedures. Despite concerns over the value of stories in promoting the use of the mathematics register (see, for example, Schleppegrell, 2007), story writing, which is a type of creative writing, can be an effective way of working through challenging concepts and problems because it requires the writer to pay close attention to details, experience

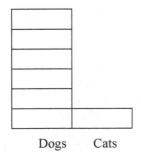

Dogs   Cats

Figure 5.10 Comparing the Number of Lost Dogs and Cats
Source: MacGregor (2002)

mathematical process and content, and develop motivation for problem solving. As humans, we need a "plot" that helps us comprehend specific information or experience the significance of an argument (Newkirk, 2014). As Wells (1986) observed, "Constructing stories in mind—or storying, as it has been called—is one of the fundamental means of making meaning; as such, it is an activity that pervades all aspects of learning" (p. 194). In other words, stories are invaluable to learning, problem solving, and sense making in disciplinary learning. They help organize, provide coherence to, and claim meaning for our experience. As such, they are a reliable means of making sense of complex issues and phenomena. Authoring a mathematics story may provide an opportunity "to generate and elaborate mathematical ideas, set and solve problems, and make decisions that highlight the key role of context, values, and so on in mathematical reasoning", giving learners "an insider's understanding of the nature of stories, which will subsequently influence their approach to reading stories" (Borasi, Sheedy, & Siegel, 1990, p. 183). It is recommended that students have ample experience with whole group modeling and peer interaction with a mathematics concept or idea before they are asked to write a story about it.

Conclusion

Engagement with mathematics is a challenging but creative process that develops rational and logical thought (Hoffmann & Even, 2018). The secondary mathematics curriculum focuses on the transition from concrete to conceptual mathematics, moving "from numbers to variables, from description to proof, and from special cases to general equations" (National Academies, 1989, p. 48). Effecting this transition requires active engagement with a variety of mathematics texts, the vast majority of which are simultaneously multisemiotic and multimodal. As Adams and Lowery (2007) pointed out, "doing mathematics is not just about manipulating numerals and symbols, but is also about developing and sharing mathematical ideas through a variety of means that support deeper learning" (p. 165). Reading can be a way of helping students gain ideas, build content knowledge, seek clarification, develop motivation, deepen conceptual understanding, increase mathematics competence, and support independent learning of mathematics (Adams, Pegg, & Case, 2015). Teachers can support students' engagement with text by teaching them how to read and interpret mathematical language, symbols, and images, as well as how to use these meaning-making resources in mathematical problem solving and communication. With the ability to read mathematics texts proficiently, students stand a better chance of developing mathematical literacy that prepares them to pursue advanced study and meet their personal and professional needs.

Reflection and Application

1 What is mathematics? Why is understanding the nature of mathematics important to the teaching and learning of mathematics?
2 What does disciplinary literacy mean in relation to mathematics? What does it mean to be reading like a mathematician?
3 What are the specific challenges involved in mathematics reading? How can these challenges be addressed?
4 What does a disciplinary literacy approach to mathematics reading instruction look like? In what ways does the approach promote mathematical literacy?
5 Design a unit of instruction for a specific grade level aimed at developing students' mathematical literacy. Be sure to identify/describe the disciplinary standards and curriculum goals to be addressed, the textual resources to be utilized, the activities and strategies to be used to promote mathematical reading and problem solving, the assessment tools to be employed to monitor and evaluate student progress toward the unit objectives, and a reasonable timeline for implementing the unit.

References

Abedi, J., & Lord, C. (2001). The language factor in mathematics tests. *Applied Measurement in Education, 14*(3), 219–234.

Abramson, J. (2017). *Precalculus*. Houston, TX: Rice University.

Adams, T. (2003). Reading mathematics: More than words can say. *Reading Teacher, 56*(8), 786–795.

Adams, T., & Lowery, R. (2007). An analysis of children's strategies for reading mathematics. *Reading & Writing Quarterly, 23*, 161–177.

Adams, A., Pegg, J., & Case, M. (2015). Anticipation guides: Reading for mathematics understanding. *Mathematics Teacher, 108*(7), 498–504.

Avalos, M., Medina, E., & Secada, W. (2015). Planning for instruction: Increasing multilingual learners' access to algebraic word problems and visual graphics. In A. Bright, H. Hansen-Thomas, & L. de Oliveira (Eds.), *The common core state standards in mathematics for English language learners: High school* (pp. 5–28). Alexandria, VA: TESOL.

Barbu, O., & Beal, C. (2010). Effects of linguistic complexity and math difficulty on word problem solving by English learners. *International Journal of Education, 2*(2), 1–19.

Bass, H. (2011). Vignette of doing mathematics: A meta-cognitive tour of the production of some elementary mathematics. *The Mathematics Enthusiast, 8*(1), Article 2. https://scholarworks.umt.edu/tme/vol8/iss1/2

Beal, C. R., & Galan, F. C. (2015). Math word problem solving by English learners and English primary students in an intelligent tutoring system. *International Journal of Learning Technology, 10,* 170–184.

Bernstein, B. (2000). *Pedagogy, symbolic control and identity: Theory, research, critique* (rev. ed.). London: Rowman & Littlefield.

Borasi, R. & Siegel, M. (2000). *Reading counts: Expanding the role of reading in mathematics classrooms.* New York: Teachers College Press.

Borasi, R., Sheedy, J., & Siegel, M. (1990). The power of stories in learning mathematics. *Language Arts, 67*(2), 174–189.

Burton, L., & Morgan, C. (2000). Mathematicians writing. *Journal for Research in Mathematics Education, 31*(4), 429–453.

Caffarelli, L., Jerison, D., & Kenig, C. (2002). Some new monotonicity theorems with applications to free boundary problems. *Annals of Mathematics, 155*(2), 369–404.

Capraro, R. & Capraro, M. (2006). Are you really going to read us a story? Learning geometry through children's mathematics literature. *Reading Psychology, 27*(1), 21–36.

Capraro, M., & Joffrion, H. (2006). Algebraic equations: Can middle-school students meaningfully translate from words to mathematical symbols? *Reading Psychology, 27,* 147–164.

Chandler-Olcott, K., Doerr, H., Hinchman, K., & Masingila, J. (2015). Bypass, augment, or integrate: How secondary mathematics teachers address the literacy demands of standards-based curriculum materials. *Journal of Literacy Research, 47*(4), 439–472.

Chapman, A. (1993). Language and learning in school mathematics: A social semiotic perspective. *Issues in Educational Research, 3*(1), 35–46.

Chapman, A. (2003). *Language practices in school mathematics: A social semiotic approach.* New York: Edwin Mellen Press.

Clinton, V., Basaraba, D., & Walkington, C. (2018). English learners and mathematical word problem solving: A systematic review. *Educational Foundations and Research Faculty Publications, 6.* https://commons.und.edu/efr-fac/6

de Lange, J. (2006). Mathematical literacy for living from OECD-PISA perspective. *Tsukuba Journal of Educational Study in Mathematics, 25,* 13–35.

Draper, R. (2002). School mathematics reform, constructivism, and literacy: A case for literacy instruction in the reform-oriented mathematics classroom. *Journal of Adolescent and Adult Literacy, 45*(6), 520–529.

Espinas, D., & Fuchs, L. (2022). The effects of language instruction on math development. *Child Development Perspectives, 16*(2), 69–75.

Fang, Z. (2012). Language correlates of disciplinary literacy. *Topics in Language Disorders, 32*(1), 19–34.

Fang, Z. (2021). *Demystifying academic writing: Genres, moves, skills, and strategies.* New York: Routledge.

Fang, Z., & Chapman, S. (2020). Disciplinary literacy in mathematics: One mathematician's reading practices. *Journal of Mathematical Behavior, 59.* https://doi.org/10.1016/j.jmathb.2020.100799

Fang, Z., Chapman, S., Kellogg, G., & Commeret, M. (2023). Beyond content: Exploring the neglected dimensions of mathematics literacy. *Journal of World Languages,* https://doi.org/10.1515/jwl-2023-0015.

Fang, Z., & Schleppegrell, M. (2008). *Reading in secondary content areas: A language-based pedagogy.* Ann Arbor, MI: University of Michigan Press.

Fang, Z., & Schleppegrell, M. (2010). Disciplinary literacies across content areas: Supporting secondary reading through functional language analysis. *Journal of Adolescent and Adult Literacy, 53*(7), 587–597.

Gabriel, Y. (2000). *Storytelling in organizations: Facts, fictions, and fantasies.* New York: Oxford University Press.

Galloway, E., & Uccelli, P. (2015). Modeling the relationship between lexico-grammatical and discourse organizational skills in middle grade writers: Insights into later productive language skills that support academic writing. *Reading and Writing, 28,* 797–828.

Gantert, A. (2008). *Geometry.* New York: Amsco.

Gantert, A. (2007). *Integrated Algebra 1.* New York: Amsco.

Gini, G., Benelli, B., & Belacchi, C. (2004). Children's definitional skills and their relations with metalinguistic awareness and school achievement. *School Psychology, s*(1–2), 239–267.

Glenberg, A., Willford, J., Gibson, B., Goldberg, A., & Zhu, X. (2012). Improving reading to improve math. *Scientific Studies of Reading, 16*(4), 316–340.

Gonzalez, G. (2021). A geometry teacher's actions for engaging students in mathematizing from real-world contexts: A linguistic analysis. In M. Brisk & M. Schleppegrell (Eds.), *Language in action: SFL theory across contexts* (pp. 87–116). London: Equinox.

Grimm, K. J. (2008). Longitudinal associations between reading and mathematics achievement. *Developmental Neuropsychology, 33*(3), 410–426.

Gunbas, N. (2015). Students' mathematics word problem-solving achievement in a computer-based story. *Journal of Computer Assisted Learning, 31*(1), 78–95.

Halliday, M. (1978). *Language as social semiotic*. London: Edward Arnold.

Herbel-Eisenmann, B. (2002). Using student contributions and multiple representations to develop mathematical language. *Mathematics Teaching in the Middle School*, 8(2), 100–105.

Herbel-Eisenmann, B., Steele, M., & Cirillo, M. (2013). (Developing) teacher discourse moves: A framework for professional development. *Mathematics Teacher Educator*, 1(2), 181–195.

Hoffmann, A., & Even, R. (2018). What do mathematicians wish to teach teachers in secondary school about mathematics? In E. Bergqvist, M. Osterholm, C. Granberg, & L. Sumpter (Eds.), *Proceedings of the 42nd conference of the international group for the psychology of mathematics education* (Vol. 3, pp. 99–106). Umea, Sweden: PME.

Huang, H. (2019). *The role of language in middle school students' mathematics performance*. Unpublished doctoral dissertation, University of Florida, Gainesville, Florida.

Inglis, M., & Alcock, L. (2012). Expert and novice approaches to reading mathematical proofs. *Journal of Research in Mathematics Education*, 43(4), 358–390.

Inglis, M., & Mejia-Ramos, P. (2009). The effect of authority on the persuasiveness of mathematical argumentation. *Cognition and Instruction*, 27(1), 25–50.

Johnson, H., Watson, P., with Delahunty, T., McSwiggen, P., & Smith, T. (2011). What it is they do: Differentiating knowledge and literacy practices across content disciplines. *Journal of Adolescent and Adult Literacy*, 55(2), 100–109.

Jurgensen, R., Brown, R., & Jurgensen, J. (2004). *Geometry*. Evanston, IL: McDougal Littell.

Krawitz, J., Chang, Y., Yang, K., & Schukajlow, S. (2022). The role of reading comprehension in mathematical modelling: Improving the construction of a real-world model and interest in Germany and Taiwan. *Educational Studies in Mathematics*, 109, 337–359.

Lager, C.A. (2006). Types of mathematics-language reading interactions that unnecessarily hinder algebra learning and assessment. *Reading Psychology*, 27, 165–204.

Lemke, J. (2003). Mathematics in the middle: Measure, picture, gesture, sign, and word. In M. Anderson, A. Saenz-Ludlow, S. Zellweger, & V. Cifarellis (Eds.), *Educational perspectives on mathematics as semiosis: From thinking to interpreting to knowing* (pp. 215–234). Brooklyn, NY and Ottawa, Ontario: Legas.

MacGregor, M. (2002). Using words to explain mathematical ideas. *Australian Journal of Language and Literacy*, 25(1), 78–88.

Martiniello, M. (2008). Language and the performance of English-language learners in math word problems. *Harvard Educational Review*, 78, 333–368.

Mejia-Ramos, J., & Weber, K. (2014). Why and how mathematicians read proofs: Further evidence from a survey study. *Educational Studies in Mathematics, 85*(2), 161–173.

Morgan, C. (1998). *Writing mathematically: The discourse of investigation*. London: Palmer Press.

Moschkovich, J. (1999). Supporting the participation of English language learners in mathematical discussions. *For the Learning of Mathematics, 19*(1), 11–19.

Moschkovich, J. (2010). *Language and mathematics education: Multiple perspectives and directions for research*. Charlotte, NC: Information Age Publication.

National Academies (1989). *Everybody counts: A report to the nation on the future of mathematics education*. Washington DC: National Academies Press.

National Council of Teachers of Mathematics (2000). *Principles and standards for school mathematics*. Reston, VA: Author.

National Governors Association Center for Best Practices (NGA) & Council of Chief State School Officers (CCSSO) (2010). *Common core state standards for English language arts & literacy for history/social studies, science, and technical subjects: Appendix A*. Washington, DC: Author.

Newkirk, T. (2014). *Minds made for stories: How we really read and write informational and persuasive texts*. Portsmouth, NH: Heinemann.

Neuschwander, C., & Weber, A. (2019). *Sir Cumference and the dragon of Pi*. Watertown, MA: Charlesbridge Publishing.

Oczuks, L. (2003). *Reciprocal teaching at work: Strategies for improving reading comprehension*. Newark, DE: International Reading Association.

O'Halloran, K. (2000). Classroom discourse in mathematics: A multisemiotic analysis. *Linguistics & Education, 10* (3), 359–388.

O'Halloran, K. (2005). *Mathematical discourse: Language, symbolism and visual images*. London: Continuum.

O'Halloran, K. (2011). The semantic hyperspace: Accumulating mathematical knowledge across semiotic resources and modalities. In F. Christie & K. Maton (Eds.), *Disciplinarity: Functional linguistic and sociological perspectives* (pp. 217–236). London: Bloomsbury.

Ojose, B. (2011). Mathematics literacy: Are we able to put the mathematics we learn into everyday use? *Journal of Mathematics Education, 4*(1), 89–100.

Organization for Economic Cooperation and Development (2002). *Framework for mathematics assessment*. Paris, France: Author.

Palincsar, A., & Brown, A. (1984). Reciprocal teaching of comprehension-fostering and comprehension-monitoring activities. *Cognition and Instruction, 1*(2), 117–175.

Picot, C., & Schneider, J. (2021). Word problems in the mathematics textbook: An instructional resource guide to support writing instruction. *Transformations*, 7(1). Article 3. https://nsuworks.nova.edu/transformations/vol7/iss1/3

Pimm, D. (1987). *Speaking mathematically: Communication in mathematics classrooms.* London: Routledge.

Pugalee, D. (2005). *Writing to develop mathematical understanding.* Norwood, MA: Christopher-Gordon.

Rowe, M. (1974). Wait-time and rewards as instructional variables, their influence on language, logic, and fate control: Part one—wait-time. *Journal of Research in Science Teaching, 11*(4), 81–94.

Rubenstein, R., & Thompson, D. (2001). Learning mathematical symbolism: Challenges and instructional strategies. *Mathematics Teacher, 94*(4), 265–271.

Rusczyk, R., & Crawford, M. (2013). *Intermediate algebra.* Alpine, CA: AoPS Inc.

Schleppegrell, M. (2007). The linguistic challenges of mathematics teaching and learning: A research review. *Reading & Writing Quarterly, 23*, 139–159.

Schoenfeld, A. (2022). Why are learning and teaching mathematics so difficult? In M. Danesi (Ed.), *Handbook of cognitive mathematics* (pp. 1–35). Springer, Cham. https://doi.org/10.1007/978-3-030-44982-7_10-1

Shanahan, C., Shanahan, T., & Misischia, C. (2011). Analysis of expert readers in three disciplines: History, mathematics, and chemistry. *Journal of Literacy Research, 43*(4), 393–429.

Siebert, J., & Draper, R. (2012). Reconceptualizing literacy and instruction for mathematics classroom. In T. Jetton & C. Shanahan (Eds.), *Adolescent literacy in the academic disciplines* (pp. 172–198). New York: Guilford.

Snow, C., Cancini, H., Gonzalez, P., & Shriberg, E. (1989). Giving formal definitions: An oral language correlate of school literacy. In D. Bloome (Ed.), *Classrooms and literacy* (pp. 233–249). Norwood, NJ: Ablex.

Stewart, I. (2017). *Significant figures: The lives and work of great mathematicians.* New York: Basic Books.

Thompson, D., & Rubenstein, R. (2014). Literacy in language and mathematics: More in common than you think. *Journal of Adolescent and Adult Literacy, 58*(2), 105–108.

Thompson, D., Kersaint, G., Richards, J., Hunsader, P., & Rubenstein, R. (2008). *Mathematical literacy: Helping students make meaning in the middle grades.* Portsmouth, NH: Heinemann.

Veel, R. (1999). Language, knowledge and authority in school mathematics. In F. Christie (Ed.), *Pedagogy and the shaping of consciousness: Linguistic and social processes* (pp. 185–216). London: Continuum.

Walkington, C., Clinton, V., & Shivraj, P. (2018). How readability factors are differentially associated with performance for students of different backgrounds when solving mathematics word problems. *American Educational Research Journal, 55*(2), 362–414.

Weber, K. (2008). How mathematicians determine if an argument is a valid proof. *Journal of Research in Mathematics Education, 39*, 431–459.

Weber, K., & Mejia-Ramos, J. (2011). Why and how mathematicians read proofs: An exploratory study. *Educational Studies in Mathematics, 76*, 329–344.

Weber, K., & Mejia-Ramos, J. (2013a). On influence of sources in the reading of mathematical text: A reply to Shanahan, Shanahan, and Misischia. *Journal of Literacy Research, 45*, 87–96.

Weber, K., & Mejia-Ramos, J. (2013b). On mathematicians' proof skimming: A reply to Inglis and Alcock. *Journal of Research in Mathematics Education, 44* (2), 464–474.

Wells, G. (1986). *The meaning makers: Learning to talk and talking to learn.* Portsmouth, NH: Heinemann.

Wilkerson-Jerde, M., & Wilensky, U. (2011). How do mathematicians learn math?: Resources and acts for constructing and understanding mathematics. *Education Studies in Mathematics, 78*, 21–43.

Wilkinson, L. (2018). Teaching the language of mathematics: What the research tells us teachers need to know and do. *Journal of Mathematical Behavior, 51*, 167–174.

Zagata, E., Payne, B., & Arsenault, T. (2021). *Intensive intervention practice guide: Literacy supports for math content instruction for students with reading and language difficulty.* Washington, DC: US Department of Education, Office of Special Education Programs.

6

Developing Teacher Expertise for Academic Reading Instruction

Continuing Reading Instruction Beyond Elementary School

As students move from elementary school through middle school and into high school and college, they are expected to engage with texts in academic content areas that become increasingly technical and complex. These disciplinary texts are demanding because they present specialized topics and complex ideas about which students have limited background knowledge and employ a form of language that is typically much more technical, dense, abstract, and metaphorical than the one(s) with which students are familiar. Comprehending and interpreting these texts requires not only recognition and understanding of vocabulary and syntax, but also familiarity with disciplinary norms and habits of mind that guide the creation and consumption of texts. Adolescent learners are often not well prepared for this challenge. The "basic" and "intermediate" literacy skills and strategies (Shanahan & Shanahan, 2008) they have developed during elementary schooling are, while foundational, rarely adequate for dealing with the more advanced texts of disciplinary learning. Despite this problem, students do not typically receive further reading instruction in middle and high schools because the process of "learning to read" is commonly believed to be complete by the end of elementary schooling, and students are expected to be able to "read to learn" from content area materials in secondary (middle/high) schools and beyond. The lack of reading instruction in secondary schools has contributed to the struggle many adolescent learners experience when reading academic texts in curriculum content areas. These students clearly need support to help them navigate across disciplinary boundaries and meet the new literacy demands of disciplinary learning.

DOI: 10.4324/9781003432258-6

Who is Responsible for Teaching Academic Reading?

But whose job is it to provide the reading support for adolescent learners? Unlike in elementary schools, where the reading teacher is explicitly charged with the responsibility to teach reading, in secondary schools, reading is no long a core subject. Any reading instruction that is available to adolescents is typically remedial or supplementary in nature and generally disconnected from the core curricula of content areas, focusing on essentially the same set of basic and intermediate literacy skills/strategies that characterizes elementary reading instruction. Other reading needs of students are presumed to be addressed, if ever, by content area teachers. However, as Bain (2012, p. 517) pointed out,

> the culture of secondary schools, with its disciplinary divisions of labor, credits, certification, territorial space (e.g., science wing, social studies area), and the "coverage" demands of content-rich standards, have conspired to enable secondary teachers to "off-load" responsibility for teaching reading and writing to teachers of earlier grades or to English language arts departments.

Thus, it is not surprising that content area teachers generally do not consider reading to be within the ambit of their instructional responsibilities and are perennially resistant to taking up reading/literacy in their professional practice. Even English language arts (ELA) teachers rarely see themselves as reading teachers, believing instead that they are teachers of writing, literature, and/or grammar. Moreover, while many secondary schools today hire a reading or literacy coach, the coach is not a classroom teacher, but a school-level literacy specialist who works with administrators and teachers across content areas to identify reading/literacy issues with students or curriculum, set goals, and solve problems (Wexler, Swanson, & Shelton, 2021).

Despite these realities, there is no denying that content area teachers are best positioned to teach reading in their specialized domains. Content area texts of secondary schooling are much more technical and specialized. Traditionally prepared reading teachers (and literacy coaches) typically do not have the domain knowledge or disciplinary expertise needed to teach reading with these texts. It would indeed be challenging for a teacher or coach to teach reading—that is, how to construct meaning from a text—if the teacher/coach him/herself has trouble understanding what the text means, how the ideas in the text relate conceptually to one another and to those of other texts in the discipline, and how disciplinary texts are created and consumed. Teaching reading in a discipline requires that the teacher/

coach be well versed in the content, discourse patterns, literate practices, and habits of mind within that specific discipline. Given the way reading teachers and literacy coaches are traditionally prepared, it does not seem likely that they will have the requisite knowledge or experience to successfully implement a disciplinary literacy approach to academic reading instruction. Reading teacher or literacy coach candidates are currently not required to be subject-area specialists; nor do they typically receive formal training in a pertinent academic subject area besides reading or literacy. As a result, they often lack knowledge of disciplinary content (e.g., big ideas, unifying concepts, and key relationships) and may not be intimately familiar with disciplinary practices and habits of mind. Within the field of reading education, teacher candidates at both elementary and secondary levels receive heavy doses of training in the so-called "science of reading", which focuses on such topics as phonological awareness, phonics, vocabulary, fluency, and comprehension strategies. Little, if any, attention is paid in coursework to discipline-specific epistemologies, methodologies, discourse patterns, literacy strategies, and habits of mind. Consequently, reading teacher and literacy coach candidates generally lack knowledge of and expertise in teaching practices related to disciplinary reading, writing, and reasoning (Kavanagh & Rainey, 2017), making them not well-equipped to adopt a disciplinary literacy approach.

Similar arguments in favor of content area teachers, rather than reading teachers or literacy coaches, shouldering the reading instruction responsibility have also been made by scholars across content areas. According to mathematics education scholars Siebert and Draper (2012, pp. 184–186), for example, reading teachers or literacy coaches usually have limited experience with mathematics text creation and interpretation and are, thus, not fluent with the literacies in mathematics. They noted that because mathematics texts do not typically consist of traditional print in the form of words, sentences, and paragraphs, reading teachers or literacy coaches cannot draw on their vast knowledge of general print literacy strategies to suggest appropriate literacy instruction in mathematics. Likewise, science education scholar Jay Lemke (2002) asserted that science teachers may be better prepared to teach science reading and science language than are reading or language arts teachers because the former could acquire the necessary reading concepts in far less time than the latter would require to master the necessary science concepts. This belief about reading concepts taking less time to learn/master than content area concepts is, although debatable, reflected in the fact that most states in the United States require content area teachers to take only three credits of study (i.e., one course) in reading for the purpose of state certification (Romine, McKenna, & Robinson, 1996). In states (e.g., Florida) where reading endorsement is recently required for content area teachers, two such courses may be required, although the content of these courses is expected to similarly focus on the six components of reading that are considered to be "evidence-based" (to wit, consistent with what the "science of reading" recommends)—oral language, phonological awareness, phonics, fluency, vocabulary, and comprehension—rather than on discipline-specific language/literacy processes, demands, and practices (see, for example, Florida Department of Education, 2022).

Given the essential role reading plays in disciplinary learning and socialization, other scholars have gone one step further, arguing that reading should become an integral part of the disciplinary content that every content area teacher should be expected to learn. They noted that because text comprehension plays a crucial role in the acquisition, construction, and sharing of disciplinary knowledge, teaching students how to read texts in a discipline is just as important as teaching them the big ideas and key concepts of the discipline. When discussing science education, for example, Patterson et al. (2018) proposed that reading comprehension be considered an essential component of science teachers' professional knowledge base, arguing that developing a foundational knowledge about reading comprehension matters a great deal for science teachers because "science is fundamentally a set of ideas about the natural world—ideas that are not readily accessible only from empirical observation, but rather, must also be learnt through reading and writing" (p. 2). They further suggested that science teachers are best suited to develop students' competence in understanding science texts because they possess the necessary science content knowledge and can guide their students in identifying key science concepts, ideas, and relationships in written materials. They emphasized the importance of science teachers having a well-developed knowledge about the challenges of informational texts and instructional strategies to address these challenges with readers. In mathematics education, Osterholm (2006) wrote that "reading in itself can also be seen as an essential part of mathematics and mathematical knowledge, and not only viewed in relation to other types of activities" (p. 326). He argued that because the ability to interpret and understand mathematics texts is part of the competence of communication, which constitutes mathematical knowledge, reading and reading comprehension should be "more explicitly included in mathematics education, in the teaching as well as examinations" (p. 326). Referencing history education, Bain (2012) similarly contended that teachers must "develop an understanding of their responsibility in making history lessons literacy lessons, not just for the struggling readers, but for all their students" (p. 520).

He maintained that every content area lesson is "in its own way a lesson in disciplinary literacy" (p. 521) and that reading instruction "should not be an add-on, but rather is inherently connected to the study of the past" (p. 520). He called on history teachers to recognize the challenges their students face in using historical texts to learn history and develop practices to help students meet these literacy challenges. Taken together, there appears to be a growing consensus that reading should be part and parcel of content pedagogies and that content area teachers are best positioned to provide reading instruction in their own subject area.

What Sorts of Expertise are Needed to Teach Academic Reading?

What sorts of reading expertise do content area teachers need, then, in order to support their students' academic reading? Although secondary teachers are typically content experts and presumably familiar with disciplinary habits of mind, they often lack the knowledge and skills to effectively teach reading in their content areas. To teach reading in their content area, teachers need more than knowledge of disciplinary content and habits of mind, although both are undeniably crucial to effective instruction. They need first to overcome common beliefs or attitudes—such as "*I am not a reading teacher; it's not my job to teach reading*" or "*Reading is an optional extra; I can wait until I have time in my curriculum to teach it*"—that hinder their commitment to teaching reading and to developing expertise for reading instruction. In other words, content area teachers must take their responsibility to teach reading seriously, recognizing that reading is not merely a handmaiden in service of the discipline but a constitutive part and, thus, an essential component of the discipline that must be taught and learned in school. As discussed in Chapters 2–5, reading is central to disciplinary practices; it is indispensable to the creation, learning, and consumption of disciplinary knowledge, so much so that it is now widely acknowledged that without text and without reading, the social practice that propels the advances of modern disciplines cannot be effectively engaged and the teaching/learning of these disciplines cannot be productively carried out. In fact, the amount of learning in a discipline depends, to a large extent, on students' ability to access, read, understand, and use relevant texts.

Along with the recognition and appreciation of the essential role reading plays in disciplinary learning and socialization, content area teachers need to have a sound understanding of the reading process, factors impacting text comprehension and interpretation, ways of interacting with disciplinary texts, and strategies for promoting and assessing students' critical engagement with and sensemaking of disciplinary texts. Understanding what reading means in a particular discipline, how it differs from reading in other contexts, and what it takes to comprehend and interpret texts in the discipline can help teachers design reading assignments more purposefully, make their expectations explicit, anticipate students' reading needs, and plan instructional support accordingly. Teachers who know how to help students activate and develop prior knowledge before reading (e.g., via the use of a KWL chart or an anticipation guide), engage in comprehension monitoring during reading (e.g., via the use of reciprocal teaching or thinking aloud), and organize and use the information gleaned from text after reading (e.g., via the use of graphic organizer or writing)—will be better able to support their students' reading process and improve their reading outcome. At the same time, teachers who know how to conduct close reading sessions will be better able to demonstrate to students what it means to read carefully, deeply, and critically in their discipline and what sorts of benefits such reading practice affords with respect to comprehension, understanding, thinking, and learning.

Because disciplinary texts of secondary content areas are typically complex and challenging, teachers also need to develop a set of knowledge and skills related to these texts so that they can better support students' reading comprehension and learning in the content area. Teachers need to know how to access and use a variety of textual resources that are relevant to disciplinary learning, including textbooks, trade books, magazines, documents, newspapers, and web-based articles. They need to know how to use different texts in different ways and for different purposes. They need to be able to match text to students' reading proficiency, designing and implementing activities that are sufficiently challenging but do not make excessive demands on students. They also need to know how to select appropriate texts or text segments for close reading. Equally important, teachers need to understand the specific language and literacy demands of their discipline and have at their disposal a repertoire of strategies for helping students cope with these challenges. They need to know how to augment their use of curriculum materials with reading/literacy support for students, as well as how to integrate use of curriculum materials into their long-term plans for concurrent development of students' content knowledge, language skills, literacy strategies, and disciplinary habits of mind (Chandler-Olcott, Doerr, Hinchman, & Masingila, 2015).

Key to the instructional decision-making here is a solid understanding of common genres valued and used by experts in the discipline. Genres are types of discourse that catalogue the social practice of disciplinary experts (Martin, 2009). As such, they construe disciplinary knowledge, values, and habits of mind. Genre knowledge is, thus, critical to disciplinary literacy teaching and learning. Teachers need to understand how each genre is schematically structured, what its purpose is, and what sort of verbal and visual resources it privileges, as well as why it is important to the discipline. They also need to know that while genre is predictable and recognizable, it is also flexible and subject to manipulation in that it tends to respond to changes in disciplinary norms and conventions, as well as to the immediate situational context and authorial intentions (Fang, 2014a). In particular, teachers need to have deep knowledge about language as a creative resource for making meaning for different purposes and in different contexts. This knowledge includes three interrelated aspects (Schleppegrell, 2018). The first is understanding how language use varies across academic disciplines and genres within the same discipline. As is evident in Chapters 2–5, different academic disciplines draw on language in different ways, with literature relying heavily on everyday, commonsense language to describe characters' feelings and actions, science on technical language to construe theoretical explanations of the phenomena in the universe, history on abstract language to offer partial interpretations of the past, and mathematics on precise language and mathematics symbols to engage in logical reasoning. Moreover, different genres (e.g., explanation, argument, report, narration, procedure) tend to marshal somewhat different constellations of lexical and grammatical resources. Understanding the different ways lexicogrammar is used in different disciplines and genres to represent experience, structure discourse, embed perspective, and encode habits of mind can help teachers better identify and respond to potential sources of comprehension or interpretation breakdowns, providing tools that enable students to work through challenging academic texts in disciplinary learning.

For example, Morgan (2006, pp. 226–227) demonstrated how linguistic expertise can help mathematics teachers notice and interpret the effects of subtle changes in lexicogrammar among the following three mathematics statements:

(a) *To add and subtract decimals, line up the decimal points. Then work out as for whole numbers.*

(b) *To add and subtract decimals, line up the digits in the units column. Then calculate as for whole numbers.*

(c) *Decimals are added and subtracted in the same way as whole numbers, first lining up the digits in the units column.*

The change in mathematical participant from "*decimal points*" in (a) to "*digits in the units column*" in (b) may be interpreted as placing importance on the values of the numbers rather than on the notation. The change in the naming of the process from "*work out*" in (a) to "*calculate*" in (b) reflects a shift from everyday language to specialist language, thus impacting the positioning of the student reader and his/her relationship to the author and the subject matter. The mathematical process is constructed in (b) as a specialist mathematical operation, rather than an everyday action, likely encouraging the student reader to assume the identity of a mathematician. The use of passive voice "*decimals are added and subtracted*" and non-finite clause "*first lining up . . .*" in (c) obscures the human agency involved. This has the effect of distancing the student reader from the mathematical operations that s/he is expected to carry out and no longer positions the student reader as an active participant in mathematics problem solving. This may cause some students to not see themselves as potential mathematicians. Moreover, the use of "*decimals*" in (c), as opposed to "*to add and subtract*" in (a) and (b), to begin a sentence focuses the reader's attention on the description of the number systems rather than on procedures for calculation. In short, the way a text is presented to students (as mathematical or otherwise) is likely to have an effect on the contextual and linguistic resources they will bring to make sense of and act on the text. The implication of this discussion is that understanding how language is used in mathematics texts can help teachers identify potentially significant text features, anticipate potential reading and problem-solving difficulties, and determine appropriate strategies for addressing these difficulties and facilitating mathematics learning.

Another aspect of knowledge about language concerns understanding how language use varies across different activities and tasks. For example, in science classrooms, students regularly move among a series of firsthand and secondhand activities (e.g., experiment, observation, reading, small group discussion, whole class sharing, writing). Similarly, in mathematics classrooms, students participate in different communicative contexts—working in small groups, reporting out to the whole class, writing up a solution, and reading the written description of the problem and solution in a mathematics textbook—as they engage in learning mathematics concepts and solving mathematics problems. Different activities constitute different situational contexts, requiring participants (teacher and students) to make use of different language registers—from language of spontaneous interaction, through language of recounting experience and language of generalizing, and to disciplinary language. Understanding the language features that characterize different situational contexts enables teachers to better support their students in moving between less formal/academic and more formal/academic language, less explicit and more explicit language, less technical and more technical language, less rigorous and more rigorous language, and less structured and more structured texts. Being able to talk about and model the use of different language features that characterize different task contexts promotes more productive discussion and effective learning of concepts and ideas in disciplinary texts.

To engage students in productive discussion about text, teachers need to develop a linguistic metalanguage—a language for talking about language and text—and encourage students to use it in text exploration. A meaningful linguistic metalanguage can, according to Schleppegrell (2018), "enable consciousness-raising about English, support modeling through talk about how language works in texts of different kinds, and stimulate interaction that enables children to learn English while also learning in the subject areas" (p. 22). Systemic functional linguistics (SF) (Halliday & Matthiessen, 2014) offers a meaning-based metalanguage that teachers can use to engage students in overt discussion about how language choices present ideational content (experiential meaning), enact social relationships (interpersonal meaning), and create organized discourse (textual meaning). This metalanguage links form with meaning, giving teachers and students a powerful tool for exploring disciplinary texts (Fang, 2021). Although it is technical and seemingly forbidding, it can be adapted for use at any grade level. For example, teachers in Moore and Schleppegrell (2014) used *doing, thinking/feeling,* and *saying* verbs, instead of the more technical SFL terms (*material, mental,* and *verbal processes*), when engaging children in analyzing and discussing what happened in stories. Teachers in O'Hallaron, Palincsar, and Schleppegrell (2015) used *author's voice, helping verbs,* and *attitudinal expressions,* instead of the more technical SFL terms (*interpersonal meaning, modality,* and *appraisal resources*), when teaching students how to conduct critical reading of science texts. While the more commonplace terms may not always have exactly the same meanings as their SFL counterparts, for pedagogical purposes, these subtle differences are not significant and can be ignored. The key here is, according to Schleppegrell (2018), "to be explicit with learners about how an author infuses particular meanings into a text by making choices from what the grammar offers, and to offer learners options for making choices themselves as they speak and write" (pp. 22–23).

A somewhat different conception of language-related knowledge base for content area teaching was recently proposed by Seah, Silver, and Baildon (2022). This knowledge base has four interrelated components—knowledge of language (KL), knowledge about language (KAL), knowledge of students

(KS), and pedagogical knowledge (PK). Knowledge of language refers to a teacher's implicit knowledge of, or linguistic competence related to, the language of classroom instruction (e.g., academic language) and the language of the discipline under study (e.g., literary language, mathematical language). It represents the essentials of what a teacher needs in order to communicate effectively in the language of instruction and to represent the content of his/her subject in ways that align with disciplinary standards and norms. Knowledge about language is a teacher's explicit, or conscious, knowledge about the discursive features of instructional language and disciplinary language. This knowledge, which is declarative in nature, enables the teacher to clearly explain the forms, structures, meanings, and functions of language patterns in disciplinary texts. Knowledge of students refers to the knowledge a teacher has of his/her students in terms of their language backgrounds, including home language practices, prior knowledge of and about disciplinary language, difficulties with disciplinary language and its use, differences in ability across language skills, differences in language ability across subject areas, and learning progress in language use over time. This knowledge helps the teacher develop students' proficiency in instructional language and disciplinary language. Pedagogical knowledge includes "the declarative knowledge of the pedagogical strategies and approaches that are available for supporting instructional and disciplinary language learning as well as the instructional knowledge that is manifested when a teacher engages in teaching in the classroom" (Seah, Silver, & Baildon, 2022, p. 7). Together, these four components of language-related knowledge base enable content area teachers to be language users, language analysts, and language teachers in the context of their classrooms.

Understanding how visual resources make meaning is, likewise, important knowledge for teachers to develop. Texts in academic content areas are often multimodal, meaning that they incorporate written language, visual images, and design features. To competently scaffold reading and comprehension of these texts, teachers need to "extend their understanding of perspectives, theories, and practices used to comprehend visual images, graphic design, and multimodal texts" (Serafini, 2011, p. 341). In particular, they need to become familiar with the grammar, or structures, of visual design (Kress & van Leeuwen, 2021) and equip students with tools for reading and interpreting images and design features in multimodal texts. Three components of this grammar are essential for this purpose: perspective, composition, and visual symbols. Specifically, teachers need to understand that how participants (characters, actors, objects) in an image are positioned in relation to the viewer/reader—close, far away, face-to-face, above, below—can evoke more or less strong connections between the reader and the participants and affect the reader's perception of the power relationship among the participants in the image. They also need to understand the compositional techniques the artist/writer uses to organize and position various participants in an image (e.g., relative size, color and contrast, foregrounding and focus), as the arrangement and placement of these participants determine their relative importance/value and impact how they interact with other elements in an image and the surrounding linguistic prose. They need to be able to identify and interpret visual symbols (e.g., a rose signifies love or caring) and motifs (e.g., a recurring visual like a cross means human mortality) so that they can help students move beyond literal understanding to consider deeper, more nuanced meanings.

Equally important, teachers need to understand the features and affordances of different modes of representation, how these modes need to be coordinated to make persuasive claims about target topics, how key concepts and processes in content areas are represented within and across modes, the role of transduction—"the creative interpretive work whereby the meaning of a sign in one mode is remade into a sign in a different mode"—in supporting students' reasoning and sense making, and what is entailed in the cognitive process of integrating modes for disciplinary meaning making (Prain, 2022, p. 144). Teachers also need a visual metalanguage for exploring multimodal texts with students, and this metalanguage can draw on visual grammar concepts such as salience, image zone, information value, motif, vector, materiality, symbolism, framing, narrative process, modality, realization, and positioning (Kress & van Leeuwen, 2021). In short, knowledge of how visual images and design features contribute to text meaning enables teachers to better support students' reading of multimodal texts, helping expand their interpretive repertoires and develop their proficiency in multimodal meaning making.

Ultimately, teachers must demonstrate expertise for designing and implementing units of instruction in which they draw on their knowledge about reading, language, text, and disciplinary norms to motivate and support students in disciplinary reading and learning. To teach academic reading using a disciplinary literacy approach, teachers need to involve learners in inquiry that allows them to "gain insight into how questions are asked and examined and how conclusions are drawn, supported, communicated, contested, and defended" in specific disciplines (Moje, 2015, p. 257). This means that an essential skill content area teachers need to have is knowing how to engage students in meaningful discipline-specific inquiries. This requires not only knowledge of the big ideas, core concepts, key relationships, and essential practices in the discipline, but also how to select and prepare texts of appropriate complexity for instruction, how to teach students to access, read, use, and produce discipline-specific texts, and how to assess both their students' progress and their own instruction.

More specifically, Moje (2015) suggested that teachers need to be able to support students in learning both disciplinary ideas/concepts and disciplinary literacy practices through the use of a pedagogical heuristic called 4Es—Engage, Elicit/Engineer, Examine, and Evaluate. The first E requires teachers to create classroom environments where students can engage in the everyday practices of the discipline under study, that is, authentic practices similar to those undertaken by disciplinary experts. These overarching inquiry practices typically include generating significant problems or compelling questions to be explored; working with data (e.g., text, tool, observation, phenomenon, interview); reading and writing a wide range of relevant print-based and digital texts; recording, analyzing, and synthesizing data into findings related to the question(s)/problem(s) posed; examining and evaluating one's own claims and the claims of others; and communicating one's own claims orally or in writing. The specifics of these practices can and do manifest somewhat differently across different disciplines, as shown in Chapters 2–5.

The second E focuses on eliciting the knowledge and skills students bring to disciplinary inquiry and at the same time engineering the content knowledge and literacy skills students need in order to engage productively in the inquiry. This is where teachers can promote the learning and use of both generic and discipline-specific reading/language skills and strategies, allowing students to see that these strategies and skills are not abstract concepts to be memorized for test purposes but powerful tools for engaging in authentic reading and inquiry practices. The third E encourages students to examine both verbal and visual choices in disciplinary texts, paying close attention to language patterns and discourse practices of the discipline. Through detailed analysis and critique of how language (e.g., words, grammar) and other semiotic resources (e.g., images, symbols) in disciplinary texts are used by authors to communicate particular meanings and achieve particular effects, teachers help students develop as critical readers and powerful writers in disciplinary learning. The fourth E asks students to evaluate when, why, and how disciplinary discourses are and are not useful so that they become more capable of and confident in "navigating across and between their own everyday habits of mind, their identities and cultural practices, and those that are valued in the discipline" (Moje, 2015, pp. 268–269).

To use this heuristic effectively to guide students in disciplinary reading and learning, teachers need a strong knowledge of (a) disciplinary content, (b) the basic processes and skills that undergird literate practice, (c) domain-specific literacy skills and practices for their discipline, (d) how texts work in their discipline, (e) how to evaluate the challenges and affordances of disciplinary texts, and (f) how to assess what students have learned from these texts and about the literate practices of their discipline (Moje, 2015). They also need to develop knowledge of youth/ family cultures and youth development, recognizing "how social identities and cultural backgrounds mediate student learning of the new cultural practices demanded by disciplines" (Moje, 2015, p. 271). In other words, teachers need to learn about their students' experiences, backgrounds, and uses of texts so that they can draw on what students have already known and experienced to make academic reading/literacy instruction and disciplinary learning more relevant, engaging, and inspiring. These sorts of expertise take time, experience, and resources to develop, demanding sustained attention, unwavering commitment, and steadfast support, as recent professional development work with teachers (e.g., Patrick & Fang, 2022; Rodriguez, 2015) has suggested.

Preparing Teachers for Academic Reading Instruction

What can teacher educators do to help content area teacher candidates develop the sorts of expertise detailed above? A disciplinary literacy approach to academic reading requires that teacher education programs promote knowledge building related to not only disciplinary content and habits of mind but also discipline-specific language and literacy skills, strategies, and practices. This work must involve both content-area teacher educators (CTEs) and reading/literacy teacher educators (RTEs), as each has expertise that the other party does not typically possess. CTEs are content experts, knowledgeable about the big ideas, core concepts, unifying themes, essential practices, and ways of thinking and reasoning within their discipline, as well as effective pedagogies for facilitating the learning of disciplinary content. RTEs, on the other hand, are reading/literacy experts, familiar with the reading process, text genres, and the comprehension or interpretive demands of these texts, as well as strategies for addressing these challenges. Teacher education programs need to draw on the expertise of both teacher educators, as well as promote collaboration between them, to better prepare content area teacher candidates for the critically important work of teaching the language and literacy practices of their discipline to students (Fang, 2014b). The rest of this section describes some ways this mission can be accomplished in the context of existing teacher preparation structures.

Cohorting the Reading/Literacy Methods Course by Discipline

Most states in the U.S. now require secondary teacher candidates (TCs) to take at least one content area reading/literacy methods course as part of their planned program of study for state professional certification (Romine, McKenna, & Robinson, 1996). Traditionally, TCs from all content areas (e.g., English, science, social studies, mathematics, business, music, agriculture, arts) are mixed and take the same reading/literacy methods course together. The course typically focuses on learning to teach the same set of generic (basic/intermediate) reading skills (e.g., decoding, fluency, vocabulary) and strategies (e.g., concept mapping, summarizing, questioning, and note taking) for application pell-mell to different content areas. Regardless of majors, TCs read the same textbook(s) and complete the same assignments. This course has rarely been popular with TCs and done little to improve reading instruction in content area classrooms (Moje, 2008). As Scott et al. (2018) concluded based on their review of five decades of research on teacher preparation in literacy across content areas, "despite noble intentions, large-scale inclusion in teacher preparation programs, and decades of research, the concerted results of [content area literacy instruction] have been underwhelming . . . [and] doing more of the same will not yield the desired results" (p. 2).

A disciplinary literacy approach suggests the need to cohort TCs by content areas for reading instruction so that RTEs can better foreground, differentiate, and address the unique language and literacy demands related to specific disciplines. As Chapters 2–5 have shown, different disciplines use genres, registers, and literacy practices in different ways. These differences, which both reflect and shape disciplinary assumptions about knowledge and knowledge production, can be brought out and explored more fully in discipline-specific cohorts. The new cohort structure will enable RTEs to craft learning goals, select instructional materials, and design assignments and field experiences in ways that are more appropriate to and focused on specific disciplines. It will also facilitate collaboration between RTEs and CTEs, as well as tracking and support of TCs during their program of study. At the same time, TCs will be more likely to embrace—and become more motivated to learn about—reading/literacy because they can see more closely the value and uses of reading/literacy in their particular discipline and are afforded more time to explore the reading/literacy-content connections in greater depth and in more substantive, discipline-specific ways.

For example, Bain (2012) reported that cohorting the reading/literacy methods course by discipline enabled history/social studies teacher educators and reading/literacy teacher educators to make curricular modifications in their respective reading/literacy methods course and content methods course in ways that helped eliminate unnecessary repetitions and forge new links across semesters, courses, and fieldwork; deepen disciplinary inquiry and understanding; and enhance programmatic coherence. It also encouraged his history/social studies teacher candidates to think more deeply and pro-actively about selecting, preparing, and using texts for instruction. The re-form, according to Bain (2012), "improved our ability to make more explicit connections between work in our students' major field, literacy and learn-ing theory, instructional practice, professional courses, and their field-based experiences in secondary classrooms" (p. 523). More specifically, the new cohort structure resulted in less fragmentation and compartmentalization and more coherence in TCs' learning experiences, allowing them to develop a greater sense of responsibility for teaching reading/literacy in history and greater expertise in using history texts to promote historical literacy. They became more attentive to text features (e.g., vocabulary, sentence struc-ture, knowledge demands, seductive details, subtexts) that present potential comprehension or interpretive challenges to students and were able to draw on their disciplinary content knowledge, reading/literacy knowledge, and knowledge of students to plan and enact reading instruction that promotes historical literacy.

One of the challenges in cohorting by disciplines is finding instructional materials for content areas outside the core subjects of science, history, literature, and mathematics, as there seem to be far fewer literacy-related resources for subjects such as physical education, music, business studies, and agriculture. Another challenge is that enrollment numbers or institu-tional resources may not always permit the forming of disciplinary cohorts for the content area reading/literacy methods course. In places where (or at times when) this is the case, it is still possible to enact a disciplinary literacy focus that enables TCs in each discipline to learn about discipline-specific language/literacy practices and pedagogies while also developing an appreciation for how disciplines differ (Fang, Sun, et al., 2014). RTEs can assign common, as well as discipline-specific, readings and experiences. Such cross-disciplinary interaction and discussion can help TCs see connections across disciplines, engender deeper understand-ing of the literate practices within their own discipline, and stimulate further inquiry into disciplinary ways with words. Moreover, an under-standing of how texts and text practices, as well as linguistic, rhetorical, and discursive conventions, vary by disciplines will enable TCs to do a more explicit and complete job of explaining the language and literacy practices of their own discipline.

Broadening Conceptions of Text and Literacy

Adopting a disciplinary literacy approach to academic reading also requires that RTEs pay due respect to how text and literacy are conceptualized and used across disciplines. Each discipline has its own ways of defining and using text and literacy, as shown in Chapters 2–5. What counts as text and literacy varies considerably across disciplines. For example, history is constructed primarily through language in primary sources, textbooks, and other written documents. However, other historical residuals in the form of nonprint text—such as paintings, maps, photographs, oral recordings, music, and architecture—are also important to historical understanding (Draper et al., 2012). Becoming historically literate means not just learning about events, facts, and historical figures through reading and comprehending written texts but, more importantly, developing a sophisticated understanding of historical time, agency, and causality by asking historically significant questions, assessing author's perspectives, evaluating evidence across multiple sources, making judgments within the confines of the historical context in question, and determining the reliability of different accounts on the same historical event (VanSledright, 2012). Moreover, because images in historical texts may communicate particular disciplinary norms and ideological positionings (see, for example, Burke, 2006 and Kress & van Leeuwen, 2021), understanding the ways images are used to promote or marginalize the perspectives of particular social groups is, likewise, an essential component of historical literacy.

The texts that mathematics students read are, on the other hand, typically multimodal and multisemiotic, consisting of written language, mathematics symbols, and images. These resources are interdependent, working in close partnership with one another to create mathematical meanings, with mathematical symbols providing a highly concise but rigorously accurate description of the nature of the relationship among mathematical entities, images rendering this abstract description concrete to human perception through visual representation, and written language offering contextual information related to the symbolically and visually described situation (O'Halloran, 2000). Becoming literate in mathematics means the ability to read, comprehend, interpret, and act on these three meaning-making resources.

Because the texts students encounter in disciplinary learning are varied, with some predominantly verbal and most multimodal, Serafini (2015) has proposed to view text not merely as a linguistic entity, but also simultaneously as a visual object, a multimodal event, and a sociocultural artifact. Approaching a text as a linguistic entity highlights the primary role language plays in disciplinary discourse and the power of lexicogrammar in fashioning meaning. Approaching a text as a visual object encourages the reader to move beyond words to consider its visual images and design features. Approaching a text as a multimodal event invites the reader to attend to not only what is in an image but also how various objects in the image are positioned in relation to one another and interact with other elements surrounding the image. Approaching a text as a sociocultural artifact "allows students to consider the artistic, structural, cultural, historical, political, and ideological ramifications of the production and reception of the texts students experience in and out of school contexts" (Serafini, 2015, p. 419). This expanded conception of text promotes the expansion of students' interpretive repertoires beyond the strategies commonly employed to comprehend verbal texts, enabling them to develop multiple literacies across disciplines.

RTEs need to be aware of the varied conceptions and uses of text and literacy in different disciplines when designing and delivering their reading/literacy methods course for TCs. They need to understand the challenges and opportunities entailed in promoting student transduction of meanings in content area learning. In short, RTEs need to go beyond the traditional conceptions of text, literacy, and literacy pedagogy, recognizing the different cultures and different demands of different disciplines and tailoring instruction to the ethos and goals of each discipline. This broadening of conception of what counts as text, genre, language, and literacy has, as Fowler-Amato et al. (2019) have argued, the potential to increase access to disciplinary knowledge and habits of mind and participation in discipline-legitimated ways of producing, consuming, and renovating knowledge. In other words, an expanded definition of text and literacy creates new opportunities for engaging and empowering students in productive disciplinary learning, which is the essence of what Moje (2007) called "socially just subject-matter instruction" (p. 1).

Enriching Literacy Pedagogical Content Knowledge

Effective preparation of TCs for a disciplinary literacy approach to academic reading requires that RTEs demonstrate strong "pedagogical content knowledge" (Shulman, 1986). They need, first and foremost, a basic understanding of "the conceptual domains of each discipline, how the conceptual domains are pedagogically framed to support learning, and how [TCs] construct their understanding of literacy practices within disciplines" (Dillon et al., 2010, p. 641). This understanding provides the foundation on which language and literacy instruction can be more meaningfully built and effectively promoted.

Equally important, RTEs need to know a range of teaching practices that are effective for making disciplinary texts accessible to diverse groups of learners and for developing their advanced literacies. More specifically, they need to be able to "represent, decompose, or approximate aspects of teaching practice related to disciplinary reading, writing, and reasoning" in ways that support students' participation in disciplinary learning and inquiry (Kavanagh & Rainey, 2017, p. 931).

A key component of this ability is a deep understanding of the role language and literacy play in disciplinary learning. This knowledge is referred to by Love (2009) as "literacy pedagogical content knowledge" (LPCK). It consists of three components: (a) "knowledge about how spoken and written language can be best structured for effective learning", (b) "recognition that subject areas have their own characteristic language forms and hence entail distinctive literacy practices", and (c) "capacity to design learning and teaching strategies that account for subject-specific literacies and language practices" (p. 541). It is traditionally underemphasized in teacher preparation, as the reading/literacy methods course in many U.S. institutions typically focuses (or is mandated to focus) on equipping TCs with knowledge of the often narrowly defined "science of reading", a perspective that aligns with the simple view of reading, with its emphasis on teaching basic skills such as phonological awareness and phonics (see Chapter 1). One consequence of this neglect is that many teacher candidates lack a deep understanding and control of disciplinary language. For example, MacGregor (2002) found that many preservice teachers were not familiar with language patterns associated with understanding and explaining mathematics concepts and ideas, exhibiting great difficulties with grammatical structures for expressing numerical comparison concisely, precisely, and clearly.

LPCK is especially important for RTEs, as disciplinary content in secondary schools is presented primarily through texts in language, as well as other modalities, that is often simultaneously technical, dense, abstract, and metaphorical (Fang & Schleppegrell, 2008; Fang, Schleppegrell, & Moore, 2014). These texts present new challenges for disciplinary learning; and in order to handle these challenges, adolescents need support to develop new language skills and literacy strategies beyond those they have already learned in the elementary grades. To support TCs in meeting their students' language/literacy needs, RTEs need to go beyond the traditional approach that typically emphasizes the teaching of basic language skills and generic literacy strategies. They need to become familiar with a range of discipline-specific language/literacy skills, strategies, and practices, helping TCs not only understand how language and other semiotic uses vary across disciplines in ways that are functional for making discipline-specific meanings but also develop effective strategies for assisting students to cope with the verbal and visual demands of disciplinary reading and writing. Acquiring this new knowledge is also crucial for TCs to productively enact close reading in their own classrooms, support diverse learners' language and literacy development, and promote disciplinary learning and inquiry.

Love (2010) described a short but intense training course (18 hours in 6 weeks) titled "Language and Teaching" in a two-year Master of Teaching program at the University of Melbourne (Australia) aimed at preparing middle and high school teachers with no prior linguistic subject knowledge to be "master teachers" capable of supporting content area learning through literacy. The course was structured into eight units that addressed the three components of LPCK identified earlier. These units offered a rich array of virtual clinics, electronic and face-to-face tutorials, workshops, and reflective tasks. They were packaged into an interactive, video-based multimedia resource (DVD). Besides the DVD, teacher candidates were placed in a school two days each week and attended school-based seminars designed by clinical specialists in conjunction with teaching fellows. Throughout the course, they were expected to relate what they had learned from the DVD to their ongoing teaching practice in school, drawing on systematically collected evidence from their own classrooms. A cohort of over 300 teacher candidates enrolled in the course. They came from disciplines ranging from the humanities (e.g., English, history, psychology) and visual and performing arts (e.g., music, art, media studies, drama) to mathematics, sciences, physical education, business studies, and information technology. They succeeded in developing a capacity to plan content area instruction with an informed understanding of the role language and literacy play in disciplinary learning and inquiry. Specifically, they were able to identify the literacy demands inherent in a unit of work they had planned and to outline strategies for supporting learning through literacy. The finding, according to Love (2010), illustrates how even a little linguistic subject knowledge can "provide a strong foundation for subject specialists to further scaffold their diverse learners into the advanced literacies required of their specializations" (p. 346).

One way for RTEs to help TCs develop LPCK is by drawing on a functional, meaning-based metalanguage provided by systemic functional linguistics (SFL) (Halliday & Matthiessen, 2014, see also Fang, 2021 and Fang & Schleppegrell, 2008) and by engaging them in close, functional analysis of text. In a recent review of relevant research literature, Accurso and Gebhard (2021) reported that professional development drawing on SFL tools positively impacts preservice and inservice teachers in several ways. First, it increases teachers' awareness of how language and other semiotic resources operate in the disciplinary genres (e.g., literary critique, scientific explanation, mathematical proof, historical argument) that students are expected to regularly read and write in school. Second, it enhances teachers' ability to design and enact language-focused curriculum, instruction, and assessment in their content areas. Specifically, teachers who learn to use a functional metalanguage are better able to lead more in-depth class discussion about disciplinary texts, assess students' disciplinary writing (e.g., evaluating how students make meaning through verbal and visual choices), and guide students' literacy learning. Third, it increases teachers' understanding of how text, context, ideology, and power are interrelated, helping them recognize how verbal and visual choices construe value and construct subjectivities in texts in different ways across different genres and disciplines. As a result of these improvements, teachers become more confident in their ability to support language learning and promote literacy growth in disciplinary contexts.

A case in point can be found in Accurso and Levasseur (2022), which describes how learning a functional metalanguage enabled one science teacher to develop linguistic expertise for disciplinary literacy instruction. The development involves four stages. In the first stage, the teacher was introduced to a set of functional metalanguage terms based in SFL (e.g., *clause, genre, register, field, tenor, mode, theme, rheme*). This metalanguage allowed the teacher to see how language is structured to fulfil specific functions in scientific meaning-making. In the second stage, the teacher applied his understanding of the functional metalanguage by conducting genre and register analyses of a passage on gas laws from a high school chemistry textbook. The analyses involved identifying how text is structured to achieve its purpose, how information is constructed and condensed through the choices of nouns and verbs, and how discursive flow is created in text through the choice of clause themes (i.e., what begins each clause). In the third stage, the teacher applied the functional metalanguage to examine language choices in the texts written by multilingual students in his chemistry class. This gave him insights into his students' language repertoire and the diverse meaning-making tools they brought to scientific meaning making. In the final stage, the teacher drew on the functional metalanguage to design and implement a language-focused science curriculum that included more extended writing and explicit teaching of strategies for creating discursive flow when presenting information or argument. Taken together, the four stages helped the science teacher move from being a science language user to a language analyst and ultimately a language/literacy teacher.

Seah, Tan, and Adams (2022) provided another example of how a meta-language informed by SFL helps improve content area teachers' LPCK, or more specifically, their language awareness and literacy understanding. They described how science teacher educators and language/literacy teacher educators in Singapore worked with elementary and secondary science teachers to increase their understanding of the role and nature of language in science learning and their ability to integrate this knowledge in science instruction. Teacher educators used an inquiry approach to introduce the SFL metalanguage to teachers in an incidental but intentional manner. The inquiry cycle began with a pre-lesson inquiry session, where teacher educators and teachers discussed student writing samples that teachers had selected for failing to meet curricular expectations. Each teacher discussed the samples they brought to the meeting, focusing on why these samples were chosen, what issues each of the samples had, and why they believed the samples to be conceptually and/or linguistically problematic. Teacher educators then shared their own analyses of the samples, using SFL metalanguage to identify and characterize students' language and discursive challenges. They focused on language features consequential to the representation of scientific meanings instead of syntactic errors from a traditional grammar perspective. In the second phase of the inquiry, teachers planned lessons and emailed lesson plans and associated teaching materials to teacher educators for feedback. The feedback typically focused on the language support in lesson plans. The inquiry cycle ended with a post-lesson inquiry session, during which teacher educators and teachers engaged in a reflective dialogue on what had transpired during the lessons, the challenges involved, the extent to which the language issues had been addressed, and follow-up actions proposed. The reflections provided the foundation for engaging in deeper inquiry in subsequent cycles. As a result of the experience with the inquiry cycle, participating teachers believed in the role of language in disciplinary learning, developed greater knowledge of and sensitivity to language, and increased their capacities for language instruction in the science classroom. Specifically, they were able to use SFL metalanguage to engage students in productive discussion about science content, identify and address specific linguistic challenges of their students, provide specific feedback on students' language use, and unpack the representational demands of science tasks.

A related component of LPCK that is important for RTEs to have is understanding how to help TCs develop classroom discourse moves—such as waiting, inviting student participation, revoicing, asking students to revoice, probing a student's thinking, creating opportunity to engage with another student's reasoning (Herbel-Eisenmann et al., 2013)—that promote students' learning of disciplinary language and content. In content area classrooms, students participate in a range of activities. These activities call for use of different language registers, including the language of spontaneous interaction in small group discussion, the language of oral recounting when reporting out to the whole class, disciplinary language when reading academic texts in content areas, and written (or academic) language when writing in response to these texts or assigned activities. RTEs need to be able to show TCs how they can engage students in classroom talks that provide rich opportunities for using language that is more or less formal, more or less explicit, or more or less rigorous for different communicative purposes and contexts. To do this, RTEs need to encourage TCs to consider how classroom contexts help students construct identities, develop dispositions about a discipline, and gain facility over time with discipline-based ways of communicating. More specifically, RTEs can engage TCs in analyzing transcripts of classroom discourse across a range of activities: Together, they identify discourse moves that are more or less powerful/productive, contemplate how these moves position students as more or less agentive learners and competent readers, and examine the linguistic and paralinguistic features that instantiate each move.

Supporting Content Area Teacher Educators for Reading/ Literacy Instruction

The development of modern Western disciplines is heavily dependent on language and text (Christie & Maton, 2011). Being literate in a discipline, thus, means not only knowledge of disciplinary content but also the ability to read, write, and reason with texts in discipline-legitimated ways. Traditionally, content area teacher educators (CTEs) focused their job on helping TCs learn how to teach the body of specialized disciplinary content these candidates are expected to have mastered in their baccalaureate studies. With little formal training in the reading and writing demands of their disciplines, CTEs rarely make reading/literacy an explicit or central part of their courses; nor do they typically consider language/literacy pedagogy within the purview of their responsibilities. As one middle school science teacher revealed about her teacher preparation program:

> As a first-year teacher, I came straight from a collegiate education program that stressed hands-on, inquiry-based activities. When being observed by my advisors, I felt they would be most impressed with lessons that involved labs and other hands-on activities. I felt that these advisors would frown upon textbook-based lessons. This led me to believe

that teaching using the text was not ideal. Therefore, I used the text very little and even tried to avoid it. (Fang et al., 2008, p. 2079)

RTEs can help ameliorate this situation by raising their CTE colleagues' awareness of the essential and pervasive role of language/literacy in disciplinary practices and the critical role of TCs in promoting students' advanced literacy development, encouraging them to take up language and literacy instruction in their courses, and offering assistance in a supportive manner. TCs are more likely to embrace language/literacy and implement language/literacy instruction when the same message preached by RTEs is also emphasized by CTEs. Draper et al. (2012) described an institution-wide effort at Brigham Young University (USA), where one RTE worked with a dozen CTEs to address issues of central concerns in their preparation of secondary teachers. These teacher educators met bimonthly as a literacy study group to explore answers to questions such as "How can teacher educators adequately prepare prospective teachers to support the literacy development of adolescents? What does literacy instruction look like for content area classrooms? How can literacy instruction remain true to the basic principles and values of the various disciplines? How can harmony be created between the work of the literacy teacher educator and content teacher educators?" (p. 368). During these meetings, the RTE selected materials for common readings, facilitated discussion of these materials, and modeled literacy strategies. She also interviewed CTEs, observed their classrooms, and provided feedback about their teaching. As a result of this collaborative work, CTEs were able to revise their preexisiting theories about text, literacy, and literacy pedagogies, and made positive changes to their teacher preparation programs, course designs, classroom instruction, and assessment practices. They enacted and supported literacy instruction in their content area methods courses, reinforcing the central message from the reading/literacy methods course that language/literacy and language/literacy instruction are essential to developing academic reading proficiency and disciplinary literacy.

An example of the efforts by CTEs to embed literacy instruction in their content methods course is presented in Nokes (2010). The article describes how a secondary history/social studies methods course instructor revised, with the support of a RTE, his practice to include literacy as a theme in the content area methods course and during the accompanying practicum experience for TCs. Specifically, the CTE explicitly taught TCs how to identify, select, and use text resources (e.g., textbook, primary sources, historical fictions) that are appropriate for teaching history and modeled instructional strategies that can be used with these resources (e.g., reciprocal teaching, jigsaw, close reading). He also taught the tools of historical inquiry by demonstrating how to use sourcing, corroborating, contextualizing, and other meaning-making heuristics used by historians to engage in the complex process of document analysis and interpretation. He assigned TCs to create a text set related to a single historical event and develop lesson ideas for using the texts. He also provided explicit instruction in general reading comprehension strategies (e.g., summarizing, activating prior knowledge, visualizing, identifying text structure) and discipline-specific interpretive strategies (e.g., sourcing, using a map legend, contextualization), modeling strategy use and providing opportunities for TCs to try out these strategies on their own. Out-of-class reading assignments for TCs include completing a double entry journal, constructing a graphic organizer, writing summaries, making intertexual connections, completing an anticipation guide before and after reading, searching for main ideas, and creating observation-inference charts. In the practicum, TCs conducted classroom observations and taught some history lessons under the mentorship of a practicing social studies teacher. They also wrote reflection papers discussing their thoughts on the literacy practices they observed and/or provided. Nokes reported that this literacy-infused history/social studies methods course produced positive results, with TCs becoming better prepared and more committed to providing reading/literacy instruction in their classrooms.

Schall-Leckrone and McQuillan (2012) described how a history education professor worked with a RTE to prepare TCs to teach the academic language of historical analysis in history lessons. Together, they designed four modules of explicit language instruction for infusion into an existing secondary history methods course. These modules engaged TCs in exploring the complexity and functionality of historical language and learning strategies for identifying and teaching the language demands of history. The first module introduced TCs to features of historical language (e.g., nominalization) and the challenges these features present to students. The second module introduced TCs to strategies for analyzing and interpreting historical text, helping them understand how language constructs content (e.g., who does what to whom, where, and how), infuses perspective (e.g., whose ideas are or are not represented in the text, what is evaluated positively or negatively by the author), and organizes text (e.g., topic sentences, words/phrases that link clauses/sentences/paragraphs). The third module introduced TCs to the differences between academic language and interpersonal language and strategies for increasing student participation in text-based discussions (e.g., think-pair-share, jigsaw). The fourth module introduced TCs to representative genres of historical writing (e.g., accounts, explanations, arguments) and an instructional cycle for teaching students to write these genres. To-gether, these modules aimed to equip prospective history teachers with the knowledge and skills needed to promote close reading, functional language analysis, and critical interpretation of historical texts in their classrooms. TCs who were exposed to these modules reported an enhanced sense of preparedness to teach students in need of language support and considered themselves both language teachers and content teachers, although they also acknowledged the need for additional modeling, coaching, and practice in using the linguistically informed strategies for doing history with their own students. In a subsequent article, Schall-Leckrone (2017) described how a genre-based pedagogy discussed in Chapter 3 can be used to prepare history teachers to teach the key historical genres of recording, explaining, and argu-ing through a functional focus on language and the introduction of cognitive scaffolds (i.e., timeline, concept web, Venn diagram) that align with the three genres.

Similar efforts were reported by Pessoa, Mitchell, and Jacobson (2021), which describes how two applied linguists collaborated with one history professor at an English-medium university in the Middle East to address the language and literacy demands of historical reading and writing. The study demonstrated that with sustained support from language experts, the history professor was able to overcome anxiety and lack of confidence to teach the language of history. Specifically, he increased his understanding over time of the genre and register features of common text types in history, drew on this new understanding in designing and delivering language-supportive instruction and assessment, provided more explicit expecta-tions and precise guidelines for writing assignments, and played a more active role in using high-leverage language resources in teaching histori-cal writing. As a result of these instructional improvements, his students became more proficient at producing historical argument essays that meet disciplinary expectations.

Building Connections Between Content Area Methods and Reading/Literacy Methods Courses

A key feature of an effective teacher preparation program is coherence (Darling-Hammond, 2006). One way to achieve programmatic coherence is to build connections between the reading/literacy methods course and the content area methods course. This requires that RTEs and CTEs col-laborate to design a sequence of coursework that provides TCs with the knowledge, skills, experiences, and disposition needed to support their students' learning of discipline-specific, as well as discipline-relevant, reading/literacy skills, strategies, and practices. Together, they can identify disciplinary knowledge, skills, standards, habits of mind, and other research-based practices that are valued in the target discipline or recommended by relevant professional organizations and government/industrial agencies. They then discuss how these standards and competencies are to be distributed, cross-referenced, and reinforced across various courses, tasks, and experiences in the program. They can also devise an instructional plan that makes explicit the sort of texts to be read/written, specific ways of reading/writing these texts, and other assignments to be completed across courses. These efforts help build an iterative, spiraling curriculum where key knowledge, skills, and dispositions are systematically introduced, developed, revisited, mastered, and refined over the entire secondary teacher preparation program. They also enable both RTEs and CTEs to "consider and understand programmatic trajectories, sequences, and learning progressions, while collaboratively working on curriculum and problems of professional practice" (Bain, 2012, p. 525).

The collaboration between the RTE and the CTE is necessary for another reason—the RTE and the CTE each has the expertise, or "pedagogic and knowledge capitals" (Creese, 2010, p. 105), that the other does not typically have. The RTE usually has limited experience in producing and interpreting texts in academic disciplines (e.g., mathematics, science) and cannot draw on their knowledge of general print literacy strategies to suggest appropriate literacy instruction for these disciplines. The CTE, on the other hand, is, while familiar with the content and habits of mind in his/her discipline, often neither adequately aware of the role text plays in disciplinary learning nor sufficiently sensitive to text features that may present reading/writing challenges to students. By working together, the RTE can draw on the CTE's expertise with disciplinary texts, content, and habits of mind "to target specific texts and literacies and to protect against instruction that promotes ways of using texts that violate the norms and practices of the discipline" (Siebert & Draper, 2012, pp. 184–185). At the same time, the RTE can contribute to the collaboration by helping the CTE select texts for instruction, identify salient or challenging text features, suggest strategies for addressing reading/writing challenges, find ways of engaging students in productive text exploration and content learning, and devise tools for assessing students' understanding and use of disciplinary language.

Given the need to foreground the disciplines in a disciplinary literacy approach to academic reading instruction, it is important that what is taught in the reading/literacy methods course serves the goals of the target discipline.

This means that "[c]onceptual and instructional frameworks that originate from within the field of literacy no longer enjoy an elevated status" (Dillon et al., 2010, p. 641). Instead, RTEs need to think about how the language and literacy knowledge, strategies, skills, and practices that they expect TCs to master can in fact support adolescents in developing the essential knowledge (e.g., core ideas, key relationships, unifying themes) and habits of mind (e.g., ways of reading, writing, thinking, reasoning) in the target discipline. To this end, RTEs would benefit from consulting with their CTE colleagues to identify concepts, skills, practices, and dispositions that are central to the discipline. For example, if sourcing, contextualizing, and corroborating are essential tools for historical inquiry, then RTEs need to design reading/writing assignments that highlight these heuristics, providing opportunities for TCs to identify text sets consisting of primary and secondary sources, read and analyze multiple accounts of the same historical event, compare perspectives, and create (orally and in writing) evidence-based arguments about the issues involved.

Because TCs are not likely to try to apprentice or be successful in apprenticing their students into disciplinary ways of reading and writing unless they themselves have had experience doing the same, it is important that RTEs and CTEs provide opportunities for TCs to "work with members of disciplinary communities, to conduct inquiry, and to practice speaking, reading, and writing within the discipline", as well as "to read and discuss discipline-based research and to read and think together with other subject-area teachers about the practices of disciplinary inquiry through firsthand (physical inquiry) and secondhand (text-based inquiry) investigation" (Moje, 2015, p. 273). In other words, TCs need to be given tasks and experiences that provide opportunities for them to read, write, think, reason, and inquire with substantive content presented through discipline-relevant texts of multiple genres, modalities, registers, and sources, in the same way that their students will be asked to engage in these disciplinary activities. To provide such experiences, RTEs and CTEs need to work together to develop a shared vision and goals. They can do so by observing each other's classes and discussing how each could build on, reinforce, or extend what the other is doing. They can also design common assignments and experiences that repeatedly expose TCs to core concepts and practices in the target discipline across multiple courses. For example, TCs can be asked to develop one unit plan that satisfies the learning objectives of both the content area methods course and the reading/literacy methods course. Specifically, TCs assemble an annotated bibliography of rich, significant texts on a grade-appropriate topic that is important to a particular discipline. They then analyze sample texts from the list in terms of their discursive features and their reading challenges, explore the functionalities of these features in disciplinary meaning-making, and discuss ways to address these challenges pedagogically. Next, TCs plan sample lessons that achieve the content goals while also addressing the reading challenges identified earlier. Finally, the unit is implemented in a common field placement and evaluated by both the CTE and the RTE for its significance to the discipline, appropriateness and appeal of lesson activities, strength of reading/literacy-content connections, conceptual coherence, effectiveness of delivery, and impact on student learning.

Conclusion

Academic texts of secondary content areas are complex and challenging. Students need support when reading, comprehending, interpreting, and pro-ducing these texts. This support is best provided by content area teachers who are familiar with disciplinary content and habits of mind. However, they need additional expertise in order to provide the support. Such exper-tise includes, at the very least, an understanding of how verbal and visual resources are used to make meaning in discipline-specific ways, the capacity to identify and address linguistic/semiotic and conceptual sources of reading challenges, and the ability to plan and facilitate productive discussion about text by using a meaning-based metalanguage.

If reading is the process through which disciplinary knowledge and habits of mind are principally learned in school, then teachers' understanding of this process is essential if they are to support students in developing the knowl-edge and habits of mind. A disciplinary literacy approach to academic reading development requires that teacher education programs provide coursework and experience that help content area (and reading/literacy) teachers de-velop knowledge and expertise in at least three interrelated areas outlined below by Carney and Indrisano (2013):

- subject matter content knowledge: knowledge of the basic concepts and the-ories in a given discipline and of ways these concepts/theories are organized and validated
- disciplinary literacy pedagogical content knowledge: understanding how teaching and learning vary in response to changing disciplinary content and ways of reading, thinking, and knowing, the developmental progression of readers as they gain proficiency in learning from text, and the sociocultural influences on the learner and learning
- process knowledge: cognitive processes used by skilled readers to construct meaning from texts across genres and disciplines, including developing and

activating schema, understanding academic registers, metacognition, awareness of text structures and genre, adopting a reader stance (critical/analytic),
and engagement in goal-directed learning.

To achieve these goals, teacher education programs need to reenvision and
redesign their curriculum in ways that support TCs' understanding and teaching of discipline-legitimated ways of reading and creating texts. It needs to
underscore the notion that promoting academic reading/literacy instruction
is a shared responsibility between RTEs and CTEs and that the ultimate
goal of reading/literacy instruction in content areas is to support adolescents'
learning and socialization across disciplines.

In this context, the relationship between reading and content must be
reconceptualized. Instead of seeing reading merely in a supportive role
serving content learning, we should consider reading as not only central
to but an equal partner with content in disciplinary learning and inquiry.
Teacher preparation programs can promote the development of expertise in
reading instruction among teacher candidates by designing a spiraling, coherent curriculum that expands traditional conceptions of language, text,
and literacy; embraces necessary repetition of skills, strategies, and practices; builds connections across courses and experiences; encourages collaboration between RTEs and CTEs; and provides TCs with opportunities
to experience ways of reading/writing, learning, and teaching disciplinary
texts consistent with those carried out by experts in their discipline. That
is, a disciplinary literacy approach to academic reading/literacy instruction
requires that teacher educators equip teacher candidates with deep understanding of the role of language and literacy in content pedagogies so that
they can better support their students in attaining advanced literacy and
discipline-specific literacies at the same time that they engage them in the
process of building content knowledge and developing disciplinary habits
of mind.

Reflection and Application

1. Why is reading instruction still needed in secondary school? Who is best positioned to assume the responsibility, and why?
2. What sorts of expertise do teachers need in order to provide effective reading
   instruction in academic content areas? How can such expertise be developed?
3. What can teacher educators do to prepare teacher candidates for academic
   reading instruction? What challenges do teacher education programs face
   if they are to promote a disciplinary literacy approach to academic reading?
   How can these challenges be addressed?

4. Think back to your high school or college days. How were classes in science, history, mathematics, literature, and other content areas taught? Was reading/literacy ever an explicit, consistent focus of instruction then? In what ways did that focus or the lack thereof affect your learning of and engagement with these content areas? How committed or prepared do you think your content area teachers were for reading/literacy instruction?

5. Suppose you are tasked with designing a professional development program aimed at enhancing content area teachers' expertise in disciplinary literacy instruction. What would the program look like? How would you go about setting up the program? What are the core principles guiding your development of the program? What processes and procedures would you follow in designing the program? What are the key elements you consider worthy of inclusion in the program? What activities and experiences would you provide in the program in order to engage, motivate, and empower teachers? What specific outcomes (knowledge, understanding, skills, strategies, dispositions) do you expect of the participating teachers? How would you monitor and assess the teachers' progress toward these outcomes?

References

Accurso, K., & Gebhardt, M. (2021). SFL praxis in U.S. teacher education: A critical literature review. *Language and Education, 35*(5), 402–428.

Accurso, K., & Levasseur, J. (2022). Building science teacher disciplinary linguistic knowledge with SFL. In L. Seah, R. Silver, & M. Baildon (Eds.), *The role of language in content pedagogy* (pp. 87–114). Singapore: Springer.

Bain, R. (2012). Using disciplinary literacy to develop coherence in history teacher education: the clinical rounds project. *The History Teacher, 45*(4), 513–532.

Burke, P. (2006). *Eyewitnessing: The uses of images as historical evidence.* Ithaca, NY: Cornell University Press.

Carney, M., & Indrisano, R. (2013). Disciplinary literacy and pedagogical content knowledge. *Journal of Education, 193*(3), 39–49.

Chandler-Olcott, K., Doerr, H., Hinchman, K., & Masingila, J. (2015). Bypass, augment, or integrate: How secondary mathematics teachers address the literacy demands of standards-based curriculum materials. *Journal of Literacy Research, 47*(4), 439–472.

Christie, F. & Maton, K. (2011), *Disciplinarity: Functional linguistic and sociological perspectives.* London: Bloomsbury.

Creese, A. (2010). Content-focused classrooms and learning English: How teachers collaborate. *Theory into Practice, 49,* 99–105.

Darling-Hammond, L. (2006). *Powerful teacher education.* San Francisco: John Wiley.

Dillon, D., O'Brien, D., Sato, M., & Kelly, C. (2010). Professional development and teacher education for reading instruction. In M. Kamil, D. Pearson, E. Moje, & P. Afflerbach (Eds.), *Handbook of reading research* (Vol. 4, pp. 629–660). New York: Routledge.

Draper, R., Broomhead, P., Jensen, A., & Nokes, J. (2012). (Re)imagining literacy and teacher preparation through collaboration. *Reading Psychology, 33,* 367–398.

Fang, Z. (2014a). Writing a report: A study of preadolescents' use of informational language. *Linguistics and the Human Sciences, 10*(2), 103–131.

Fang, Z. (2014b). Preparing content-area teachers for disciplinary literacy instruction: The role of literacy teacher educators. *Journal of Adolescent and Adult Literacy, 57*(6), 444–448.

Fang, Z. (2021). *Using functional grammar in English literacy teaching and learning.* Beijing: Foreign Language Teaching and Research Press.

Fang, Z., & Schleppegrell, M.J. (2008). *Reading in secondary content areas: A language-based pedagogy.* Ann Arbor, MI: University of Michigan Press.

Fang, Z., Schleppegrell, M., & Moore, J. (2014). The linguistic challenges of learning across academic disciplines. In A. Stone, E. Silliman, B. Ehren, & G. Wallace (Eds.), *Handbook of language and literacy: Development and disorders* (2nd ed., pp. 302–322). New York: Guilford.

Fang, Z., Lamme, L., Pringle, R., Patrick, J., Sanders, J., Zmach, C., Charbonnet, S., & Henkel, M. (2008). Integrating reading into middle school science: What we did, found, and learned. *International Journal of Science Education, 30*(15), 2067–2089.

Fang, Z., Sun, Y., Chiu, C., & Trutschel, B. (2014). Inservice teachers' perception of a language-based approach to content area reading instruction. *Australian Journal of Language and Literacy, 37*(1), 55–66.

Florida Department of Education (2022). *Florida reading endorsement matrix.* Tallahassee, FL: Author.

Fowler-Amato, M., LeeKeenan, K., Warrington, A., Nash, B., & Brady, R. (2019). Working toward a socially just future in the ELA methods class. *Journal of Literacy Research, 51*(2), 158–176.

Halliday, M., & Matthiessen, C. (2014). *An introduction to functional grammar* (4th ed.). London: Routledge.

Herbel-Eisenmann, B., Steele, M., & Cirillo, M. (2013). (Developing) teacher discourse moves: A framework for professional development. *Mathematics Teacher Educator, 1*(2), pp. 181–196.

Kavanagh, S., & Rainey, E. (2017). Learning to support adolescent literacy: Teacher educator pedagogy and novice teacher take up in secondary English language arts teacher preparation. *American Educational Research Journal, 54*(5), 904–937.

Kress, G., & van Leeuwen, T. (2021). *Reading images: The grammar of visual design* (3rd ed.). London: Routledge.

Lemke, J. (2002). Multimedia semiotics: Genres for science education and science literacy. In M. Schleppegrell & C. Colombi (Eds.), *Developing advanced literacy in first and second languages* (pp. 21–44). Mahwah, NJ: Erlbaum.

Love, K. (2009). Literacy pedagogical content knowledge in secondary teacher education: Reflecting on oral language and learning across the disciplines. *Language and Education, 23*(6), 541–560.

Love, K. (2010). Literacy pedagogical content knowledge in the secondary curriculum. *Pedagogies: An International Journal, 5*(4), 338–355.

MacGregor, M. (2002). Using words to explain mathematical ideas. *Australian Journal of Language and Literacy, 25*(1), 78–88.

Martin, J. (2009). Genre and language learning: A social semiotic perspective. *Linguistics and Education, 20*, 10–21.

Moje, E. (2007). Developing socially just subject-matter instruction: A review of the literature on disciplinary literacy teaching. *Review of Research in Education, 31*, 1–44.

Moje, E. (2008). Foregrounding the disciplines in secondary literacy teaching and learning: A call for change. *Journal of Adolescent and Adult Literacy, 52*(2), 96–107.

Moje, E. (2015). Doing and teaching disciplinary literacy with adolescent learners: A social and cultural enterprise. *Harvard Educational Review, 85*(2), 254–278.

Moore, J., & Schleppegrell, M. (2014). Using a functional linguistic metalanguage to support academic language development in the English Language Arts. *Linguistics and Education, 26*, 92–105.

Morgan, C. (2006). What does social semiotics have to offer mathematics education research? *Educational Studies in Mathematics, 61*(1), 219–245.

Nokes, J. (2010). Preparing novice history teachers to meet students' literacy needs. *Reading Psychology, 31*(6), 493–523.

O'Halloran, K. (2000). Classroom discourse in mathematics: A multisemiotic analysis. *Linguistics & Education, 10*(3), 359–388.

O'Hallaron, C., Palincsar, A., & Schleppegrell, M. (2015). Reading science: Using systemic functional linguistics to support critical language awareness. *Linguistics and Education, 32*, 55–67.

Osterholm, M. (2006). Characterizing reading comprehension of mathematical texts. *Educational Studies in Mathematics, 63*, 325–346.

Patterson, A., Roman, D., Friend, M., Osborne, J., & Donovan, B. (2018). Reading for meaning: The foundational knowledge every teacher of science should have. *International Journal of Science Education, 40*(3), 291–307.

Patrick, J., & Fang, Z. (2022). High school science teachers learning to teach reading through a functional focus on language: Toward a grounded theory of teacher learning. In L. Seah, R. Silver, & M. Baildon (Eds.), *The role of language in content pedagogy* (pp. 61–85). Singapore: Springer.

Pessoa, S., Mitchell, T., & Jacobson, A. (2021). Scaffolding argument writing in history: The evolution of an interdisciplinary collaboration. In M. Brisk & M. Schleppegrell (Eds.), *Language in action: SFL theory across contexts* (pp. 207–233). London: Equinox.

Prain, V. (2022). Teachers' language-based knowledge to support students' science learning. In L. Seah, R. Silver, & M. Baildon (Eds.), *The role of language in content pedagogy: A framework for teachers' knowledge* (pp. 137–158). Singapore: Springer.

Rodriguez, T. (2015). A content area reading course re-imagined: A situated case study of disciplinary literacies pedagogy in secondary English teacher education. *Literacy Research and Instruction, 54*(2), 163–184.

Romine, B., McKenna, M., & Robinson, R. (1996). Reading coursework requirements for middle and high school content area teachers: A U.S. survey. *Journal of Adolescent and Adult Literacy, 40*(3), 194–198.

Schall-Leckrone, L. (2017). Genre pedagogy: A framework to prepare history teachers to teach language. *TESOL Quarterly, 51*(2), 358–382.

Schall-Leckrone, L., & McQuillan, P. (2012). Preparing history teachers to work with English learners through a focus on the academic language of historical analysis. *Journal of English for Academic Purposes, 11*, 246–266.

Schleppegrell, M. (2018). The knowledge base for language teaching: What is the English to be taught as content? *Language Teaching Research, 24*(1), 1–11.

Scott, C., McTigue, E., Miller, D., & Washburn, E. (2018). The what, when, and how of preservice teachers and literacy across the disciplines: A systematic literature review of nearly 50 years of research. *Teaching and Teacher Education, 73*, 1–13.

Seah, L., Silver, R., & Baildon, M. (2022). *The role of language in content pedagogy*. London: Springer.

Seah, L., Tan, A., & Adams, J. (2022). Developing content teachers' language awareness through practitioner-researcher inquiry into student writing. *Teaching and Teacher Education, 119*, 1–11.

Serafini, F. (2011). Expanding perspectives for comprehending visual images in multimodal texts. *Journal of Adolescent and Adult Literacy, 54*(5), 342–350.

Serafini, F. (2015). Multimodal literacy: From theories to practices. *Language Arts, 92*(6), 412–423.

Shanahan, T. & Shanahan, C. (2008). Teaching disciplinary literacy to adolescents: Rethinking content-area literacy. *Harvard Educational Review, 78*(1), 40–59.

Shulman, L. (1986). Those who understand: Knowledge growth in teaching. *Educational Researcher, 15*(2), 4–14.

Siebert, J., & Draper, R. (2012). Reconceptualizing literacy and instruction for mathematics classroom. In T. Jetton & C. Shanahan (Eds.), *Adolescent literacy in the academic disciplines* (pp. 172–198). New York: Guilford.

VanSledright, B. (2012). Learning with texts in history: Protocols for reading and practical strategies. In T. Jetton & C. Shanahan (Eds.), *Adolescent literacy in the academic disciplines: General principles and practical strategies* (pp. 199–226). New York: Guilford.

Wexler, J., Swanson, E., & Shelton, A. (2021). *Literacy coaching in the secondary grades*. New York: Guilford.

Index

academic reading: challenges of 17–21; definition of 13
anticipation guide 187
author's generalizations 45
author studies 135

biographical studies 135
book studies 135

classroom discourse framework 194–5
classroom discourse moves 195–6, 233–4
Common Core State Standards 57, 77, 104, 122, 145, 167
content area literacy 28–31
critical language awareness 142–3
C3 Framework for Social Studies State Standards 76–7

decoding 4–8, 21–3; see also word recognition
developing historical literacy through reading: conducting close reading 104–9; document-based lesson 95; Sourcer's Apprentice 103–4; teaching historical reading strategies 95–104; using multiple sources 91–5; writing argument from sources 110–4
disciplinary literacy 30–4; see also advanced literacy

4Es pedagogical heuristic 224–5
5Es pedagogical heuristic 143–55
English language arts: critical literacy ideology 43–4; cultural literacy ideology 43; functional literacy ideology 42; goals of 42–4

expertise needed to teach academic reading 217–25, 240–1
Explanation Chart 202–3

fourth-grade slump 17–18
Frayer Model 186
functional language analysis 62–3, 104–9, 137–8, 149–54, 196–9

genre studies 135
genre teaching-learning cycle 111–4
gradual release of responsibility model 96
grammatical metaphor 25–6

history: definition of 73–5
historical literacy 75–7
historical materials: arguing text 80–1; explaining text 79–80; primary sources 78; recording text 78–9; secondary sources 78; tertiary sources 78; types of 78–81
historical reading: challenges of 81–7; close reading 88; contextualizing 88; corroborating 88; expert reading 88–9; historical empathy see perspective taking; inferring 89; perspective taking 88–9; sourcing 88
home science reading program 135

improving science reading ability: building science content knowledge 132–6; close reading 149–53; developing science language proficiency and multimodal competence 137–40; image-to-writing 138–9; learning to read like a scientist 140–3

knowledge about language 219–21
knowledge structure 74, 123

language comprehension 5–8
language development: three critical
    moments of 25–7; see also literacy
    development
language-related knowledge base for content
    area teaching 221–2; see also knowledge
    about language
learning to read 22, 213
linguistic comprehension see language
    comprehension
linguistic metalanguage 221; see also
    knowledge about language
listening comprehension see language
    comprehension
literacy development: advanced literacy
    26–7; basic literacy 26; preliteracy 26
literacy pedagogical content knowledge
    230–1, 233–4
literary devices 44, 46–7
literary literacy 56–8
literary reading: challenges of 44–51;
    definition of 45, 55; expert reading 52–6;
    interpretation 55; reattention 56
literary techniques see literary devices
literature: crossover literature 59; definition
    of 44–5, 68; drama 48–9; Great Books
    42–3; poetry 47–9; prose fiction 44, 48–9

mathematics: characteristics of 163–6;
    definition of 163
mathematical literacy 166–9
mathematics problem-solving heuristic
    188–90
mathematics reading: challenges of 169–79;
    expert reading 179–85; relationship to
    mathematical literacy 167–9; storying
    184, 205; translation 168, 176–7; see also
    resemiotization
mathematics register 165, 178, 191–9, 202
mathematics word problem: types of 202–3
mathematics writing: types of 199–200
multimodal texts 20–1, 142, 222–3; see also
    science multimedia genres

National Assessment of Educational
    Progress 29, 90, 123, 169, 192

Next Generation Science Standards 122,
    154
NSTA Outstanding Science Trade Books for
    Students K-12 134

Principles and Standards for School
    Mathematics 164
preparing teachers for academic reading
    instruction: broadening conceptions
    of text and literacy 228–9; building
    connections between content area
    methods and reading methods courses
    237–40; cohorting the reading methods
    course by discipline 226–7; enriching
    literacy pedagogical content knowledge
    229–34; supporting content area teacher
    educators for reading instruction 234–7
promoting reading in mathematics
    teaching and learning: communicating
    mathematics through writing 199–205;
    creating opportunities to read and discuss
    mathematics texts 185–91; linguistic
    simplification 192–4; teaching the
    mathematics register 191–9

reading: definition of 1, 4; elements of 1–4;
    relationship with language and learning
    24–8
reading alouds 135, 148, 187
reading comprehension: construction-
    integration theory of 13–14; definition of
    5; factors impacting 13–17
reading development: pyramid model of
    23–4; stages of 21–3; see also literacy
    development
reading process: complex view of reading
    8–13; DRIVE model 11–12; models of
    5–13; multidimensional view of
    reading 11; Rope Model, 6–7; simple view
    of reading 5–8
reading to learn 22, 213
reciprocal teaching 187–8

science: definition of 121
science of reading 7, 42, 215–6, 230
science literacy: fundamental sense of 121;
    derived sense of 121
science reading: challenges of 123–8; critical
    reading 140–3; expert reading 128–32;

importance of 121–3; resemiotization 139–40; science multimedia genres 127–8

sentence completion 138, 154

sketchnote 139–40

social studies 73

structural generalizations 47

teaching literature: close reading 62–3; communal reading 58–61; critical inquiry 59; cultural modeling 60–1; examples of 63–8; general principles and approaches 56–63; guided discussion 58–61; literary theories 61–2

text: definition of 1, 228–9; genre 3; hypertexts 3; paratext 55; screen-based texts 2–3; verbal texts 2; visual texts 2

transduction 138–9, 223; *see also* resemiotization

unit studies 59, 65–6, 135

visual grammar 20–1, 222–3; *see also* multimodal texts

visual metalanguage 223

who is responsible for teaching academic reading 214–7

word recognition 5–8, 12–13

zoom-in strategy 179–80; *see also* close reading

zoom-out strategy 179–80

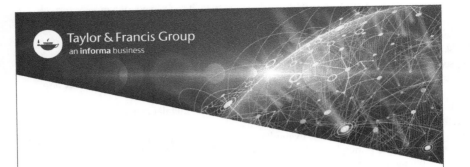